KING OF THE GYPSIES

KING OF
THE GYPSIES

Bartley Gorman
with Peter Walsh

First published in hardback in 2002 by Milo Books Ltd

Paperback edition first published in August 2003
by Milo Books Ltd

ISBN 1 903854 16 4

Typeset in Sabon by Avon DataSet Ltd,
Bidford-on-Avon, Warwickshire
www.avondataset.com

Printed and bound in Great Britain by
Cox & Wyman Ltd, Reading, Berkshire

MILO BOOKS LTD
10 Park Street
Lytham
Lancs FY8 5LU
info@milobooks.com

In memory of my dear brother Sam Gorman,
the best travelling man who ever took off his shirt.

Acknowledgments

I am indebted to boxing record compiler Harold Alderman for supplying details on Benny Marshall, to prize-ring historian Tony Gee, author of the book *Up To Scratch* (Queen Anne Press) and to the keepers of the MacFie collection at Liverpool University. Many friends and relatives also provided photographs and helped with recollections, particularly Caley and Kathleen Botton, Alan Bowers, Ken Cooper, Bob Dawson, Simon Docherty, Henry Francis, Mick Harper, Tommy Lee, Frank McAleer, Dave Russell, Siddy Smith, John Taylor, John Walton and Pat Wilson.

Contents

Prologue

MY NAME IS Bartley Gorman and I am the King of the Gypsies. What does that mean? Well, sometimes it describes a Romany political leader or the head of an extended family: a spokesman, a figurehead. Occasionally it is a fancy title adopted by a gypsy to impress the *gorgis* (house-dwellers). But for the fighting men of the travelling world, it has a different meaning: it is a title earned in blood, snot, sweat and gore. For them, the King of the Gypsies is the best bareknuckle fighter of his day. And if you are the best man among the travellers, then you are a very good man indeed.

Travelling men fight. Not all of them and not all the time, but many, and often. They would rather settle a row with knuckles than resort to the courts or call the police. Their contests may be held at fairs like Appleby in Cumbria, Musselburgh in Scotland or Ballinasloe in Ireland; at race meetings like Doncaster or Epsom; in a field or encampment; on the spur of the moment in a pub or club, at a wedding or a funeral. The fighters may have trained for months or be as drunk as lords. Sometimes there are rules: no biting, no butting, no gouging, no kicking, no hitting a man when he is down. Often there are not. When a fight is 'all-in', anything goes.

I was born into this tradition. My great-grandfather and grandfather were Gypsy Kings and my uncle too was perhaps the best man of his day. I felt from childhood that it was my destiny to succeed them – indeed, to go one further: I wanted to be the most famous and most feared of them all. I achieved this, but at a terrible cost.

For twenty years, I reigned as champion. I have beaten dozens of opponents; fought some of the hardest men in Britain and Ireland and knocked them flat. I have cleared more bar rooms than John L. Sullivan, seen blood run down the lanes. I have been attacked by mobs, been hospitalised five times and have stood in the dock in four crown courts. Many times I have regretted it. For years, I lived on a razor's edge and it scarred me. Yet knuckle fighting is so strongly a part of the gypsy heritage – so tied up with family pride and honour – that I felt I had to do it.

Though I no longer claim the bareknuckle heavyweight championship, I will be King of the Gypsies until I die. Then, if one man can gain recognition as the current champion, he will take over the title. He will be looked up to, admired, feared – and hunted – by all other gypsies. He will draw crowds wherever he goes. Even now, if Mike Tyson was boxing Lennox Lewis down at Doncaster racecourse and I was fighting Henry Francis 100 yards away, every gypsy man would come to see me. They wouldn't look at the other bout.

I should explain here that the word gypsy has two meanings. In its precise sense, it describes the descendants of a nomadic people who migrated to Europe from the region between India and Iran around 700 years ago (is it coincidence that some of the oldest pictures of fist-fighting, on pottery and clay tablets, come from that area?). The Europeans thought they were Egyptians, which they shortened to 'gypsies'. They were also known as Romanies after the language they spoke. They survived by peddling, music-making and fortune-telling. Some came to believe they were the descendants of the Biblical Cain, banished by Our Lord for slaying his brother Abel: God said to Cain, 'For what you have done you shall wander the world until the end of time and the land shall never yield its fruit up to you.' Cain's people lived in tents and played flutes and were coppersmiths.

Some also say the man who made the nails for Jesus's cross was the first gypsy because afterwards he was banished to the wilderness.

In a broader sense, a gypsy is anyone who lives the gypsy lifestyle and adopts their wandering ways, habits and appearance. Most Irish travellers – the background from which I come – are not Romanies but they are still gypsies. So are the Scottish travellers and a small group called the Kale in North Wales. Altogether there are said to be 120,000 travelling people in Britain, though this includes the more recent New Age Travellers, who are mainly people seeking an alternative lifestyle.

The gypsies have kept alive a tradition of barefist fighting that goes back to the dawn of man. The ancient Africans, Chinese, Egyptians and Indians all held such contests and the Greeks made boxers one of three classes of athletes at the Olympic Games (the others were wrestlers and runners). Many history books state that, as a sport and a spectacle, boxing died with the decline of the Roman Empire, but that it not true. It survived in pockets around the world. I believe the travelling people, the gypsies, also kept it alive.

When pugilism 're-emerged' in England in the late seventeenth century – it had never been away but before then there had been no newspapers to report it – the first recorded champion was James Figg, a shaven-headed bruiser who was also expert with sword and cudgel. He clobbered all comers at his amphitheatre in London. Less well known was his contemporary Benjamin Boswell, who claimed to be the son of the King of the Gypsies. The Boswells were among the elite of the Romany clans and 'Prince' Boswell came from an encampment on Finchley Common in London. He was said to have been a highwayman as well as a superb fighter. Captain John Godfrey, the first scribe of the prize-ring, wrote that he had 'a particular blow with his left hand at the jaw, which comes almost as hard as a little horse kicks. Praise be to his power of fighting, his excellent choice of time and measure, his superior judgement, dispatching forth his executing arm!' But Godfrey also claimed Boswell was a coward: 'Though I am charmed with the idea of his power and manner of fighting, I am sick at the thoughts of his nurse-wanting courage.' He does not say why this was; perhaps he was just prejudiced against gypsies, as so many people were in those days. Certainly Boswell was a top man of his day and often appeared at the Great Booth at Tottenham Court in London. His opponents included title claimant George Taylor, whom he beat at least once, sailor James Field and Jack Slack, who later became champion of England. Boswell was later rumoured to have returned to life as a highway robber.

Another notorious fighter of this time was Billy Marshall, who was born in Ayrshire around 1672 and who reputedly lived to be 120. He was of tinker stock and earned notoriety as a boxer and a bandit, becoming 'king' of the tinkers of Galloway and terrorising much of the countryside. His legendary exploits included deserting from the Army no less than seven times and from the Navy three times. He is reputed to have married on seventeen occasions and had countless children (both in and out of wedlock), fathering at least four after the age of 100! His gravestone stands in a cemetery in Kirkcudbright. As the Book of Genesis says, 'There were giants in the Earth in those days.'

The next 200 years saw the Golden Age of pugilism in England. The 'sport' was bloody, cruel and dangerous but became a cult, patronised by peers and even royalty. Bouts were held within a square ring made of staked-out rope. Though rules were devised they were often ignored, particularly in the north of the country. Fighters would hit and hold, wrestle, trip and throw, fall on their foe with elbow or forearm, gouge, throttle, strangle against the ropes and even kick with their spiked shoes. Terrible injuries were routine and deaths commonplace.

Many of the men who chanced their arm in these brutal contests were gypsies. Most of them have been forgotten: their fights were never recorded and many hid their true background to avoid prejudice – you could be hanged for being a gypsy in the Middle Ages. One who did become well known was Bill Hooper, or 'Hooper the Tinman', who came from the Bristol area and worked as a tinsmith in London. He was discovered by Lord Barrymore and worked for him as a minder. Hooper was good enough to fight a draw with the giant Big Ben Brain but his career fell apart after a victory over Bill Wood, who was also said to be a gypsy. He ended up destitute and died in the workhouse shortly after being found slumped in a doorway.

Gypsy pugilists were noted for their cleverness and a certain showboating arrogance. One who flaunted his ancestry was Jack Cooper. He became so renowned among his people that even today travelling men will say, 'Who do you think you are, Gypsy Jack?' The Coopers were and still are a famous fighting tribe from Hampshire, and in the early 1800s they included Jack's brothers Jem and Tom and cousins George and Tom. Gypsy Jack was the best of them and one of the foremost ten-stone men in the country. The head of the clan was his father, described (in the old magazine *Famous Fights Past and Present*) as 'a big man with an immense black beard which nearly covered his face and wearing a broad-brimmed black beaver hat and an elaborately embroidered white slop [smock] which made him look more like an Armenian High Priest than a gypsy horse dealer.'

When the Coopers turned up for a fight, they were some sight. When Jack fought Young Dutch Sam, one of the best pugilists who ever drew breath, at Andover, there were several expensively dressed lords among the aristocratic crowd, but it was the arrival of Cooper's backers that caused a stir. They were 'three as remarkable men as were ever seen at a prize-fight.'

They were Romany ryes – in English, 'gypsy gentlemen' – and had come on the ground superbly mounted. The tallest, and at first sight the most interesting, was almost a giant, for his height could not have been less than 6ft 3in. It would be impossible for the imagination to conceive a more splendid specimen of humanity. His face was singularly handsome, the features as regular and perfect as those of a Greek statue. Among his own people he was known as Tawno Chinko, but to the general world he was George Lee.

With him was his friend and captain, the notorious Gypsy Will, who was hanged for murder five years later in front of the gaol at Bury St Edmunds. He, too, was a man of great strength and stature – 6ft – and built far more massively than his companion, with bushy, black hair, a face so swarthy it was almost the colour of a negro's, and big black eyes. His dress consisted of a loose, blue jockey coat, top-boots and breeches and on his head he wore a broad-brimmed, high-peaked Spanish hat.

The third member of the group was Ralph Bosville, said to be the cleverest horse-doctor, horse-dealer and horse-stealer in England. This description tells you the kind of colourful people the gypsies were. Though Gypsy Jack was a great fighter, he lost that particular fight to an even better man. Jack liked the drink too much – the downfall of many a travelling man – later killed Paddy O'Leary in a prize-fight and was convicted of manslaughter.

No relation to the Hampshire Coopers but also said to have some gypsy blood was the heavyweight George Cooper. He was born in Stone, Staffordshire, in 1791 and is said to be the man on whom George Borrow based his character 'the Flaming Tinman' in his book *Romany Rye*. A sketch of Cooper shows him with kiss curls on his forehead, just like my grandfather wore. He was known as 'The Bargeman' because he worked on the canal boats and was highly rated: Bill Richmond, the great black pugilist, called him 'the best natural fighter I have worked with'.

His most famous contest was against the Irish champion Dan Donnelly at the Curragh in County Kildare in 1815. Cooper was holding his own until Donnelly hurled him with what was described as 'one of the most dreadful cross-buttocks ever witnessed' (the cross-buttock is a throw over the hips). For extra impact, the Irishman fell on Cooper with all his weight. After eleven rounds, lasting twenty-two minutes, Cooper finally fell from two thundering smashes, the last of which broke his jaw. Today the site of the battle is known as Donnelly's Hollow and is marked by a monument and by the footprints of Donnelly, which were dug out after the fight by his fanatical followers and which are still visible. A street poem was composed – *The Ballad of Donnelly and Cooper* – and became instantly popular. My cousin Maria can still sing it today. It begins:

Come all you true bred Irishmen, I hope you will draw near,
And likewise pay attention to these few lines I have here;
It is as true a story as ever you did hear
Of how Donnelly fought Cooper on the Curragh of Kildare.

Cooper fought in the prize-ring for thirteen years and opened a school for the Noble Art of Self Defence in Edinburgh. His opponents included the best men of the time such as Tom Oliver and Hickman. He died in 1834.

Thomas Britton, the 'terror of Somersetshire', is unknown today but was one of the best and most feared fighters among all gypsies. In the 1820s, he and John Burton led England's most dangerous gang of highway robbers. Two of their victims died when they were brutally waylaid on their way back from a fair. Burton was caught and later executed at Taunton gaol but Britton, said in contemporary newspaper accounts to be a 'remarkably powerful man', escaped and fled the county. He became a horse dealer, amassed a fortune and was the scourge of Leicestershire, where he boasted he could 'master twenty men at a time' in pugilistic combat. He was eventually recognised by an astute peeler and in 1843 was committed to Shepton Mallet for trial. I don't know what became of him but believe he was hanged.

Other great champions of the prize-ring days are said to have had gypsy blood: Posh Price (the name Posh means a half-bred gypsy), Tom Spring (whose real name was Tom Winters), featherweight Tom Smith and Joe Goss. Jem Ward, who was known as the 'Black Diamond' and was said to be of early Irish traveller stock, became champion of England in the 1820s, as did his brother Nick a decade later. So important did fighting become to the gypsies that many started naming their children after famous fighters such as Mendoza and Bendigo.

Perhaps the best-known was Jem Mace, who was born in the village of Beeston, Norfolk, in 1831, the son of a blacksmith. He learned to play the violin and left home in his teens, hanging around gypsy camps and earning a living playing at weddings. He also fought for money in the booths at fairs and eventually became a pugilist. He was known as the 'Swaffham Gypsy' but vehemently denied having Romany blood, perhaps because it was frowned upon in those days. Certainly he had the dark looks, his uncle Barney married a Romany, and some of his early opponents were travellers like Charlie Pinfold and Farden Smith, who Mace said in his book *Fifty Years A Fighter* was 'known as the King of the Gypsies and was a regular giant, standing 6ft 2in in his stocking feet and broad in proportion.' He and Smith fought on Norwich Hill for several rounds (a round ended when one fighter was punched or thrown to the ground) until the police arrived and they had to flee. They reconvened the next day on a nearby heath but Smith refused to fight, declaring, 'I give you best, Jem.'

Mace's cousin Pooley also fought a fellow Romany called Louis Gray in a field near King's Lynn in Norfolk. Gray, who camped near Norwich, had been giving an exhibition at a boxing booth at nearby Fakenham – where I would later fight – when Pooley's dad and uncle made some unfavourable remarks about him. One thing led to another and he was matched to fight Pooley, who won after seventeen brutal rounds.

But the age of the knuckle men was drawing to a close. In the 1860s the Marquess of Queensberry wrote the first rules for boxing with gloves. Soon it would replace barefist fighting, which was persecuted and driven underground. Only the travellers and a few other groups – such as the miners of the Welsh valleys and the Potteries – would keep it alive, holding bouts in secret, on hilltops and in hollows, away from prying eyes. Jem Mace would be the last British bareknuckle champion of the world and is known today as the Father of Modern Scientific Boxing. It is in his time that my story really begins.

CHAPTER I

In the Days of Giants

DONNYBROOK FAIR, DUBLIN, 1854. Blind Jimmy Gorman sat amid the din and chaos of a bustling alehouse, drinking stout. He was pleased with himself. Though sightless since birth, Jimmy had never let his affliction stop him doing business and had just bought and sold a horse in a matter of minutes. Now the profit was burning a hole in the pocket of his topcoat, and he intended to celebrate in the time-honoured tradition of the Irish travelling man: by getting drunk.

The annual fair at the village of Donnybrook on the outskirts of Dublin was a lawless event; so much so that an affray in Ireland became known as a 'donnybrook'. Itinerants, merchants, entertainers, cattlemen, farmers, con-men and rogues came from all over the country for an orgy of horse trading, dealing, drinking, wenching and thieving. Travelling theatres and freak shows, as well as bareknuckle matches, added to the atmosphere. The people were rough, illiterate and lived for the moment: one newspaper writer, visiting the fair in 1822, had reported that 'the Irishman is the only man in the world that fights for amusement.' Life and limb were cheap.

As Blind Jimmy lifted his tankard to his lips, he was unaware of the giant, black-headed man shouldering his way through the crowded bar. But he heard the room falling quiet, and could sense the figure looming over him.

'You, man, that has just sold me that horse,' came a growl.

Jimmy recognised the voice. This was the fellow he had slapped palms with a few minutes earlier to seal the deal.

'Yes?' said Jimmy.

'You're a blaggarding bastard. That horse is lame.'

'Never.'

'It has a swollen spavin. I'm Jack Ward, the best travelling man in Ireland. And I'm going to make you pay hot and heavy for this.'

Before Blind Jimmy could say another word, Ward wrenched him by the collar and dragged him through the crowd of drinkers, punching him to the face as he went. He threw Jimmy outside and set about him with his huge fists. Each time Jimmy was knocked to the floor, he tried to crawl away, and each time Ward pulled him up and knocked him down again. Men crowded around to watch but no one dared interfere. Ward was the meanest fighting man in Ireland: the King of the Tinkers.

Ward left Jimmy unconscious in a heap. Some people who knew the blind man lifted him into a barrow and pushed him nearly dead to the small circle of wagons where his family was staying. The Gormans rarely stopped in the middle of a throng, preferring to stay on the outskirts or by a crossroads; they thought themselves a cut above the general rabble. His bearers shouted for help and the women came rushing out. They saw a bloodied pulp, barely conscious. There were wails and oaths. Wet towels were fetched and placed gently on Blind Jimmy's swollen face.

Most of the Gorman men were at the fair or drinking in the pubs but Jimmy's younger brother was still in his wagon. Bartholomew Gorman didn't care for drink. He heard the commotion and came down the steps of his barreltop. He was eighteen years old, his shirt collar and cuffs undone, his shoulders broad in a collarless shirt. His family called him Bartley.

'Who has done this?' he asked.

'It was Jack Ward,' someone replied.

They carried Jimmy gently to his wagon. One of the women went to make a poultice to apply to his wounds. There was no thought of fetching a physician – they couldn't afford one. They were their own doctors. As they tended their barely conscious relative, no-one noticed young Bartley slip away.

The King of the Tinkers was still laughing when the saloon door swung open and Bartley Gorman walked in.

'Which man is Jack Ward?' he asked.

For the second time in an hour, the bar fell silent.

'I am,' said the huge, black-headed man. 'Who wants to know?'

'Step outside,' said Bartley.

Ward looked him over and snorted. He put down his drink and strode outside, his men eagerly following. Bartley was alone, facing a powerful giant surrounded by cronies, but he was unafraid. He neither knew nor cared who Ward was. He believed that God was on his side, so who could harm him? They were taking bets on how long Bartley would last when he laid into Ward like a whirlwind. The big man swung back but his cumbersome blows were easily ducked. For the next ten minutes, young Bartley Gorman gave the King of the Tinkers the hammering of his life, until the vanquished giant could rise no more.

Donnybrook Fair was closed down a few years later because it was too rowdy. By then, Bartholomew Gorman had become the most renowned fighter among the travelling fraternity. That encounter with Ward had changed the course of his life; a century later, it would set the course of mine. Bartley was my great-grandfather. I would inherit both his name and his violent calling.

*

A WARLIKE SPIRIT runs through the bloodline of my family like a curse. A thousand years ago and more, Ireland was a Celtic kingdom ruled by warrior clans, or septs. The Mac Gormains were one of these ancient tribes and ruled lands around what is now the town of Carlow in County Leix. Their name came from the word *gorm*, meaning blue. Some say it signified woad, the blue plant dye that Gaelic warriors painted onto their bodies before battle to intimidate their foes; a prominent warlord would be renowned for his body decoration and his sons and daughters would be known as 'children of the blue one' – Mac Gormain. Certainly they were fighters: our family motto is 'First and Last in War' (in Gaelic, *Tosach Catha Agus Deire Air*).

Like many Celtic chiefs, the Mac Gormains were driven from their fiefdom during the Norman invasion and dispersed, eventually settling in Clare to the west and Monaghan in the north. Some became noted for their wealth, hospitality and patronage of the Gaelic poets. But eventually my branch of the family was forced off the land again. What put them back on the road? There are various theories about the origins of the Irish travellers. Some say they are the remnants of an ancient class of wandering poets, joined by those dispossessed during times of upheaval such as Oliver Cromwell's campaign of slaughter in the 1600s and the battles of the Boyne and Aughrim in the 1690s. Perhaps they were overthrown by a neighbouring chief, put to flight with their servants, their children and their dogs, and never again allowed to settle. Perhaps I am the King of Ireland in exile! Others were people left homeless by the Great Famine of the mid-nineteenth century, when the potato blight destroyed the staple crop and one-third of the population perished or fled abroad.

Many of them earned their living by crafts such as metalworking: until not so long ago, all Irish travellers were referred to as tinkers, the word deriving from the Irish *tinceard* (tinsmith). Today it is often seen as an insult and many get upset if you call them tinkers. I am proud of it. In those days, people could not afford to buy a new pot or kettle if they found a hole in their old one. They had to repair things, a skill that has almost disappeared in our modern consumer society. How many young women – or men, for that matter – can even darn a sock today? Most of the travellers' traditional crafts – spoon-mending, tinsmithing, flower-making – have gone by the way, destroyed by new inventions and mass production, but in those days they were vital.

My great-grandfather, Bartley Gorman – who took the mantle King of the Tinkers after beating Jack Ward – was a genuine travelling tinsmith. I have a treasured photograph of him as an old man, mending a pot, his great fists and his battered face bearing testimony to a lifetime of fighting. He was born in Ireland in 1836 and named after Saint Bartholomew, one of the Apostles (Hebrew names run in my family). He was educated by monks and unlike many travellers could read and write. He was also an athletic young man but not known to be a fighter until the beating he gave Ward. He was certainly no thug. The wagon in which he lived was virtually a shrine to the Blessed Virgin and Our Blessed Sacred Heart and he would let no man enter it that used bad language or conducted himself improperly. Into old age he would read the Divine Offices in Latin every night.

The stories that follow have been passed down orally from generation to generation in my family and others. My great-grandfather is known in our family as Bartley I. His son, my grandfather, was Bartley II, and one of *his* sons, my uncle, was Bartley III. My cousin, another Bartholomew, is Bartley IV and so I am Bartley Gorman V. All were knuckle men except my cousin – he says he was a lover, not a fighter.

Bareknuckle boxing is often described as an English sport, but the Gaels of Ireland had staged fighting contests at their annual Tailteann Games, at the site of the ancient queen Tailte, until the twelfth century. With the re-emergence of prize-fighting from the seventeenth century onwards, many Irish pugilists made their mark. The most famous was Dan Donnelly but there were many others, and most of the heavyweight champions of the American prize-ring were of Irish immigrant stock, including the great John L. Sullivan. Bartley never competed in the organised prize-ring; he was a tinker, on the margins of society, and stayed within his own world. There his fame quickly spread – the tinkers called him 'Boxing Bartley' – and his right-hand punch was christened the 'Dublin ox-dropper'.

By the time Bartley I reached manhood, the top fighter in England was, by coincidence, also of gypsy background: Jem Mace. He was flash, with silk tie, top hat and silk handkerchief (our word for neckerchief). He never paid for anything because of his fame and, even today, 'to mace' means to get something without paying or to take someone for a ride. He won the heavyweight championship of England against Sam Hurst in 1861, but lost it a year later to the bigger and heavier Tom King. King refused to give him a return match so instead Mace fought Joe Goss – whose wife, Helen Gray, was a Romany – and beat him in nineteen rounds for the middleweight championship of England.

Next he was matched against an American of Irish birth, Joe Coburn. The American's backers wouldn't let him fight in England, claiming they would not get fair treatment, so the bout was arranged for Pierstown, Ireland, on October 4, 1864. Both men travelled there but at the last minute they argued over the choice of referee and the match fell through. It was re-arranged for October 14 but was again abandoned. The Irish were all for Coburn, who hailed originally from Armagh, and accused Mace of backing out. A ballad was later written about it, *The Cowardly Englishman*, including the verse:

The Englishmen bet five to one that Mace would gain the
   day,
But indeed they were mistaken for poor Jem he ran away,
Our champion boldly stood the ring without either dread
   or fear,
But he was disappointed Jem Mace did not appear.

The travellers were also upset with Mace; they believed he had let them down. And so it was that he was drinking in a Dublin saloon when in walked my great-grandfather and challenged him out. Mace was then the most famous bare-knuckler in the world but my great-grandfather was now King of the Tinkers and feared no man. He was twenty-eight and Mace was thirty-four, so both were in their prime.

Mace knew the *craic* with the travellers; there was no backing down. He took off his coat, went outside on the cobbles and squared off. Mace was a master – he invented half of the moves boxers use today – but my great-grandfather went at him hell for leather. The *garda* intervened and stopped it, so we shall never know who was best, but Boxing Bartley always believed he would have won. The contest was later written about in an old boxing magazine called *Famous Fights*; it had a pencil sketch of my great-grandfather calling out Mace, with his cap in his hand. Speaking many years later at a Liverpool sporting club supper, Mace recalled that the only punches which had troubled him in his prime were the 'temple-tickler' of Bob Brettle and Bartley Gorman's 'ox-dropper'.

Two years later Mace regained the English heavyweight title and in 1870 he beat the American champion, Tom Allen, in Louisiana for the heavyweight championship of the world. He went on to travel the globe, conducting tournaments and teaching the scientific skills that enabled him to beat men nearly twice his size. But he never forgot the power of the punch that Boxing Bartley landed on his jaw. Mace died in 1910, and lies in an unmarked grave at Anfield Cemetery in Liverpool. With the help of the Merseyside Ex-Boxers' Association, I intend to erect a proper headstone on his grave in recognition of one of the most important figures in boxing history.

This same period saw an exodus of Irish tinkers in the wake of the savage Potato Famine. Many sailed to the British mainland, where they encountered the English and Welsh Romanies. At first there was a clash of cultures, and the Romanies developed a somewhat jaundiced view of the Irish tinker:

He is by nature a fighter, and he fights with a cold fury and a fixed desire to maim that is rather frightening. When the travelling Irish first invaded Wales and the Welsh border counties they came in rough contact with the Gypsies, and the Gypsies very definitely had the worst of it. So much so, in fact, that they would rather move camp than risk a fight, unless they were in greatly superior numbers. All that was long ago, and the Irish tinker, with the passage of time . . . has softened, if he has not entirely disappeared. But the memory lingers in the Gypsy mind.

(*Gypsies of Britain*, Vesey-Fitzgerald, p 184)

My breed were part of this exodus. They brought with them their secret language, Shelta, also known as Cant, which goes back hundreds of years. The Romanies, of course, had their own tongue: for example, they say *gry* for a horse, we say *curry*; their word for dog is *juckle*, ours is *camra*. There are hundreds of such words and they are still used today. Eventually, the travellers of both communities mixed more freely. They were not alone on the open road. Many people lived rough in those days: deserting soldiers, dispossessed tenants, seasonal labourers, orphans, vagrants, highwaymen and brigands. Fistfights were an everyday occurrence.

Bartley I observed a strict ritual on the eve of every fight. During the day he would sit for hours in the nearest Catholic church, praying. He would return at supper time, wash outside his wagon in a bowl of cold water and shave with a cut-throat razor. Then he would put his spindle-backed chair in front of a stick fire and sit up all night with his wife's shawl over his shoulders, staring into the flames. No one could approach him: the women and children would watch him in awe from the windows of their wagons. 'He's going to carib the juck,' they would whisper to each other, meaning, 'He's going to fight the man.' As dawn broke, he would go to his opponent's wagon, knock on his door and challenge him out in the time-honoured way. Gypsies did it that way so they would be fighting when sober, and God help the man if he had a hangover – he had to come out anyway. They always did. Sometimes a ring was made up but more often they would fight in a hollow or the corner of a field or even right there amongst the wagons and horses.

The English travellers thought they had found the man to beat Boxing Bartley in Caleb Wenman, a tearaway from the Bristol area, traditionally home to many of the best pugilists. He and Bartley met at the Black Patch at Smethwick, Birmingham, a vast camp which at any one time would have 1,000 horse-drawn wagons. Their fight was one of the most vicious in history. No quarter was asked or given. Finally Wenman, who was getting the worst of it, aimed a desperate right cross. The punch landed on my great-grandfather's neck with a sickening crack: the force was so great that Wenman's forearm broke and the bone stuck out through his skin. In agony and shock, he could not continue. Boxing Bartley was also in a terrible state; the punch had dislocated his neck. An old gypsy herbalist put a pony collar around his neck and strapped it to hold his head still. He had to wear that for three months. Wenman fared much worse; his broken arm became infected and had to be amputated at the elbow.

The ferocity of the Wenman bout deterred most challengers: who wanted to fight a man whose jaw was so strong that you broke your arm punching him? Boxing Bartley was now in his prime, six feet tall, strong and fearless. He looked like a human version of the bull terriers he kept for dog fighting. But one man was not afraid of him. Moses 'Moe' Smith was one of the great unheralded prizefighters, a pure-bred Romany from Wilmslow in Cheshire and the pride of the English gypsies. They said that even Mace avoided him. He and Bartley were similar, both gentlemen with manners, but a clash had to come.

The Englishman and the Irishman were finally matched in an outdoor cockfighting pit in Cheshire before a great crowd of gypsy elders. As the fight began, a terrible thunderstorm broke, with torrents of rain and great flashes of lightning blasting branches from the trees.

'Bartley, we will have to stop,' said Moe.

'I'll stop this fight only if the lightning strikes and kills me,' replied Bartley.

Ankle deep in rainwater and mud, they punched each other to a bloody standstill. In the end, with darkness closing in, the storm still raging and both men barely able to stand, their supporters pulled them apart. They chair-carried Smith out of the pit, while my great-grandfather had to be led away, completely blind; they slit the swellings on his cheeks with a peg knife so he could see.

Several years later, he and Smith met by chance at a fair and shook hands. 'We have some unfinished business to settle, Moses,' said Bartley. 'I would like to finish it.'

'Well I wouldn't, Bartholomew,' said Smith. 'But I tell you what I will do. If any man says to me that he can beat Bartley Gorman, I'll fight that man. And if any man tells you he can beat Moses Smith, I want you to fight him.' They agreed and parted as friends.

Those fights were conducted largely under the old London Prize Ring Rules, with a round ending when one man was knocked down and a new one beginning when he was fit to resume. The floored man had thirty seconds to come up to 'scratch' – a line in the middle of the ring. Throws like the cross-buttock were allowed; my great-grandfather was expert at it. The fighters were like lions, with manes of long hair, and were famed throughout the land. But they were fast becoming outdated: the prize ring was in its twilight period. The Queensberry Rules for boxing with gloves were published in 1867. Fifteen years later, an eleven-judge British court ruled in a landmark legal case that prize-fighting was unlawful but that 'sparring' with gloves was lawful. Within a few years, knuckle fighting had all but disappeared on both sides of the Atlantic: the last world heavyweight title fight without gloves was in 1889, when John L. Sullivan beat Jake Kilrain over seventy-five rounds in Mississippi, USA.

Fights did persist in secret, though the participants and spectators were liable to arrest. The gypsies had always obeyed their own laws and were not about to abandon one of their strongest traditions just because the police or Government said so. The *Sporting Life* in June 1887 recorded one such contest before 100 spectators at Chingford, Essex, between a local boxer called James and a Romany called Gypsy Lee, which arose from a quarrel:

Round 1 – No time was lost, James being the first to get home, and showing himself the superior at outfighting, and at the end of 2½ min. the Enfield man had the first fall in his favour. In the second round the gypsy was determined to get to close quarters, and in doing so had his claret tapped. After this he was a bit cautious, and in the struggle that ensued both went down side by side.

Round 3 – This round in fact decided the battle. The gypsy forced conclusions, punishing his man severely, and at the finish, after some severe fighting, threw his man heavily. Some seven more rounds were fought that need little description. As soon as the boxer was hurt he seemed to lose all heart, and contented himself with fighting for the body, going in with his head down. [Lee], seeing this, kept jabbing him with the left on the right eye, which soon became useless. In the tenth round 'James' was knocked down, and refused to fight any longer. Time, 37 min.

Prizefighting also survived for many years in the tough mining communities of Wales and other areas, and it was here that the next great fighter of the Gorman dynasty would have many of his most famous contests.

Boxing Bartley had ten children: two boys, Bartholomew and Jimmy, and eight girls, Mary, Helen, Julie, Ann, Winnie, Delia, Maggie and Catherine, who burned to death as a child in a barreltop wagon. The eldest son would be known as Bartley II and would become, in my opinion, the best fighting man ever. He was born in 1883 and took after his mother's family, the Maguires: while the Gormans were tall and dark, he would be only five feet eight and had blood red hair. He was very dapper and very vain: always smartly dressed, clean and neat, shaved with a razor and strap and with a checked cap pushed back on his head to show his three kiss-curls.

He was very handsome; all the women were after him. He was also a bold and fiery young man and, unlike his father, loved to drink and carouse. One night he came home drunk and challenged out the old man. Boxing Bartley came down the steps of the wagon in his nightshirt and hit his son so hard that he would say he felt the pain of it until the day he died. I thought he was exaggerating when he told me that story on his knee; then, many years later, a boxer called Don Halden hit me so hard as I was bending down to pick up my vest that I still feel the pain of it twenty years on. So I know my grandfather was telling the truth.

Bartley II would not let anyone, man or woman, touch him when he was dressed. He wore a silk handkerchief around his neck, a three-quarter-length shooting coat with leather buttons, a waistcoat, a gold watch and chain with a £5 piece on it, britches and leggings, shoes shining like a glass bottle – he would clean them for an hour before he'd go out – and a cane stick. He thought he was the bee's knees, and he was.

He could lilt:

> Riddle-diddle da, riddle diddle diddle diddle-dum
> Riddle-diddle da, riddle-diddle diddle dum
> Riddle-diddle da, riddle diddle diddle diddle-dum
> Ooh-ra-ra, riddle diddle diddle dum

He was also one of the finest step-dancers in Ireland and would lilt while he danced. His favourite song was *Willie Riley and His Own Sweet Colleen Born*:

> Oh rise up Willie Riley, and it's come along with me
> I mean to go along with you and leave this country
> For to leave my father's dwellings, his houses and free
>   lands
> And away goes Willie Riley and his own sweet colleen
>   bawn

The fourteen verses were passed down in my family by word of mouth. An Irish lord once heard my great-grandmother, Bridget, trilling it by a roadside fire as he went past in a carriage and paid her a guinea to sing it right through. Bartley II learned and loved all of these old campfire songs. He was a fine lilter and a fine dancer and it was nobody's business how he could fight.

He beat Walter Lee, a tough English Romany; Matt Carroll, the scourge of Ireland; Tom Daley, another rugged Irish traveller; Chasey Price, a man-mountain from South Wales; Will Rosamount, a Welshman; Wiggy Lee; fought Black Martin Fury, the most feared man in Wales; and drew with Irishman Andy Riley after two hours. He never lost.

He was staying on a heath near London when Walter Lee came to challenge him. 'You can't come onto the British mainland and say you are the champion, you Irish so-and-so,' said Lee. He had brought a ring with him and they staked it out the night before the fight in the middle of dozens of gypsy wagons. Bartley's wife, Caroline Brian, was a brush-wagon woman – someone who sold scrubbing brushes, wicker baskets, enamel pans and kettles. She and his sisters didn't want him to fight, so while he was resting they locked him in his wagon. But this was for the title. He smashed the wagon to pieces with his fists to get out; smashed the doors, windows, the lot, got out and fought Lee for an hour and knocked him out. He said Lee was some man, about seventeen stone; my grandfather was fifteen-and-a-half stone. 'Walter Lee wasn't a man, he was a South African gorilla,' was his comment.

Bartley II could bounce three yards at a time – sideways, forwards, backwards – and perfected a left hook on the temple followed by a right to the chin or another left hook to the jaw. If he landed cleanly, he could put anyone away. He was also very hard to hit, a ghost, though he would have so many fights that his nose ended up like a piece of putty and his head like a bulldog's, hence his nickname: Bulldog Bartley. He treated my grandmother like a white slave – many travelling men were the same. An old man told me years later that my grandad used to lie in the lanes all day, eating and drinking, tending to the horses, and if anyone upset him it was like waking a bull.

His fight with Matt Carroll came about after Carroll's sister Maggie hit Bartley I with a soldering iron outside a Dublin pub and broke his nose. Boxing Bartley's daughter Ann vowed to get this Maggie and went looking for her. So Maggie told *her* brother Matt, a notorious knuckle man, who warned that if Ann came anywhere near his sister he would break her jaw. When Bartley II, who was then twenty-seven, heard of this threat to his sister, he sailed for Ireland with his siblings to settle it.

Carroll and his supporters were waiting on the quayside. As my grandfather came down the ship's gangway, Carroll stepped forward. 'I'm the best man in the thirty-two counties of Ireland,' he roared.

Bulldog Bartley paused on the last step. 'Only until I step off this ship,' he replied.

They went to a nearby spot and fought as the peelers stood by and watched. Carroll knocked my grandad over a wall but he clambered back and kept hitting him with punches under the heart, wearing him down. At one stage, Carroll's sister was shouting so much that my grandfather sidestepped him and knocked her out. It is said they fought for seventy-two rounds and then he knocked out Carroll as well. Now he was King of the Gypsies of Britain and Ireland.

They say that people have grown bigger over the past century but there were giants in those days too. The biggest man he ever fought was Joseph 'Chasey' Price, known as 'the Blackbird'. Price was only eighteen but already enormous. They met on Bryn Mawr mountain in South Wales and Bartley II knocked him out in one minute. Ten years later, he went back and Price was six foot eight. He put my grandfather on his knee like a child and said, 'This is Bartley Gorman, the only man ever to beat me.' Bartley said he wouldn't have stood a chance with him when Price was older, though I reckon he was just being polite – he always thought he could beat anyone.

My grandfather spent a lot of time in South Wales and said some of the best men he came across were colliers. They would fight in what they called 'blood hollows', out of the way of prying eyes, and even the little boys took part. This was the golden age of Welsh boxing, when the country produced champions like 'Peerless' Jem Driscoll, Freddie Welsh and Jimmy Wilde. My grandfather said Driscoll, the great featherweight whose mother was an Irish traveller woman, was the best boxer he ever saw.

Outside the ring, the best man in the region was another traveller of Irish descent: Martin Fury, known as 'Black Martin' or sometimes 'The Giant'. He was related by marriage to my grandfather – his brother Hughie married Bartley II's sister Ann. Fury had gained much notoriety by beating Jack Hearn when he was outweighed by almost four stone, according to this account – under the headline 'Gypsy "King" Dethroned' – in the *South Wales Echo*:

Hearn was a very fine man, about 15 stone in weight, about 5ft 10in in height and all strength and ruggedness from head to foot, while Fury was only about 11st 6lb. None of the gypsies could believe that Hearn could be beaten, for he had licked all the gypsy fighters that came his way, and those gypsies in those days didn't fight for money, for there was nobody about to offer them purses, but just for the love of fighting. But this Fury turned out to be a very fast and clever fighter. He kept on ducking and dodging in and out, and playing on Hearn's face, until it was dreadfully swollen and battered.

They fought for an hour and a half until Fury closed both of Hearn's eyes and he could no longer see.

The gypsy women were now shouting to go for the police, and the fight was stopped, but a gypsy shouted, 'We will lance his eyes and get him to see, and he can fight again.'

They did it and the fight went on, but Hearn was blinded again, and the man could fight no more. Five minutes after the fight the police came, and an old gypsy woman said to them, 'My dear men, you're too late.'

Fury must have been young when that took place because he grew to be a very big man. He and my grandfather fought to a draw. Our two families would remain close and, like the Gormans, the Furys would have a long fighting pedigree: my cousin Gypsy John Fury is a successful boxer, fighting an eliminator for the British heavyweight title in 1991 and beating the champion of Italy. John is 6ft 4in and weighs nearly twenty stone and is, in my opinion, the best man currently among all travellers and the best streetfighter in Britain. Black Martin was his great-uncle.

The best man Bulldog Bartley ever met, so he said, was another Irish traveller called Andy Riley. They fought in the Old Country for two hours to a draw. Those Irish could really mix it: even the great John L. Sullivan's father once said, 'There's at least a dozen men in the Emerald Isle have got the beating of my son.'

In England, the Gormans met another travelling family of Irish descent called the Wilsons. Jack Wilson was born in Pine Street, Toronto, Canada, in 1873, and would become my maternal grandfather. His family were horse dealers: they would take the train to the railhead at Winnipeg, then go out by coach and horseback into the North West Territories, buy Mustangs from the Indians, bring them back, rest them, put them on the train to Montreal, then ship them by cattle boat to England to sell to the British Army. Jack was once kicked in the head by a mule; he was unconscious for three months and carried a dent in his head for the rest of his life. He came to Liverpool when he was fifteen and stayed, eventually marrying Bulldog Bartley's sister Mary. He was a hard man: he made his sons box each other and would take a bullwhip to them for any disobedience. One of them, known as 'Ballinasloe Joe', became a good boxer. Jack Wilson made a fortune horse-dealing and always wore a derby hat, a navy suit and gold watch chain set with £5 pieces. He looked like a cross between Winston Churchill and Sidney Greenstreet, with a hole in his head.

The Gorman and Wilson families became very close and grandfather Jack was prepared to back his brother-in-law against any fighter in the world. In the winter of 1907, the Canadian-born world heavyweight champion, Tommy Burns, arrived in the British Isles to pick up some easy money defending his boxing title. He breezed through several challenges, including a one-round knockout over Irishman Jem Roche in Dublin. Wilson met Burns in a Dublin hostelry and said, 'You were fighting the wrong man when you fought Roche, it should have been Bartley Gorman.' He offered £5,000, a fortune then, as a straight bet, winner-takes-all, to fight bareknuckle against the heavyweight champion of the travellers, Bulldog Bartley, in Dan Donnelly's Hollow on the Curragh. Burns declined but Wilson followed him to London and repeated the offer. Again he declined. Before twelve months were out, Burns had sailed to Australia and lost his title to Jack Johnson, the first black champion, for a purse of £6,000. The gypsies said he would sooner fight the giant negro than Bartley Gorman II. I'm sure my grandfather would have beaten him.

Jack Johnson, the first black heavyweight champion, has a special place in the affection of the gypsies, perhaps because, like them, he was an outsider. The Irish travellers were up all night singing *camorlias* before he beat Burns. He was an all-time great – some say the best ever – and even now, gypsy fighters will declare, 'I'm not scared of Jack Johnson or any man.' Johnson used to stand with one hand on his hip, a habit my grandfather shared; it is something I do too.

They could fight then. People shouldn't make the mistake of thinking that Mike Tyson or Lennox Lewis could beat the likes of Johnson or Jim Jeffries. Those were the days when a man would walk with a plough behind a horse all day long, not sit on a tractor. You couldn't beat a farmer in those days, never mind a prizefighter. My grandfather used to practise

17

on a gate: he would tie rags around it to save his knuckles and would then have someone swing it towards him while he hit it back with his bare hands.

Even though knuckle fighting was now strictly illegal it was a regular event at fairs. The police weren't interested – they weren't about to raid a big gypsy gathering and cause a riot. Tom Daley, another traveller of Irish descent, had fallen out with Bulldog Bartley and bumped into one of his sisters at Oswestry horse fair.

'Tell that brother of yours that when I see him I will beat the living daylights out of him,' said Daley.

'I'll make sure you have that opportunity,' she replied.

She went back to Wrexham and told him, and Bartley II walked the eighty miles to Llangefni Fair, an annual event at a small village on the Isle of Anglesey, to fight him. Daley put one hand on a five-bar gate and jumped straight over it. All the Welsh horse dealers were saying, 'Oh, what a man Tom Daley is.'

My grandfather, a fearsome drinker, pretended to stagger up to the gate and trip over it. But when he stripped off they couldn't believe it. He sparked out Daley with a tremendous leaping left hook but it took him an hour.

Though my grandfather was never beaten one-to-one, such a violent life had its price. Later that year he had an argument with six farmer brothers in a pub in Anglesey and drew off and hit the biggest of them. He couldn't help himself – he was a terror for 'drawing the box', which means hitting someone before they know it. Anyway, the brothers ganged up on him, kicked him unmercifully and left him draped over a stone wall. He was in hospital for two months and they reckon he passed little bits of bone through him until the day he died.

You could hear grandad coming from two miles away when he had been drinking: he would be challenging out everybody, especially on the tough grounds. 'You couldn't trust him,' my dad used to say. He fell foul of the law on several occasions. He did twelve months in Walton Prison in Liverpool for hitting a man. Another time, the family was stopping at a wood near Rhyl when the estate keeper came, rattled the front of the wagon with his cane and said, 'I want you gypsies out of here when I come back from the pub.' They were still there when he returned and he hit the wagon again.

My grandad came out with a candle and said, 'We will go in the morning, sir.' As he said it, his son, my Uncle Bartley (yet another Bartholomew in the family) came from the side and sparked out the keeper. My uncle fled and my grandfather took the blame, spending six months in Ruth in jail, near Denbigh, sewing mailbags all day long. I remember passing the jail and my father saying, 'That's where your grandfather did time. Your grandmother and I would stand outside on the bridge and he would wave to us from his cell window.'

In 1912, my great-grandfather, Boxing Bartley, died at the age of seventy-six. His body was taken on a ship from Liverpool back to Ireland and was buried by the Roman Catholic Brothers of the Brown Scapula in Greenland Cemetery, Larne. Two years later, the world was at war. Like many travellers, my grandfather tried to avoid military service, but was caught and conscripted into the Black Watch, the famous 'Ladies from Hell', so-called because of their kilts. They were in camp in Scotland and there is a stile on an old road out of Stranraer where the family used to meet him when he got leave. He suffered a wound to his leg in training and opened it up a little to get invalided out, which a lot of gypsy men did.

It was around this period that he met his most famous opponent. Johnny Basham was a former British champion, the first man to win the Lonsdale Belt outright at welterweight. He had a famous series of fights with Ted 'Kid' Lewis, who in my opinion was the best boxer Britain has ever had. Basham also boxed in the booths occasionally and one day was appearing in a marquee at Wrexham Beast Fair, offering £5 to anyone who could last three rounds with him. Bulldog Bartley was there with his former opponent Tom Daley, both in checked caps and spotted handkerchiefs. The barker asked if any man would fight Basham – who was in military uniform himself at the time – and Daley shouted up, 'I will.'

The old tent was bulging. When the barker looked to see who had shouted, Daley whipped off his cap and pointed to my grandfather.

'It wasn't me,' said Bulldog Bartley.

'Come on, Ginger. It's only an exhibition,' said the barker. 'Are you afraid?'

'No, I'm not afraid of anyone.'

He didn't know who Basham was. Boxers didn't mean anything to him, not when he'd fought the likes of Chasey Price and Martin Fury. So he got in the ring. He had an old railwayman's waistcoat on with long silk sleeves. He took his hat and coat off but kept the waistcoat, and they commenced boxing with gloves on. From the first bell, it was no exhibition. Basham nearly killed my grandad, and after a couple of minutes Bulldog Bartley was completely exasperated.

'I can't pick a chicken with gloves,' he said. 'I've got to get these off.'

'You can have it any way you want,' said Basham and, being the man he was, took off his gloves. My grandad did the same, removed his waistcoat and they went at it bare-knuckle. In the second round my grandfather knocked Basham down with a left hook-right cross. Someone cut the lights, a riot broke out in the crowd and my grandad grabbed his coat and left.

Fifteen years later, he was in a café in Wrexham with some of his sons having a fry-up when a man at next table said, 'I'll buy that for you, Ginger.'

'What do you mean, sir?'

'I'll pay for that.'

'It is very kind of you but I don't know you.'

'Well I remember you. Do you remember boxing a soldier on the beast market? You broke my jaw, you red-headed bugger.'

It was Basham. They shook hands and had a laugh.

In the Days of Giants

Of course, there were many fine gypsy men whom Bulldog Bartley never got down to business with: you couldn't fight everyone. One of the best was Bill Elliott (pronounced *Ellit*), who was born around 1888 and whose family were originally sheep drovers in Scotland. He was the same size and weight as my grandfather and was also never beaten. He travelled from county to county to fight, wearing a silk around his waist, and after beating another sheep drover at the big gathering at Appleby Fair in Cumbria declared, 'I'm the best gypsy man ever.'

A Welsh traveller took issue with him. 'No, there is a man called Martin Fury down in our part of the country.'

So Elliott upped sticks and went to fight Fury. They met at Merthyr Tydfil, Fury arriving on a landau with a load of men behind him. Apparently it was a draw, because Elliott later said to Fury, 'You never bet [beat] me Martin, I never bet you.' He gave Fury great respect for coming to fight him. They were supposed to have a second fight at a donkey fair at Gloucester but it never came off. Elliot, who died in 1953, could still fight into his sixties and had a saying: 'Never mind my old round shoulders and my old splaw feet, I'm old Bill Ellit, the best unscienced travelling man that ever slept in a van.'

Each family of gypsies say that their own folk were the greatest fighters. Travellers are like American Indians: the Cheyenne, Blackfoot, Sioux, Apache and Comanche. They are breeds. Travellers are the same. My *jeal* (a Cant word meaning kin) consists of seven families: the Bryans, Furys, Gormans, Kellys, Maguires, O'Neills and Wilsons. Others are just as tribal and won't admit anyone else is champion because of the pride of their breed. When I fight, it is for the ghosts of my grandfather and great-grandfather, the memories of my breed. It is deeper than people know. It is not a man having a fight for money: it's for honour and valour and glory.

CHAPTER 2

Born to Fight

I WAS BORN with the cry of the banshee on me. My mother was ten years old, a little barefoot girl in Ireland, when she saw this strange apparition. She was with her two brothers late one midsummer evening and they were sneaking the horses into a farmer's field for the night. Little Katy Wilson was skipping down this lane when she came across a broken stone wall overgrown with brambles and thorns. She looked through a dip in the wall and saw this small creature-woman sitting in the ruined gable end of a cottage. She had no clothes, just her long hair coming down over her body, and was using a piece of the thorny briar to comb it. 'She was racking her hair and it was pulling on the plugs of her hair and she pulled it that hard that it caused her to cry out,' my mother would later tell us. The sound, a shriek, caused the horses to bolt down the lane.

I would hear that story countless times at campfires late at night. Perhaps I'm crazy to believe it but I do. It is why I have had bad luck: the wail of the banshee is supposed to herald death, and I have seen more than my share of that.

My parents could have not have been more different in appearance. Kathryn 'Katy' Wilson was a gentle woman with auburn hair, fair skin and freckles. Samuel Gorman, the son of Bulldog Bartley, was a dark, upright man with hair as thick and shiny as black plastic. Though he was fierce-looking and came from a line of renowned knuckle men, he was not himself a fighter. He was a law-abiding man, a strict church-going Catholic and rigid disciplinarian. He only ever fell foul of the law once in his life, for not having a dog licence, and to hear him dwell on it you would think he had committed murder. He was always turned out in a suit, collar and tie and set high standards for his family.

Samuel was twenty-seven years old when he married Katy and she was thirty-three. She came from Newry in County Down and was one of the Wilson travelling clan, close friends of the Gormans: in fact my mother and father were first cousins. They had a big travellers' wedding with an outdoor banquet laid out on long tables near Nottingham. Katy was married in black, still in mourning for her mother who had died six months before.

Neither of the newly-weds had been to school and neither could read or write. They lived with a posse of brothers and sisters, uncles, aunts and cousins in a farm field down Black Lane at Giltbrook on the outskirts of Nottingham – the land of Robin Hood. And that's where I was born, on St David's Day, March 1, 1944. It was a stormy night and the scene was like something from a romantic novel: as the women fussed around and my mother cried out in labour, my father jumped on a half-blind black stallion called One-Eyed Jack and rode him bareback through the gale for the midwife. The nurse climbed on the horse with my father, hanging on for her life, the wind howling around them, and they arrived at the camp in time for her to deliver me right there, in a gypsy trailer with little round windows in the back.

I was christened Bartholomew and was baptised at the Church of Our Lady of Good Counsel at Eastwood. Old Bulldog Bartley, the greatest-ever gypsy fighter, held me in his battered mitts.

'Ah, pretty little boy,' he said, 'my jeal all over.'

I looked like a carbon copy of him, with flame-red hair and blue-green eyes and my mother's fair skin. Perhaps my future path was mapped out for me there and then. I would be told many times that I was the image of my grandfather. It was a good job I ended up six feet one and fifteen stone and had a knockout punch in each hand. But my real strength as a fighter came from within: it's spiritual.

On my birth certificate, my dad put his occupation as 'scrap iron and rag dealer'. I don't know why: he was a carpet salesman. Perhaps he was worried the taxman would come after him. He bought rolls of carpet and webs of oil cloth (lino) and hawked them door-to-door, wearing out his shoe leather tramping up driveway after driveway. He was never wealthy but made a living and put food on the table and clothes on our backs. Even in the post-war years of rationing, we never went without.

Eleven months after me, on February 5, 1945, my brother Samuel arrived, born in a barreltop wagon. He was dark like dad, with the same black hair. We became inseparable, as close as two brothers could be, watched over always by my mother. She never left us, day or night. We thought she was the most beautiful woman in the world – and the finest cook.

My first conscious memory is of standing by a water trough watching a horse drink. I was a waist deep in long grass, with bees buzzing and the sun shining and the horse flicking its tail to keep away the flies. My head was wet where my godmother, Aunt Nudi, had dipped it in water to make my hair curly. Our site was typical of many small gypsy encampments of that time. Relatives surrounded us in eight or nine caravans – or trailers, as we call them – some with tents nearby. Ours was one of the first aluminium trailers, known as a 'tank'. We had an eight-by-eight tent with a wooden floor and a three-ply stable door. The tent had a wooden frame that folded like a concertina and red wooden knobs in each corner to peg it out. Fixed to the ceiling was a paraffin tilly lamp. We had a queen stove, painted aluminium because it doesn't burn, with old enamel advertising signs for Woodbines and Ovaltine fixed at the back of the stove to keep the heat in. On the wooden floor was a lovely carpet, nice chairs, a dining table and curtains all the way round so you couldn't see the frame. The tank had a chrome chimney with a cowl on top of it, and little fancy mudguards, and the four of us lived in it. Some lived in cottage wagons made of wood. There were also some flash cars: before World War Two, my grandfather Jack Wilson had a Chrysler Richmond with silver bugle horns on each side, while my dad had a Chrysler Q, a smaller version. During the war they couldn't get petrol, so they sold them.

The women ran the domestic side of the camp, constantly washing and cleaning and cooking – always cooking. At Christmas, my mother and the other women would take their turkeys to the local bakery in big meat dishes to be roasted. Each one would have a string tag to identify it. Gypsy women are very particular about food hygiene; you rarely get food poisoning among travellers. Meat was always washed in salt water. The Christmas pudding would be like a football laced with Guinness, rum and currants and raisins soaked in brandy, with old silver and brass thru'penny bits washed and sterilised and put in it, and would be boiled in a cast-iron pot. They sometimes cut a big slice off the pud and fried it up in a pan.

We lived an outdoor life, ate fresh food, stayed up late and never went to school. We had no playpens so sometimes toddlers would be tied with a length of rope to the towbar of a trailer to stop them wandering off. It sounds idyllic but the travelling way can be harsh. My father was brutal, and I mean *brutal*. He had a thick leather belt with two big metal rings in it and he would hit me for the slightest reason, wrapping the belt around his hand to get a proper grip and flogging me without mercy, even when I was a toddler. He hit me everywhere with it: head, ears, eyes. I carried weals and bruises all the time. That is how it was in those days. I admit I was a reprobate, always up to mischief, and I would eat dirt before I would give in, even when he was lashing me. I also think he beat me because it was the way he had been brought up himself; he had been thrashed and, with my bright red hair, I reminded him of his father. It was a kind of revenge. He never hit our Sam the same way. Sometimes it would get so bad that Uncle Bartley, my dad's brother, a very fair man and a mean fighter, would intervene. 'Sam, if you touch that boy I will break every bone in your body because he is only a baby,' he once said when my dad took the belt to me.

Gypsy children also see and hear things that town and city children don't. Death touched me from an early age and has never been far away since. When I was four, I was outside the tent and saw a big bird coming towards me. The nearer it came, the bigger – and lower – it got: it was an aeroplane and it was coming down. I was sure it was going to hit me. It passed no more than twenty feet above me, the whoosh of air nearly sending me off my feet as I gazed up open-mouthed, and hit the ground with a terrible crash in the next field. The pilot was killed. It was a military plane and soldiers came and sealed off the area. My father later took me to the pilot's funeral. I didn't really understand what had happened except that this brave man must have fought the controls to keep the aircraft from hitting me.

On another occasion, I saw eight cows and two horses struck dead by lightning under a tree near Rugby in Warwickshire. I remember the stench of the charred animal hide, the blackened legs and the skulls where crows had pecked out the eyes. Those sights make an impression on a young child.

Like our parents, neither Sam nor I could read or write. Instead of going to school, we would accompany my mam and dad on the road. Dad would pull into a street and hawk every house while we had to sit for hours in the van. Dad took sugar, milk and tea in an enamel billy can and I had to go and ask for hot water. We also had our chores on the site. We had to wash up and clean all of the chrome on the trailers. I used to do it listening to my favourite, *Jet Morgan and the Red Planet*, on the radio, imagining I was a space hero. It was so real you didn't have to see it.

There were always comings and goings: tears and crying when friends left the site, backslapping and drinking when newcomers arrived. When I was seven, we moved to North Wales, to Bala Lake. We stopped with eight trailers on the

Dead Pig Common, so-called because an old pig had been thrown out there years before. Gypsy stopping places often have such names: you might say, 'We're stopping at the iron gate,' because there was an iron gate there years ago, or 'the grassy corner'. Tin Kettle Lane was another one, so named because there was a lot of scrap iron thrown down there.

I had a dog, Rustler, a cross between an Alsatian and a greyhound, and was forever on the move, exploring the woods and fields and streams. Sam and I filled our days with adventure. We coursed for hares, learning that the best lurcher dogs often had catgut stitching in their bellies and legs – it meant they had been brave enough to run through barbed wire fences to chase their prey – and training them to a pitch. Competition was fierce to have the best dog.

As I say, strange things happen to travellers. I was walking along a river with Rustler and spotted a snake six feet long tangled around a tree. It had escaped from a circus a few weeks before. I killed it, took it back and hung it from the 'flying lady' silver mascot on my father's Bedford van. It reached down to the ground. A snake is a detested thing among gypsies, a symbol of evil since the Garden of Eden, for God said to the serpent, 'From henceforth man will strike out at your head and you will strike at his heel. From henceforth you shall crawl on your belly and eat the dust of the earth to the end of time.'

My main sport was fishing; not with a rod but by hand, wading into the water and tickling the fish and then gently getting them by the gills. I loved it more than anything and could get two trout in one hand. Of course, often it was poaching but who cared unless you got caught?

One day I must have spent too long in the water and when I got back to the trailer I was shivering uncontrollably. Within an hour, I was seriously ill. Someone was sent to fetch an old doctor down from the mountains.

'He wants to be left in a room on his own,' the doctor instructed my father. 'Put him in the caravan, pull the blinds to and leave him quiet.'

Dad did as the man said, but within a short time I was almost comatose. 'I'm not leaving my lad here like this,' said my father. 'He's dying.'

He carried me into one of the tanks, laid me on the bed, coupled the trailer up to his van and said to my grandfather, 'I'm taking him to the hospital at Wrexham.'

Grandad sat on the bed with me in the back as we drove the forty miles to Wrexham. I was barely conscious as the old tank bounced up and down on the road. I will never forget that journey with my poor grandfather holding my hand, old Bulldog Bartley, with his broken hands and his putty nose, his old coat with the leather buttons and knotted handkerchief and his bit of beard going grey, trying to comfort me, softly singing songs. He did his best.

When they got me to Wrexham I was rushed straight into the hospital with double pneumonia. Relations arrived in old Buicks, my grandfather Wilson and aunts and uncles, but I was so weak I couldn't even wave to them. For several days I lingered at death's door.

Gradually I began to recover. I knew I was getting better when they took me out in a wheelchair onto the green outside the hospital and gave me a bit of ice cream. My legs had turned into sticks. When I finally managed to crawl out of bed and on top of the blankets, the other children were shouting, 'Look, Bartley Gorman's out of bed.' I used to complain to my mum, laying it on thick: 'You never bring me anything nice to eat, you never bring me a spotted dick.' It was my favourite. The next time she came, she shouted from the end of the ward, 'Bartley, look what I've got for you.' She held up this big pudding she had cooked specially, covered in muslin. I hid myself under the blankets and wouldn't show my face, I was so embarrassed at everyone staring.

I was in hospital for three months until I was well enough to go home but was a sickly kid after that. I had a succession of earaches, toothaches, coughs and viruses. I seemed to spend half my life in bed and, being gypsies, my family were not always able to get me the best treatment. Not long after leaving hospital, I came down with a chest infection and my father went to the chemist. Dad spoke in a funny way, deep and gruff, and he wasn't always easy to understand.

'My son has bronchitis,' he said.

The chemist thought he said, *My son has a brown carthorse.*

'What's up with him?' he asked.

'He's hoarse,' said my dad.

Again, the man thought he said, *He has a horse.*

It sounds ever so ridiculous. Anyway, the chemist gave my dad some horse liniment. My father came back, thinking it was medicine, and gave me a tablespoon of this yellow liquid which you were supposed to rub on horses. God almighty! I leapt in the air, hit the tilly lamp and almost brought the tent down. My eyes came out like balls. I went into a fit and ran to the tap, gargling water. Dad took a dose himself and it nearly killed him. He went back up to the chemist and had murders with him. But somehow it cured me.

No sooner was I back on my feet than I was in the wars again. I tried to jump a galvanised fence and missed my footing; the edge of the corrugated iron went straight up my leg and opened it like a zip. I needed eight stitches. The doctors never even gave me an anaesthetic. They were trying to tell me stories to take my mind off it, tales about giant spiders in South America, but you could hear me yelling all over the hospital.

Even with my scrapes and illnesses, I was a bold little bastard and dad would still punish me just as harshly. He had very strict rules. He wouldn't let me wear a belt because he said it weakens your back; we had to wear braces. That is why the gypsies used to take their handkerchiefs off and tie them around their waist to fight – because they didn't wear belts. Although the family were close and self-supportive, it was still a tough old world, where disputes were settled the simple, direct way. Even my dad had to raise his fists when the occasion demanded.

He and Black Bob Evans, a close friend, were watching over some horses while their wives were out hawking. My dad looked over at Evans and said, 'Who do you reckon would win out of you and me?' The next thing, they were fighting in the street. Bob's son ran to get his mum while I stood and watched. The women came running and broke it up. Black Bob was the best man in North Wales. He had a saying: 'I'll fight with a lion that roars in my face but not with a snake that crawls at my feet.'

Grandad could still fight like the devil. Just before my dad came out of Wales, he was sleeping under the four-wheel dray one night, with a sheet over the top, when my grandad returned from the public house.

'Get up and make me some tea,' he ordered.

Dad ignored him, so Bulldog Bartley drew off and punched him as he lay there, breaking his nose in three places.

I was too young to ever see my grandfather fight, but years later I spoke to a old man who had. Davy Stevens lived in a little cottage near Wrexham. He was nobody's fool, an old potter who knew how to bang plates together so they wouldn't break. 'Can you remember my grandfather, Uncle Dave?' I asked him.

'When your grandfather was sixty-three years old, I was with him in a pub in Chester,' he said. 'He could still lilt and step-dance and sing old Irish songs. There was this travelling man and he had about six sons in the pub. I tell you Bartley, one was the biggest lad I ever did see. This man was a Romany gypsy and he caused an argument with your grandfather because he had his sons with him. Your grandfather said something back to him, so his biggest son stepped in and said, "Listen, I'm the man for you." '

My grandfather may have been sixty-three but he still had the name Bartley Gorman, undefeated, and had never been known to refuse a fight. 'Let's go outside,' he said.

They retired to a cobbled courtyard. 'Oh Bartley, I was only a young lad,' said Davy, 'and this man, black curly hair, he was about twenty-seven, he bloody didn't half give it your grandfather. Bloody hell. He knocked him up this old entry outside the pub, he was fetching the blood from down his nose, he was punching the hell out of him. Your grandfather was drunk as well.

'Then your grandfather said, "Hang on, hang on." He walked over to a horse trough and he ripped his shirt and waistcoat off and dipped his head in. He swilled water all over him. My God, Bartley, when he came back he was bouncing three yards. He hit the big lad on the point of the jaw, knocked him clean out. I never seen anything like him in my life.'

After several years in Wales, my parents decided that they wanted Sam and I to have some schooling. We upped sticks and moved to Bedworth, a tough coal-mining town north of Coventry. Our new home was Warner's Yard, a plot of land on a main road next to a pub. There were a few other travellers there, like old Tom Flanagan, who would go around the markets picking up discarded fruit to wash and sell. We had not been there long when I saw at firsthand the misery that violence can bring.

*

BOXING DAY, 1953, and a big celebration. My aunt Teresa had married Arthur Till that day and my *jeal* gathered for the reception at the Three Horseshoes hotel in Exhall, Coventry. By early evening the party was in full swing. There was drinking and laughter and singing and dancing. Christmas decorations hung down from the ceiling and a big fir tree stood in one corner, festooned with tinsel. I ran around with our Sam and the other children, like little wild things. Some of the younger men and women were looking forward to going on later to a dance at Bedworth.

At around 9pm, a hard-looking stranger came into the bar. His name was Sid Roper. He was a travelling fairground operator and a notorious brawler, one of the hardest showmen in the country; he once tried to hit a man at a fair, missed and splintered the jamb of a wooden swing. Showmen and gypsies generally don't mix but this was Roper's home

31

turf and I suppose he thought he could go wherever he wanted. He was drunk and dangerous.

He sat down near my cousin Kathleen and put his bottle of Guinness on the floor. Kathleen pulled her chair away because she didn't like the look of him and the bottle spilled. Whether this was the cause of what happened next, I will never know. Roper got up and walked towards my uncle Jimmy Wilson, who was dancing with his arms around my mother while the band played *The Tennessee Waltz*. Jimmy was a lovely man who wouldn't hurt a fly, but without warning Roper punched him full in the face. Uncle Jimmy spun like a top across the floor. He put out his hands out to break his fall but missed and his head hit a table. Glass broke. Some women screamed and one knocked me over as she ran from the room.

Some men lifted Uncle Jimmy into a chair and put a handkerchief on his bleeding forehead. 'What did you do that for, Sid?' one shouted.

There was confusion. Roper grabbed hold of the groom's tie and was almost throttling him. One of my cousins shouted, 'Do something, Caley.'

Caley Botton was courting my cousin Kathleen. He was only twenty-one years old but built like a barn door – six foot and sixteen stone. A few months earlier he had challenged out Coventry Pot Fair but no-one would take him on. I watched, nine years old, as Caley and Roper started fighting. They struggled on the small stage and sent the drum kits flying. Caley got his right arm free, drew back and hit Roper with a ferocious punch. The showman's head banged against the wall and he crumpled in a heap, blood spattering over the turquoise dress of one of the bridesmaids. Caley went to stick a few more blows on him but was pulled back.

They dragged Roper out by the scruff of his neck. Meanwhile my uncle was still unconscious. The police and an ambulance arrived and took Roper to the cells and my uncle to hospital. The party broke up, because no-one had the stomach for it after that. But even worse was to come:

later that night, the news came back that Uncle Jimmy was dead. He had never regained consciousness. Jimmy was one of seven brothers and there was a terrible scene, with awful wailing and crying from the women.

Two days later, Roper appeared in court. One of his eyes was closed and the other was puffy with bruises where Caley had hit him. A detective superintendent told the magistrate that he should be remanded in custody for his own safety. 'But for the arrival of the police, and his arrest, Roper would possibly have been more seriously injured,' he said. 'There is a great deal of feeling between the parties.'

My breed wanted to tear him apart. He was kept in custody and the case was heard at Warwick Assizes. Roper initially pleaded not guilty but after hearing some of the evidence, admitted manslaughter. A Home Office pathologist said my uncle died from 'cerebral compression and cerebral laceration consistent with having come in contact with the ground.' He also said Jimmy's skull was thinner than normal.

Then came the sentencing. 'In some ways this was an accident,' said Mr Justice Finnemore. 'It probably never entered your head that when you struck this man, you were going to injure him seriously.' He fined Roper £30.

There was uproar. All of my aunts and uncles were shouting at once.

'Thirty pounds for a man's life?'

'It's like Judas betraying the Lord for thirty pieces of silver.'

'He murdered him.'

'We'll get you, Roper.'

Even Roper didn't feel justice had been done: he later said he wished he had got three months in prison. The police had to help clear the court and the protests continued in the street outside.

A tragedy like that in a close-knit family is devastating. Three months after Jimmy's death, one of his brothers, Johnny, was taken into hospital and stayed there for months before dying of a broken heart, though they said it was septicaemia. Uncle Henry became very ill, had to go for psychiatric treatment and eventually had a lobotomy.

Roper himself did not long avoid true justice. In October 1954, having served his sentence, he was leaving a show at Nottingham Goose Fair when he had a seizure in the cab of his truck. They took him to hospital and found he had an inoperable brain tumour. It was a pity for Roper: he never meant to kill my uncle.

We have always believed that it was Caley's punch that damaged Roper's brain and caused his death. He was some man, Caley Botton, one of the best fighters of his generation, and became part of the family when he married my cousin. He had a fighting pedigree: one of his forebears was Caleb Wenman, the man who lost his arm fighting Bartley Gorman I, while his grandfather, Old Freddie Botton, could kill you with a walking stick. Caley made his name when he fought Willy Biddle, from Leamington Spa, who claimed to be the best man among travellers in the Fifties. They fought on the fairground at Coventry and were arrested. They were put in the same jail cell and began arguing again. 'I beat you once, Willie, and I will beat you again,' said Caley, but Biddle declined, even paying Caley's £5 fine for him, and they forgot about it.

After that, Caley got up at Bedworth Fair and announced, 'I'll fight any traveller in the country.' No one accepted, so instead they arranged for him to fight Frankie Raven, a leading boxer known as the 'Coventry Wonder', in a ring at the booth over six three-minute rounds. Caley was out of shape for the ring and in the first round Raven broke his nose. Blood went everywhere. In the fourth, Raven knocked him out of the ring; my dad pushed him back in. But Caley stuck it out for the full eighteen minutes. He was tough. 'I couldn't hit him. He was too clever for me,' said Caley afterwards. It was a lesson for me: fighting is not just about strength and power.

*

I WAS NINE when I first went to school. My father and mother couldn't read but decided Sam and I needed to learn. We were sent to Saint Francis of Assisi School, a red-brick, slate-roof primary with a small tarmac playground in Bedworth. They put me just one class up from the youngest ones, so I was older than everyone else in my form. Even so, my knees were knocking under the table. I was an alien, like someone from the wild suddenly introduced to civilisation.

At playtime I would stay in the shadows of the stone porches that faced the schoolyard, watching the other children, too shy to step out. Eventually a little kid said, 'Come on, Barty,' and I ventured out. My father had bought me marbles so I could play with the other kids and make friends. He was kindhearted, even though he beat me so. We had a hole in the dirt that we played around and you had to get the glass marbles near the hole. I won the game when this lad called Joe Friel kicked all the marbles away and said he had won. He pulled me by the hair. I started fighting and thrashed him, even though he was one of the bullies of the school. From that day on, I was fighting every day.

I often fought boys bigger than me. I once tussled for a mile all the way back from school with a tall lad called Peter Hayward. I would tell these lads I could beat them before we had a fight, and I really believed it – I had been raised to believe I was an invincible Gorman. I was also a teacher's pet, however. A teacher called Miss Mornian had a lovely redheaded son who tragically died in a road accident. I was the only other redhead in the school, and every time I sat in the class I knew she was looking at me. I'm sure she gave me special affection because I reminded her of her son.

That school was the only place I ever learned anything. I had a good brain and soon picked up the basics of reading; you teach yourself afterwards. But my attendance record was dreadful and I am still a poor speller. The first book I ever read was the Bible. My mother brought a little blue one for six shillings and sixpence from a Catholic church. It was all 'thous' and 'thees' but I read that Bible every night, often to my parents. It was the only book I had but also the only one I was interested in. I wanted to know where man came from. I didn't believe in God because my parents told me to; I wanted to find out for myself. Like other kids of the time, I also used to devour the *Eagle*, *Beano* and *Dandy* comics.

Later I would read *The Ring Record Book* for hours, with the records of all the old boxers. Sam and I had boxing gloves from when we were small and had been brought up around fighters. My dad took me to the gym at Bedworth Labour Club. I was only nine, and shy at first, but eventually I was banging away at the bags and shadow-boxing. Even though I still had not fully recovered from my illness of two years earlier, I started competing as a schoolboy amateur and probably had around twenty fights. Sometimes we were trained by Les Allen, a top-ranked pro middleweight who beat several champions. My father knew Allen and also Randolph Turpin, the world middleweight champion from nearby Leamington Spa. I can remember seeing Turpin when I was a lad, out doing his roadwork.

My father never mellowed. He was the most serious of men, and very moral. 'You can always tell a trollop because she throws her hair back,' he used to say. 'And you can tell a whoremaster because he cleans his shoes on the back of his trousers.' He used to make me spar with the big lads to toughen me up when I was ten and they were fifteen. I would cry because they were hurting me so much – crying as I was fighting – but I would never give in. I had been brought up with this thing that I could not be beaten.

Dad still hit me nearly every day. I was the boldest bastard in skin and hair and used to say, 'Give me more.' One day when I was eleven, and he had beaten me, I sat on the bed and began to cry. My spirit was broken. Dad came and hugged me. Nobody has loved their father more, because he was also the kindest man in the world; he spoilt me and beat me at the same time. But those childhood scars never leave you.

I boxed for my secondary school, Nicholas Chamberlaine, but never learned a thing there. There was the usual name-calling from some of the older boys – 'gyppo' and all that – but I soon earned a reputation as a boy who could look after himself. Our Sam got in a fight one day with this lad Gerald Barker and was losing so I climbed onto the dustbins, dived on top of Barker and knocked him out. They took him away and I was ever so worried. I got the cane quite a few times and I was also hit with a plimsoll once by the games master for failing to bring in some football boots; we couldn't afford them.

When I was twelve, another brother arrived. Our John was born at the hospital in Nuneaton and I carried him out, wrapped in a shawl, in my arms. My mum was forty-five and some of her family actually turned against her for having a child so late in life; they thought it was a bad thing. Outside school we spent hours playing on the bombsites all round Coventry. I also set up a little stall outside Warner's Yard selling newts and lizards we had caught. With the money, I bought my first gamecock for five shillings. They were happy times. The old photograph men used to come round and take our pictures and I was always pulling faces and poking out my tongue. My dad would look at the pictures, costing twenty-five shillings, and say, 'Look at him, Katy. Look at the money I've wasted on this.' And he'd rip up the pictures.

My school report from 1957, when I was thirteen, recorded that I was late 'almost every day'. The headmaster's comment said I had 'a dreadful record for punctuality' and my form master noted, 'Has at least tried hard this term but has had little or no success.' I did get an 'A' for art – and I wasn't the worst in the class!

If I had started school earlier and applied myself, who knows how my life would have turned out? I love to read now and to watch documentaries on television. I have a good knowledge of current affairs and can hold my own in any conversation. But there is no doubt that my education was lacking and you do miss out on a lot. Perhaps I would have caught up with the other children at school and become an artist or even a preacher. Perhaps I would have become a professional boxer, even a champion. But I left school at thirteen and never went back. Gypsies grow up quickly. From now on I was a man and would act as such. My path was set.

CHAPTER 3

Coming of Age

WE FACED EACH other with shirts off and fists cocked, like the men we had seen in the camps, like the fabled pugilists of old. Our fists were clenched tight, the knuckles white with tension, our faces set and serious. Around us was a broken circle of travelling men. One or two urged us on. We moved closer. I felt no nerves, no fear: I was born for this. Bare fists hit bare flesh. It was my first organised bareknuckle fight. I was twelve years old.

My opponent, Pete Taylor, was about my age. Our dads had agreed to let us fight in a field at Polesworth in the West Midlands and a few men gathered round to watch: a fight always draws a crowd, no matter what the age of the participants. We flailed away at each other for twenty minutes until they declared it a draw. My reward was a slap on the back from my dad.

Within months I had fought several more lads: John Green, Freddie Turnbull, a little Geordie tough nut whose father Billy had once fought the great Johnny Winters, and Harry 'Tightskin' Smith, whom I boxed with gloves on the common at Muckley Corner, a roundabout on the A5 near Lichfield. My dad organised that. Smith hurt me – he was about sixteen and I was only thirteen – but they didn't let it come to a conclusion. His brother Ernie did say, 'Bartley's a proper minute man,' meaning a boxer.

Most I organised myself, because of my grandfather and

the name of my breed. I was Bartholomew Gorman, heir to the traditions of Boxing Bartley and Bulldog Bartley. Peter Lee, the same age as me but a bit heavier, was a descendant of Wiggy Lee, a great old-timer who had lost to my grandfather, and Peter and I re-enacted their earlier battle when we fought at Llangefni in North Wales. A small posse of young lads watched us.

'Show him what old Bartley Gorman can do,' shouted my cousin Kevin.

'Show him what old Wiggy Lee can do,' shouted Peter's brother John.

My dad had taken me out of school. I suppose he thought it was time for me to earn my keep; he had started barnpainting and needed us to help. We went back on the road, travelling a lot, mainly to East Anglia to paint agricultural buildings. We would sit in the back of the van on the paint tins – me, Sam and my cousins Clarence and Kevin – while my dad or my Uncle Bartley drove us around farming areas looking for work. We had a pedal-operated pump and a 100-foot hose to spray the paint. It was hellish work for children. We used tar on some of the roofs and in the hot summers, with my fair complexion, it would burn the skin off me. I was paid five shillings a day while the older boys got more. We painted Dutch barns, aircraft hangars, abattoirs, cattle markets, you name it. It was so lonely painting remote buildings: sometimes we didn't see another person for days. My dad would give us a pound of cheese and a loaf of bread for the whole day and if we didn't eat that, we starved. We never took anything we shouldn't have. 'If you lift so much as a nail or a screw, I'll kill you,' my dad would warn.

In my mid-teens we were working in Wales and answered my father back. He came up and put a dent in my head with a drain rod. I staggered in a daze – though I didn't go down – and some farmhands carried me into a milk parlour, smothered in blood. We had to leave the job because I was in such a state. At the hospital they wanted to put six stitches in my head but my father wouldn't allow it because he didn't want anyone to say that Samuel Gorman had given his son stitches. They bandaged me up instead and my dad was so sorry afterwards that he gave me a diamond ring and let me drive the van back, the big Bedford with bumblebee windows. When my Uncle Bartley saw what he had done, it took ten men to hold him off my dad.

Our base was a disused quarry on the edge of Welshpool, a small town in mid-Wales. We stopped our trailers under the face of the quarry, which rose in a sheer rock wall. A steam train ran by into the town to the market to fetch cattle and sheep and pigs. It was a sheltered spot and would be our home for several years. We had television and electricity and my mother would cook with a calor gas oven. In summer we sometimes had a fire outside and we would sit around listening to tales of Ireland, of leprechauns and how you could never catch them, of the crying banshee, the old songs and the old places. Travellers are terrible people for seeing ghosts, and the Irish are the worst of all. To them, Ireland was an enchanted land where inexplicable things were commonplace.

They often told the story of my great-grandfather sitting by the *gleads* (embers) of a campfire at a crossroads in Ireland when everyone was abed, and how a woman in white appeared. He bade her goodnight but she glided past silently. A few minutes later, she returned. My great-grandfather kept two bull terriers in a box under the wagon and he let them out. The woman, he said, turned into a goose in the lane and pecked the dogs' eyes out. My great-grandfather ran into the wagon and the yelping dogs bolted and were never seen again. The next morning they found feathers all around the lane.

These stories might seem absurd to house-dwellers but, believe me, you see strange things when you camp in isolated fields and travel down deserted lanes and bridleways. We would huddle around the flames to listen and then would have to go back to our beds, trembling.

I made my first trip to Ireland on a cattle boat with my father when I was fourteen. As we came in and could see the lights of Dublin, a man was singing *I'll Take You Home Again, Kathleen*. I felt I was returning to my homeland. It struck me how poor Ireland was; there were few cars, just bikes. And I remember giant policemen walking in pairs. When I returned years later, the policemen were smaller and there were no bikes but plenty of motor vehicles.

On Sundays, after Mass, our friends the Evanses would come over with a wind-up gramophone and there would be singing and tap dancing. We also had our own sports. One was standing jumps with half-bricks in your hands, which you would swing to gain extra momentum. Some could cover over thirty feet in three jumps. Sometimes you had to clear a canal lock from a standing start, again with the bricks in your hands. We also had our version of the high-jump, which was to try to vault a five-bar gate. Occasionally you even came across a seven-bar gate, though that was real Olympic standard. My dad was very keen on 'flapping': you make a track in a field, tie a rabbit skin to a thin rope and reel it in on an upturned bicycle wheel while the dogs race to get it first. We coursed hares and rabbits, poached and fished. I was in the rivers all the time; I knew every inch of the Severn.

Some of the men liked to fight gamecocks. Though I did it too, I think now it is terribly cruel. They would cut off the legs of the cocks to see if they tried to walk again – they called it 'treading the ends' – and if they did it proved they were brave enough to mate. I learned the names of all of the different breeds and types: American Fliers, Old English Game, Black Red, Silver Duckwing, Lemon Pile, Ginger, Wheaton, Indian Asieal, Japanese Sharma. The Black Reds were the best of all, I'd say; like a fowl version of a bull terrier.

Our biggest thing was to go to the pictures: they had a singalong with the words on the screen before the main event, which we always enjoyed. Our family bonds were very close; sometimes too close. Our parents could be very possessive, even with the young men, and by now we wanted to spread our wings. We were into the fashions of the day, with quiff haircuts, pencil ties, drainpipe trousers and winkle-picker shoes.

We were also very interested in fighting and listened rapt to stories of the great knuckle men. My Uncle Bartley, who lived with us, was a top man with very quick hands. I have a very rare photo of him squaring off against Joe Lock in Lancashire, one of the few pictures of an old-time gypsy fight still in existence. Uncle Bartley won after a close contest. He had a hard life; he'd once been up in court for desertion after he'd left his wife and family to try to make some money. He told the court that he could not live without his child, and the chairman of magistrates said, 'Then you had better go back and make love to your wife,' which must be the first time in history two people have ever been ordered by a court to do so! His wife, Ivory, died when she was thirty-eight and left him with eleven children. He had called from a phone box to see how she was and fainted inside it when they told him she had died.

He, my dad and others passed on the stories of fighters around the fireside, as man has done since ancient times. They talked of men like Benny Marshall, one of the forgotten greats. He was born in 1906 in Monmouthshire, and won the British ABA welterweight title in 1926, before turning pro. He was a magical stylist who often boxed with his hands down by his sides, defying his opponents to hit him. As a professional he went unbeaten for several years, but was so good that the leading British boxers avoided him. In disgust, he sailed for Australia to fight one of the greatest Aussie boxers of all time, Jack Carroll, the number one contender for the world welterweight title. Benny was stopped in the tenth round with a badly cut eye, his first defeat. He won his next fight but was then badly knocked out in two rounds by a very good middleweight, Jack Haines. He returned to England, won a few more fights, then disappeared off the scene, travelling around the world. Even in his old age, Benny could walk on his hands for a quarter of a mile. He also fought with bare fists, though he wouldn't tackle my grandfather because he was too heavy for him.

There are many forgotten gypsy fighters of the Twenties and Thirties and one of my reasons for writing this book was to record their names before they are lost. One of my uncles says the best was a heavyweight called Jimmy O'Neill, from Lancashire, but I have been unable to find out anything about him, except that he was known as the 'Bolton Thunderbolt' and packed in boxing to go hawking. Strong John Small, the champion of Cornwall, Devon and Somerset, would always challenge his opponents at 6am, not a minute before or after, and was never beaten. Chris Royals, from Worcestershire, would walk into a field of pea-pickers and challenge them all; he had a poster at the end of his lane saying, 'All challengers welcome'.

Reilly 'Jumbo' Smith was a heavyweight boxer who some said was the best man of his day. 'I'd fight Carnera,' he used to say, referring to Primo Carnera, the giant world champion. But his favourite saying was, 'Two men meet before two mountains', meaning mountains will never fight because they are immobile, whereas men will. Smith was one of sixteen children. He did his roadwork in old army boots, running behind a horse and cart, and kept two bears that he wrestled.

Reilly beat Edwin Nunn and La-la-loo Lee, among others. His most famous fights were against Charlie Bacon, a young bull who beat Smith at Cambridge Fair in the late Thirties after a family dispute. Smith's brother, Ben, picked him up with tears in his eyes, but Reilly said, 'Don't cry over me. Next time we meet I will beat this man.'

They fought again in a field at Six Hills, near Melton Mowbray, Leicestershire. Old Bill Elliott, Reilly's uncle and one of the great fighters of my grandfather's day, was there shouting, 'Shera him, shera him', which means hit him in the head. The fight was stopped early when Smith ripped open Bacon's left eye with a right hook. Over 100 travellers had gathered to watch it and Reilly apologised for the quick finish, saying, 'Sorry, gentlemen, that the entertainment didn't last longer.'

Johnny Winters was a six-foot-three, rawboned man from the Nottinghamshire area who looked like a tougher version of Jack Palance. Many were scared of him. He never moved off the spot when he fought. Winters had two classic contests with 'Whiteface' Tommy Allen, a clever, scientific fighter from the same area. My grandad used to point out Allen and say, 'See him? He's going to the 'formatory [reformatory]', because Allen was always in trouble. And he did.

Allen was stopping on a site at Walsall and Winters's mother was there. They were queuing to get water from a tap when the old lady left her can for a minute. When she returned, Allen had moved her can and filled his own first and Mrs Winters was upset. A few words were exchanged.

'There is no good you talking to me,' said the old woman angrily. 'I've got a son can talk to you.'

'Fetch your son then,' said Allen.

Two days later, Allen was lying on his bed in a wagon when a man came to the door.

'Are you in there?' came the shout.

'What can I do for you?' said Allen.

'I'm Johnny Winters.'

'Oh aye.'

'I hear you were cheeky to the old woman the other day.'

'Yes, but she was a bit cheeky to me.'

'Well, I have come here to settle it. You don't talk to my mother, you talk to me.'

'It will be a pleasure.'

Allen was slim, about twelve stone, while Winters was fifteen stone, but Allen was confident he could beat anyone. They fought for fifteen minutes and for the first ten Allen cut Winters to ribbons. Then Winters found his weak spot. Allen had ulcers and when Winters hit him in the stomach, he started to fetch up blood. So Winters hit him in the belly again and again and they had to stop it. They met at Doncaster some time later and fought again. This time Allen hit Winters over the towbar of a trailer and cut him terribly but Winters beat him again the same way.

Sam Ward and Jim Crow were two unbeaten fighters from Darlington. Ward was wiry but hit like a mule: it was said he could break a bone wherever he hit you and his arms were

so long they nearly touched his knees. He never looked for a
fight but never reneged on one either and his sister could
fight too. Sam was fighting at a fair in 1940 when a man
crept up behind him with a shovel. His sister sparked the
man out in front of 300 witnesses. Crow was more stocky
but tough as leather: he beat a man called Jack Smith while
suffering from pneumonia. Another extraordinary, unbeaten
fighter was Little Adam Lee from Blackpool. He was fifteen
stone but only 5ft 3in, and would grab men by the waistcoat,
plant his feet on their thighs, pull himself up and nut them.

It was men like this I was raised to admire. They took
pride in themselves and the way they dressed. They stood
tall. My father used to hit me in the back many a time to
make me stand straight. Johnny Winters dressed in fifty-
bob suits, blue serge, with the seam on the outside of the
thigh loose by one inch. They had six rows of stitching
around the turn-up, patch pockets each with two pleats and
a buttoned flap, and three rows of stitching around the
lapel. The back of the jacket had a belt and two big seams.
They'd put on a grey smock when they were hauling the oil
cloth and carpets.

My uncle Ticker, also known as Tiger Gorman, was 6ft
1in and 15st and usually sported a velour hat with a twelve-
inch brim, a Crombie coat down almost to the floor and
black-and-white two-tone brogues. I believe he was the best
knuckle man of his day. He also had over 200 fights as a
boxer in the fairground booths, was never on the canvas and
once floored the future world light-heavyweight champion
Freddie Mills. The booths were then an integral part of
travelling fairs and were one way for a gutsy man to make
money in hard times. They had elaborately painted wooden
fronts and the boxers would line up while a barker challenged
men in the crowd to fight them. If you lasted say, six rounds,
you might earn £1. Many would have a go but the booth
boxers knew their stuff. If there were no takers they would
have to box each other to entertain the crowd.

Uncle Ticker once fought a booth veteran called Sam
McVey, the 'Coloured Wonder', for twelve rounds at

Nottingham Goose Fair. Ticker had been on his uppers and hadn't eaten a thing for a couple of days. At the end of the contest he shouted out, 'Feed me and I will knock him out in two rounds.' Ticker was a demon with bare fists. In his old age, he took on a fighter called Jimmy Brazil who had hit Ticker's son with a jack handle and put twenty stitches in his head. Ticker went up to sort it out and Brazil hit him in the ribs with a jackhammer. Ticker took it, said, 'Is that the best you can do?' and slaughtered him.

These were the best men in England and there were good fighters close by in Wales too. Johnny Price, a scrap dealer from Newtown and my dad's friend, was only twenty-eight when he was kicked to death by two men after a prize-fight. Black Bob Evans was another we knew well. He rarely removed his topcoat and would dig his heels in the ground in hobnail boots so they couldn't knock him back. Any one of these men would be worth a book in their own right.

My grandfather could fight until his dying day. In his old age Bulldog Bartley used to stop at Minera mountain near Wrexham. He went to the pub one night when he was sixty-five and in there was a local bully called Bill Johnston who worked in a foundry. He spotted my grandfather sitting quietly in a corner.

'You're going to buy me a drink, gypsy.'

'No I'm not,' said my grandfather.

'You are going to buy a drink or I will put you out on your ear.'

My grandfather went to the toilet and Johnston followed him. 'You're going to buy me a drink when you go back into the bar,' he said.

As Johnston turned to walk back, my grandfather hit him on the sly and knocked him flat out. He then went back through the pub, picked up his coat and left. When he got further down the road he realised he had picked up Johnston's coat by mistake and there was £3 in it. He went back to the same pub a few days later to return the jacket and they welcomed him like a hero. Johnston was never seen in there again.

Yet my grandad said that if he had his life over again he would never raise his fists. He used to sit for hours by the fire, trying to straighten his broken nose. 'That's how you're going to end up,' my dad would tell me. Bulldog Bartley died in 1955 in a Standmore trailer at Muckley Corner, near Lichfield, and was buried at Wrexham beside his mother.

The tales we heard of these men filled us with youthful enthusiasm. My wiry body was filling out, Sam was also shooting up, and we loved to spar with our battered old boxing gloves or engage in trials of strength like picking up telegraph poles. We used to speculate on what we wanted to be. Many said 'Elvis Presley' but I always said I wanted to be the best barefist fighter in the world.

*

WHEN I WAS sixteen we went hare-coursing on Cerrigydrudion mountain near Llanrwst, by the Snowdonia National Park in North Wales. I had a little Ford van, driving with learner plates in my winkle-picker shoes. A crowd of us went, dogs and all, in the van and a pick-up truck, and we met our cousins the Bryans, including Owen Bryan, said to be the best fighter in North Wales at the time.

As I have said, coursing was, and is, a popular pursuit among travellers, as this newspaper report describes:

Illegal coursing starts once the corn is off the fields in September. It usually takes place at dawn or dusk, although if the group is big enough it can happen in broad daylight with impunity. The flat lands of East Anglia provide perfect venues for opportunist gatherings. If the coast is clear they simply open a farm gate, drive in and let the dogs out.

The dogs will be large lurchers, usually greyhounds crossed with salukis. Owners decide between them whether they want to run their dogs 'single-handed' – one dog slipped alone on one hare – or 'double-handed', with two dogs. Sometimes bets are struck on how long it will take one dog to kill, say, five hares. Coursers walk the fields and slip the dog as soon as a hare breaks cover.

Let me say it takes a very good dog to kill a hare alone. Anyway, there must have been fifty of us at the mountain. After a lot of coursing and killing, Owen Bryan said to my dad, 'I will race you for four pounds.'

It was a ridiculous thing to say. Owen was sitting on the back of an old 'bouncer' lorry with the tailboard down.

My dad said, 'Fifty pound, never mind four pound.'

'Don't talk like a c**t,' said Owen.

'Who's a c**t?' said dad.

The answer was a smash straight in the mouth from Owen, the best man in North Wales. My dad was forty-three, Owen about thirty. At it they go. Neither took their shirts off, they just fought straight off. We were all dumbstruck.

Another cousin, Big Tony, put up his hand. 'Hang on Owen. He's an old man to you. I'll fight you.'

Tony wasn't a fighting man but he loved my dad. The minute he said it, another of the Bryans stepped in and said, 'No you won't. I'll fight you.'

So now there were two bareknuckle fights on this wild Welsh mountain and we were all shouting at the tops of our voices for one fighter or another. The farmers heard the commotion and came from different farms. They thought there was a riot on their land. They broke it up and we all headed back home amid bad feeling and muttered threats.

One of the Bryans had left his vehicle at our site and came back for it. My dad was waiting with no shirt on.

'Where's Owen?' he asked.

No sooner had he said that than in walked Owen, stripped off with his hands taped up, ready to fight. My dad knocked him down with the first punch. Owen got up and they went at it. It was a terrible fight; women were watching it from the trailers with their hands over their mouths in horror. Someone wrapped a dog lead round my dad's neck and I went to step in, at sixteen. Owen's brother, Dave, who was twelve years older than me, put his hand out to stop me, saying, 'Hang on.'

I destroyed him with a volley of punches.

My cousin Caroline Stevens, who was just fourteen, came out with a shotgun and stopped the fighting. No-one had really noticed what I had done to Dave, as they had all been watching my dad and Owen. As the men stood back, panting for breath, I stepped forward.

'I'll fight you,' I challenged Owen.

He looked at me with contempt. 'No,' he said, 'my brother will fight you.'

'I've just beat him.'

I saw disbelief in Owen's eyes. He looked around and saw his brother, battered. The disbelief turned to shock. Still, he refused my challenge.

'I'll wait till you grow up, old lad.'

'Never mind when I grow up. I'll fight you now.'

I was ready and I believed I could beat him. I will always regret that I hadn't stopped my father and fought Owen myself.

It wasn't over yet. Big Tony resumed his earlier fight but lost when his opponent put pennies between his fingers and cut him up. They weren't friends again for years afterwards, though now it is all forgotten. I'll say this for Owen: he was a very good fighter and afraid of no-one.

That incident made my mind up. We erected a gym in a shed and I started to train every day. I was going to be gypsy champion. The others didn't believe me but I knew I had something different, a power that others did not possess. It would take another incident to make them realise.

*

IN THE MIDDLE of Welshpool is a clock tower and across the road is a public house. One night we were standing under the tower, talking, when some men came out of the pub. They were Welsh farmers and most of them were in their forties. I was with John Stevens and Clarence Gorman, my cousins, both a few years older than me but neither of them fighters. I was sixteen, in my red jeans.

These Welshmen came around us; they fancied pushing around the gypsy lads. One of them, a notorious man called Tanner, started picking on Clarence. Another one singled me out.

'Are you eyeing my mate up?'

'No, I'm not eyeing anybody up,' I replied.

'You were.'

'What would you do if I was?'

He pushed me. I pushed him back. He fumbled for something in his pocket and I saw a glint of metal. *He's got a knife*, I thought.

Without pausing, I hit him with a single right hand shot so fast it was a blur. He flew backwards and his head hit the concrete. He was unconscious. His knife clattered on the pavement. His nose was almost cut in two between the nostrils and his mouth. One of his legs twitched. Nobody else moved a muscle. They were all in shock.

'Anybody else want any?' I asked.

Johnny Stevens, his eyes wide with wonder, stage-whispered to me in Cant, 'Let's go, we are going to get it.'

We walked back to the camp. The others were worried about comebacks, so we made a big fire in the quarry and waited all night for the gang to come and fight us. Nothing happened. I went back into town not long afterwards and I didn't get any more trouble.

My days of taking beatings from my father were also coming to an end. I couldn't love anybody more than my dad but as I got older we had terrible rows. One day he came to hit me with a stick and I took it off him, broke it and said, 'Never touch me again.' And he didn't. A few days later, I was having a boxing spar with him in the quarry and I opened up on him. He was overwhelmed. My aunt stopped it and said, 'You ought to have better sense.' I regretted it afterwards, but I had crossed a threshold.

You cannot thwart destiny. Around this time I went down to the cinema and saw a newsreel of this handsome, articulate, brash young man called Cassius Clay. He had won a gold medal at the 1960 Olympics and was standing at the top of the Empire State Building in New York, telling anyone who would listen that he was going to be the champion of the world. He was really something.

I wanted to fight him. I also wanted to do in the prize-ring what he intended to do in boxing. Ahead of Clay lay the world champion, Sonny Liston, one of the most frightening men in the history of the ring. And in my way was a champion every bit as daunting: the man they called 'Big Just'.

CHAPTER 4

Big Just

URIAH BURTON STOOD five feet ten inches tall and weighed seventeen stone. He had blond, wavy hair swept back into a pony tail, high cheekbones and a broad, open face, and wore the garb of a true travelling man: red shirt, yellow corduroy trousers and a red handkerchief around his neck. His manner was intimidating: he would talk with his face right up to yours, looking you square in the eye, smiling as he talked and giving the impression he was laughing at you. A true Romany, he believed he was a descendant of a lost tribe that Moses led over the Land of Nod. He was what we call the *root* of a gypsy.

When I was sixteen, I admired only two fighters: Rocky Marciano and Uriah Burton. Everyone had heard of Marciano, the world heavyweight champion who never took a backward step and never lost a fight. But Burton was known only in the secretive world of the travellers, a name uttered in hushed tones. He was an ogre, they said. He had the strength of five men. He beat opponents two at a time. He would stop at nothing and fight to the death. He sounded like something from the Dark Ages, more myth than man. Only when I came to know him did I realise the stories were true.

Uriah, or 'Hughie' as he was known, reigned as King of the Gypsies through the late 1950s to the early 1970s. He would claim to have been born in Liverpool in 1916, though in fact it was at least ten years later, and his grandmother Ashala was a Romany leader. He spent most of his childhood in the Irish Free State and his family, like mine, travelled in horse-drawn painted trailers, selling wicker baskets and repairing pots and pans. His mother was a brush-wagon woman.

Hughie was no stranger to trouble. One on occasion he was travelling in Ireland with his older brother Hosiah, known as 'Oathy', who was taller and leaner and a monumental fighter in his own right. They had stopped in a field for a cup of tea when the farmer appeared and told them to move. Oathy refused and started battling with the farmer and his son. The son gave an 'Irish howl' which brought men running across the fields from a nearby village. As Oathy fought desperately to fend them off, one of the villagers held up his hand.

'Steady on,' he shouted. 'One dog, one bone.'

The mob stood back, allowed Oathy to settle matters man-to-man with the farmer, and the brothers moved on relatively unscathed. Hughie always remembered the incident as an example of honour in a fair fight.

As he grew older, his family moved to a council site in Belfast. Hughie liked to box the local youngsters, Catholic and Protestant alike, and in later years would try to use his influence to bring peace to the two communities. As a fighter he remained in Oathy's shadow until the family returned to England, where his reputation took off. He would later describe how it happened in a small, privately published book, *Big Just: His Life, His Aims, His Ideals*, copies of which are prized among travellers.

When I came to England I felt a great change in my own people. I carried on my Romany life, going to horse fairs and race meetings, where all types of tinkers and gypsies would gather, but there was no rest from the continual drunks and bullies and fights would start. In order to make peace, I decided I would establish myself as a stronger man in order to become the best knuckle-fighter in Britain.

He put out a challenge to fight anybody, anywhere, under old prize-ring rules. A contest was arranged against Colin Strauch, a South African heavyweight boxer based in England, for £1,000 a side, to take place at Bolton Greyhound Stadium, but the Press got wind of the story and the authorities banned it.

In September, 1958, Hughie was matched to fight bare-knuckle against the Polynesian boxer Kitione Lave. Lave, known as the 'Tongan Torpedo', is barely remembered now but in the mid-Fifties was a young powerhouse who terrorised the British heavyweight scene, destroying men like Don Cockell. He married a British girl and settled in Doncaster, where he liked to sing Tongan songs in the clubs. He was to fight Burton for £500 a side, winner takes all. Again the plans were thwarted: both men were visited by a police superintendent, bound over to keep the peace and threatened with six months in jail if they breached the order. 'It was stated that Burton had told the police he was a better man than Lave,' *Boxing News* reported. 'Lave explained that he had a wife and child to support, wanted money and must have a fight.'

Finally, in 1959, Burton fought Strauch at a pub in a secluded part of Yorkshire near Barnsley, in a no-rules, no-holds-barred fight to the end. Strauch wore boxing gloves and a sweater while Hughie was stripped to the waist and wore light bag mitts. 'The fight moved from one end of the courtyard to the other,' Hughie wrote. 'We hit each other among the parked cars and on the steps of the pub. Strauch stumbled and I hit him with a left and eventually Strauch collapsed writhing in agony, but I hit him until he was out.' The group of men returned to the bar, where it was decided that Hughie would fight a Doncaster man called Ted Schzek. So, for the second time that night, they trekked out to a nearby field. Schzek leapt at Hughie, who ducked, tripped him, and finished him off with a knee to the face.

It was brutal, but typical of Burton. In combat he was ferocious. He would hit to the groin, punch to the kidneys, bite, gouge, kick, butt and knee. He was proud beyond all reason and refused to be beaten: you would have to kill him first. That same pride extended into all areas of his life. He wouldn't take a cup of tea or a bite to eat off any man, even if he was thirsty and starving. It is a gypsy thing, mind over matter.

The fight which won him recognition as the King of the Gypsies took place at the tiny Scottish border village of St Boswell's, Roxburghshire. Burton's challenge was accepted by 'Big Jim' Nielson, a travelling man from the North who for many years had been acknowledged as a top bareknuckle fighter – some say *the* top man. After one fracas in Skipton, Yorkshire, it took eight policemen to lock Nielson up, and even then they had to call for reinforcements. He was bigger but a fair bit older than Burton, hadn't been active for some time, and drank and smoked – unlike Hughie – but he was still a formidable man.

When they got to the village green, Hughie offered Nielson the chance to back out. Nielson refused. 'I can beat any man,' he retorted. Hughie would later claim he knocked Nielson unconscious in two minutes, but there is much dispute about this: witnesses say he was losing until he bit Nielson's tit off – actually chewed off one of his nipples – and forced him to give best. As I say, he took no prisoners.

Hughie became a living legend. He would set up a tape player at fairs and other gatherings and would hit the bag and skip rope out in the open with the tape belting out: 'I'm Uriah Burton, the best man among gypsies.' He was an awesome sight – like a more powerful version of Charlton Heston – and soon there was a common saying among travellers: 'I'm afraid of no man 'cept Hughie Burton.' He had a strange presence about him, and effectively ran the big gypsy gathering at Doncaster races for many years.

Once, during St Leger race week, an unusually large group of Irish families camped on the site beside the usual hordes of British travellers. Both groups viewed each other with suspicion and that night, after the pubs had chucked out, they shaped up for a mass brawl. Hughie, who never drank, was asleep in his trailer when he was woken by the commotion. Putting on trousers and shoes, he opened the door to see a group of English Romanies armed with golf clubs facing the Irish travellers, who were shirtless and ready to fight. With no fear, Burton stepped between the two sides and asked first the English, then the Irish, to step back and cease. There was a tense stand-off, then both sides backed down, such was his authority and presence. None but the boldest and strongest could have done such a thing.

Despite his reputation, Hughie was a nice man and very moral. He had iron principles and was known as 'Big Just' for his impartiality in sorting out disputes. He was also not above winding people up, and was often in the Press: he became the first bareknuckle fighter for 100 years to issue public challenges through the newspapers.

Perhaps his most famous fight was against Big Tom Roberts, an unbeaten prize-fighter from the south of England, outside the Organ Hotel at Epsom. One man who was there told me, 'Big Tom hit Hughie across the bonnet of a Bedford van but Hughie got up and they got to scuffling. Hughie was an all-in man and ripped half his testicles out and Roberts had to go to hospital.' Roberts had some tough men with him and a mass brawl broke out in which Hughie's brother Oathy was hit in the head with an axe. They weathered the storm with the help of friends from Manchester.

Formidable as Burton was, he had no shortage of rivals: it's the gypsy way. My Uncle Ticker was getting on in years but that didn't stop him walking all the way from the Midlands to Doncaster to challenge Burton. Big Just was in a showman's wagon and Ticker challenged him out at 6am. 'Come on in, my old Ticker, and have a cup of tea,' said Burton. He wouldn't fight him. I'm not saying Ticker would have won but, old as he was, he'd have fought Burton for tuppence. When Ticker died they buried him in his red boxing boots and red dressing gown.

Another great man that Burton never fought was Big Tom Lee, a human ox from Lancashire known as the 'Atom Bomb'. Lee did fight Oathy Burton in an old bomb crater in

Manchester. No-one else witnessed it, so it is uncertain what happened, but Oathy told my father that they fought for an hour until Lee hit him with a brick. The Atom Bomb could pick up half a ton and load it; hit a five-bar gate and split it. Some claim Big Just avoided him. Certainly Lee was a terror. He once went up to my dad at Nottingham Fair, where there were hundreds of gypsy toughs all around. 'You see all these fighters, Sam?' he said. 'Any one of them is just a walk in and a walk out to me.' He meant it; not one of them would have troubled him. The only time I met him was at ringside when Henry Cooper defended his British and Empire heavyweight titles against Johnny Prescott in Birmingham in 1965 and my father introduced me. He was getting on in years but you could tell that he had been a fighter. Years later he was apparently very badly beaten up by a group of men and never recovered.

There were others. Bob Braddock, a notorious travelling man with a face full of scars, twice fought the Atom Bomb and would not have hesitated to challenge Burton. He would later become one of my biggest backers. His first fight with Lee came when they were hop-picking in Worcestershire, and was stopped before reaching a conclusion. They met again at Mansfield auctions and Lee hit Braddock so hard that he knocked him *up* a flight of stairs. Another renowned fighter was Tucker Dunn, the best man in London in his day and king of the hill at Barnet Fair. Tucker would be in his early seventies now but can still look after himself.

Caley Botton, who flattened Sid Roper on the tragic night of my cousin's wedding, was 6ft 1in and 17st, had a granite jaw and used to spar with world champ Randolph Turpin and British heavyweight champ Johnny Williams. His grandfather was prepared to put up £50,000 for him to fight Big Just but it never happened. It would have been some encounter: they were similar in build and strength. Caley did beat another very good man called Wisdom Smith, a multimillionaire from Stratford-upon-Avon. Smith sucker-punched him backwards out of a chair, so Caley got up, put thirty-six stitches in his eye and knocked him spark out. He later emigrated to North America and travelled all over, having about thirty fights and claiming the bareknuckle championship of Canada. He befriended a lot of Scots-American travellers over there, including the Hilton family, which produced some top boxers. They nicknamed him 'Big Chuck'. He is nearly seventy now and still as tough as teak.

You won't find these men in any books. They live on only in oral tradition and family folk memory. To us children gathered around the campfires on a summer evening, they were dragonslayers.

*

MY FIRST ENCOUNTER with Big Just remains burned in my memory. His father had died and, in keeping with Romany tradition, his trailer and belongings were burned in a huge pyre. His father had been born in Wales and Hughie decided to erect a twelve-foot stone obelisk in his memory on the summit of a hill at Middletown. This was only a few miles from the quarry where we lived. Four giant blocks of Devon granite were to be hauled 1,000 feet up the hill, and to do it Big Just press-ganged a large number of men – he literally kidnapped them and forced them into labour. One bricklayer was clapped in handcuffs and taken from Manchester; another was chased into a bank when he tried to escape, with Hughie jumping over the counter to drag the man back to his car. Hughie later wrote:

> I got a bus to take the men, and got their word that if they weren't put in handcuffs they would help. The first weekend I had seventy-five men. Some didn't like it and said they would shoot us down or run us down in the road, they were mad at us because I wasn't worried by their threats, they had been taken along in good faith and I had the responsibility for them. I had to feed them and give them somewhere to sleep. I made my horsebox, a marquee and an articulated caravan into sleeping quarters. I spent good money on food for them, and another large amount on drinks.

It was hard, dangerous work. One of the lorries nearly overturned on a slope with a load of men in it. Hughie and Oathy just laughed. It got so that no-one was prepared to drive the lorry up the slope except Oathy, who was scared of nothing. Some of the men were even whipped; I saw one with a big stripe across his face. Hughie ruled with a rod of iron. 'I'm not a conventional employer,' he said. He did feed them well though; there was roast lamb on a spit.

It was the talk of the area and I went over with my friend Alfie Boswell to have a look. I was eighteen at the time, weighed thirteen stone and was ready to fight anybody: even then, I knew I was going to be the champion. We went to the Bull's Head pub where Hughie would bring the men for refreshment. Alfie and I wandered outside and saw Big Just sitting in the passenger seat of a black Zodiac. You couldn't mistake him for anyone else.

Alfie walked over and leaned at the car window. A lot of young Romany men call their elders 'uncle' even when not related. 'You want to go in the pub there, Uncle Hughie, it's full of women,' said Alfie.

He was just being friendly but it was the wrong thing to say. Burton was obsessive about his morals. He glared at poor Alfie with eyes like lightning. Hughie was wearing a red shirt and he ripped it apart with his hands.

'There's no pox on me. I'm a clean-living man,' he roared.

Here was I, at Alfie's shoulder, facing Big Just square-on, and he had pulled his shirt off in front of me. He was in his prime, perhaps twenty years older than me, but I was not afraid of him. This was what I had been waiting for. I felt the power and adrenalin swelling in my body.

Yet I didn't challenge him out. I don't know why. I wanted to fight him but I bit my lip. Perhaps it was out of respect because Alfie had called him uncle. Anyway, I did nothing and the moment passed. I later watched them put up the monument, which stands there still. Hughie also went up in an aeroplane to put his father's ashes on the mountain. I was impressed. Even though I was after his crown, I admired Big Just. He wasn't some lowlife street brawler: he had ambition and principles and wanted to leave his mark on the world.

I was making my own mark. My little band and I were the terrors of Wales. There was me, Sam, and my cousins Clarence and Kevin, John Stevens and the four Lee brothers, led by Tony, the oldest. We never had much money but we would pile into our little vans and head off to dancehalls. We were just out for a good time but we were always brawling. We had fights down in Tiger Bay in Cardiff in pubs with young lads, and out on the cobbles with blacks and miners. Tony Lee was usually the instigator but I was always the main fighter. Many a time we had to punch our way back to the vans. We also used to drive down to South Wales to fight travellers, but at the fairs people were already starting to avoid Sam and me. From being a skinny kid, Sam had shot up, even past me. We were together all the time but very different in character. He was more placid and wasn't keen on fighting until I got him interested in it. But if you hit Sam it was like giving electricity to a light bulb.

I was learning how to knuckle-fight properly. When I was nineteen I moved my trailer outside The Refresh, a former train station converted into a pub near Blaenau Ffestiniog. The construction firm Balfour Beatty was making a dam for a hydro-electric plant nearby and erecting pylons to carry the power. The Refresh was a very rough pub. Men were always in there playing cards and occasionally a knife would be pulled. I challenged out the building workers there and a big Irishman accepted. We fought near the slate quarries, in front of a crowd of navvies. I had just Sam to see me fair play and didn't even tell my dad about it. I was young and gangly but wiry, a fast light-heavy, while he was about thirty-five, a hairy-chested Irishman with big arms, the best man on the dam. In the clinches I could smell the sweat of him. Nobody knocked anybody down but I hurt him and he hurt me before they broke it up. I later had loads of fights like these, against navvies and road-diggers, so many that I can't remember them all.

From time to time I would hear about Big Just's exploits.

In 1960, the best fighter in Ireland challenged him to a death match. Barney Docherty was 5ft 8in and 15st and had beaten legends like Big James Friel from Donegal and Tom Delaney from County Mayo. He planned to sail to England to fight Burton in what would have been one of the most brutal contests of all time. But never made it. While on the night train from Limerick to Dublin, Docherty died in mysterious circumstances. 'My father had a fight with three soldiers on the train,' Barney's son Simon later told me. 'They found his body outside Thurles. We had to go and identify it. We never got to the bottom of it. Because it was a night train, there was hardly anyone in it and so there were no witnesses. He had a do with these men and, because they were soldiers and he was a travelling man, it was never investigated properly.'

At Motherwell Trots, a meet near Glasgow, Burton was walking through the crowd with his hands in his pockets when a paid strong-arm man named Curry attacked him. Hughie was dazed by several blows to the face but still had the presence of mind to jump back out of range and avoid Curry's follow-up swings, then grab his attacker in a clinch. Seeing the bookmakers gathering round, Hughie shouted, 'I'll take two-to-one that I'll put him away.' When there were no takers, he sank a left into Curry's kidneys and finished him off.

In 1964, Big Just bought a plot of land at Partington, near Manchester, and put twelve trailers on it. He would later extend the site and install drainage and hot and cold running water. It became his private fiefdom, which he ruled with his own version of the law. He would preside over open-air trials of anyone who broke the rules of the camp, dispensing fines or ordering men to do physical exercise or hard labour as punishment. Two pairs of boxing gloves hung permanently from the branch of a tree to settle disputes. A track ran round the camp and sometimes Hughie would order a miscreant to rise at 6am and run several laps. Young lads would be shackled in a shed, where they had to sleep on straw. Their families could bring them food and water but they would have to spend several days in there as punishment.

Hughie was still on the back pages a lot: he once fought two men in a single day and there was a picture of him standing over one of them. He challenged the whole of Europe and was taken up by Donny 'the Bull' Adams, a rag and bone merchant from Staines in Middlesex, who had done time in prison and was a notorious fighter. 'Let the rules blow in the wind,' said Adams. According to Big Just, he drove down to Staines with a friend to seek out Adams and found two men at a racing stables who offered to show the way. Burton put the two men in handcuffs and bundled them into the car to make sure there were no tricks. As they approached the farm where Adams was to be found, they saw what looked like a dangerous reception committee. Hughie accelerated away, taking his two hostages all the way to Birmingham. He later discovered, so he said, that the men waiting for him had been part of a group of thugs who had tried to bushwhack him at Epsom Races. Adams – who was not a gypsy, even though the Press later referred to him as 'King of the Gypsies' – was younger but, though a good man in his own class, you would not expect him to beat a maneater like Burton, the real King. Hughie didn't want to mess with London though; he was a north of England man.

I liked and admired Big Just. He was seen as pretty colourful until I came along; he would go to a line and stop whereas I would go ten miles over the top. He once told the *Daily Mirror*, 'I don't fight rounds because no man, when he starts eating dinner, wants to break off every two minutes and then start eating again. And fighting is like dinner to me.'

In contrast, I still had a yearning to be a professional boxer. My dad had already collared Mickey Duff at a promotion in Wales and told him I was the best young fighter in Britain. In 1963 I wrote a letter to the former champion Bobby Neill, who had become a top trainer, asking if he would take me on and help me get a pro licence. He wrote back, telling me to read his book *Instructions for Young Boxers*, but he didn't take me on.

I decided I could box and fight bareknuckle at the same time; I would use the one to train for the other. I reckoned I could become heavyweight champion in boxing; more importantly, I was sure I could be King of the Gypsies. For twenty years, Big Just had been the man to beat. Now I was ready to take his mantle.

CHAPTER 5

A Band of Gypsies

'YOU PUNCH TOO hard, Bartley,' said old Wogga Wood. 'I'm scared of you killing someone.'

I shrugged and resumed thumping the heavy bag. It swayed and shuddered, its rope creaking against the ceiling hook. Wogga stood back, a water bottle in one hand and a sweaty towel in the other. Two young boxers tip-tapped skip-rope beats on the wooden floor of the gymnasium. Others slid around the roped ring, shadow-boxing. Double doors connected the training area to an adjoining bar, where a line of men stood drinking beer. They would open the doors so the drinkers could watch the crazy, red-headed gypsy fighter.

I pulled a crowd every night. I could hit the light bag so hard it would fly up almost to the horizontal. Sometimes Wogga would hold the heavy bag still and I would drive dents into it with my gloved fists, the sweat running off my brow. My power was natural; I didn't have to develop it.

I became a regular at Wogga's gym when my family left Wales in 1963, the year John F. Kennedy was shot, and settled in Uttoxeter, a racecourse town halfway between Stoke-on-Trent and Derby. There was a plot at the back of a garage just off the town centre and the owner, Joe Phillips, let us pull our trailers on there. Travellers are often ostracised by townspeople but we soon made new friends. The locals could see that my parents were decent. Dad was always in suit, collar and tie and marched us to Mass every Sunday. At meal times everything had to be perfect: we had silver knives and forks and best Crown Derby. Dad wouldn't have anybody in the trailer except family, close friends and special guests. He kept an old-fashioned biscuit barrel full of gold sovereigns. Occasionally he would take the lid off and show us. 'There you are, son,' he'd say. 'I don't need a bank account.' Then he would squeeze the lid back on.

He was still selling carpets and painting barns. I helped but was also branching out on my own, learning to wheel and deal. Travellers are some of the best salesmen you'll ever meet. They know psychology, how to appeal to people's vanity or greed, how to plant a sprat to catch a mackerel.

Even more than dealing, I loved fighting. I had set my heart on boxing, though it almost cost me dear even before we had reached Uttoxeter. We had stopped for a while on a big pit bank near Telford and someone told me about a gym in Wolverhampton. I set off to find it, taking the train to Wolverhampton station and then asking the first group of men I saw where the boxing gym was.

'Why? Don't you know?' said one of these men. He had a Geordie accent and an evil look in his eye; probably a collier come down for the work.

'No, I'm a stranger here,' I said.

'Oh, you're a stranger, are you?'

He pushed me in the chest. The other men came in a circle around me. I looked around for help but the street was dark and virtually deserted. I was only eighteen years old and they were grown men. Yet I felt that strange mix of energy and calm that always settled on me before a fight. Without warning I threw a hard straight left into the face of the first man. As he stumbled, I hit the man next to him with a right cross, then the man on his other side with a left hook. Both of them hit the deck. As the others stood there, unsure of what to do, I turned and walked away – fast. They didn't come after me; I think they were too stunned.

I found the gym in the end but it wasn't really to my liking – the training was a bit soft. I went there a few times but we left the area soon after for Uttoxeter. I went looking for a new gym and soon found Wogga Wood, a former booth boxer who had forgotten more about the fight game than most trainers will ever know. He coached at the Drill Hall in the coalmining town of Rugeley. The room was large and well equipped, though it stank of sweat, stale air and liniment. The Territorial Army were based next door and went through their drills there, doing hand-to-hand combat and bayonet practice. Wogga trained some good fighters: his son Jackie won five National Coal Board championships when that title meant something in the amateur ring. One of the first things he did when I went in was to get Jackie, a light-heavyweight, to try me out but I already knew how to fight and more than held my own.

I loved it. I was soon training every Tuesday, Friday and Sunday, plus doing my roadwork every day at dawn. I liked sparring best of all: getting in there and fighting. I would do three rounds with one boxer, three with another, three with another and three with another: twelve rounds. Most pros wouldn't do that, unless they had a title fight. Wogga took me under his wing and after every training session insisted that I drink two bottles of Guinness to 'build me up'. We would sit in the bar with our glasses of stout in front of us and talk about boxing for hours: hooks, jabs and footwork, great fighters, famous fights. I was entranced. A bomb could have gone off next to us and I wouldn't have noticed.

I would have a dozen or so fights for the boxing club. I did lose the odd bout – one I remember to a man called Denis Briggs – but I learned quickly and still have a 'Best Boxer of the Night' trophy from one tournament. As I got better – and bigger – it became harder to find opponents. One slick stylist I fancied my chances against was a young black man from the Midlands called Fitzroy Johnson. We were matched to box but he refused when I weighed-in five pounds heavier than him. Later he turned pro and, as Bunny Johnson, won the British and Commonwealth heavyweight titles.

My toughest fight came when I was twenty-two. I was due to fight a man at the Metropolitan Club in Small Heath, Birmingham, but he didn't turn up, so they put me in with someone called John Mulroy. Our bout was late on, about midnight, and I was so confident that I fell asleep in the dressing room. Wogga came in and roused me. 'I've just seen your opponent,' he said. 'He's got green velvet boots on.' This Mulroy was an Irishman, had boxed for his country and had a big Birmingham-Irish contingent there to watch him. I had a load of Irish and English travellers there to see me. Suddenly the atmosphere was red hot.

I bounced into the ring like Ali, showboating, moving around, feeling the ropes, hamming it up. 'He's pissed as a newt!' said one ringside spectator. Then I saw Mulroy. He was in his thirties, a fully-fledged man, and looked about six foot three. All of the Irish were going mad, roaring. It was bedlam.

We came out for the first round and I used the ring, swaying and making him miss. He was no mug: I always had a lot of time for amateurs because they were unpaid men, fighting for the love of it, not for money like some performing *jotter* (monkey). He was also a southpaw, which made matters worse. He was long and rangy and started connecting, and I couldn't resist getting drawn into a punch-up. Soon we were at it hammer and tongs. I caught him with some cracking right hands but he took them and hit back. He was one of the hardest punchers I would ever meet, including bareknuckle. He hit me so hard with one left cross that I thought the branch of a tree had fallen on my head. I loved it because it was a rough, unorthodox fight.

By the end of round two we had been through the mincer. I went back to my stool and said to my trainer, 'Just roll them gloves up.' He pulled them right up so my knuckles were tight against the padding. The bell rang for the final round. This was war now.

'Float like a butterfly, sting like a bee,' shouted our Sam at ringside, mimicking Bundini Brown, Muhammad Ali's sidekick.

Someone at ringside took umbrage. 'Black your face before you come here and say that, mate,' he shouted back.

Sam promptly started fighting in the crowd: him and Johnny Stevens against five or six men from Birmingham. A woman hit Johnny on the head with a stiletto heel. There was uproar. I could hear the commotion but couldn't afford to take my eyes off Mulroy. He stepped back and grinned at me and I smiled. They say if a boxer smiles during a fight it is a sign of weakness but I can tell you that is not true: there was nothing weak about Mulroy. He ducked his head into my face. I gave him the shoulder. The ref tried to pull us apart and Mulroy punched me low. I hit him back, right in the foul protector. The ref was yelling. Chairs were flying at ringside. Sam had one man in a headlock and was punching another with his free hand. Someone jumped on the ring apron.

Suddenly there was a loud rending noise and the ring tilted sharply to one side; it had partly collapsed. I'm sure Sam was the cause of it. The referee had had enough. He waved his arms wildly and called the fight off. 'Referee disqualifies both fighters for dirty fighting,' read the back page of the next day's *Birmingham Post*. They reckon we made history.

I stopped taking the gloved game seriously after that, although I would have a few more bouts over the years. I felt baulked by gloves and referees. I used to get butterflies before boxing but never before a bareknuckle fight. I just felt constrained by the rules. In the lanes, you are your own referee. It was also difficult to reconcile the travelling life with the strict training needed to be a good boxer. As I got older and was on the road more and more earning a living, it was impossible to put in the hours at the gym. Occasionally I would stop in an area and if there was an amateur show on I would go along to see if they had an opponent free. They wouldn't ask too many questions about licences and the like if you were a heavyweight; they'd put you on if they could, because the crowds loved to see two heavies. They might call it an exhibition to satisfy the ABA inspector, but it would be a proper fight. I had quite a few contests like that under aliases, particularly around Norfolk, where the money was good for barn painting. It was all corn there – you wouldn't see a cow or sheep.

*

I NEVER DARED tell Wogga that I was using his boxing training to prepare me for bareknuckle fights – he would have gone mad. But by this time my reputation as a barefist fighter was spreading and young men were coming to challenge me. One morning my father was sitting in the trailer, figuring out where he was going to go hawking that day, when a wiry, dark-skinned lad showed up in the yard with his dad.

'My son can beat your son,' said the dad.

'I'm a match for Bartley, I can beat him any time,' chimed in the lad.

Our fathers started haggling. 'He'll fight him for a hundred pound,' said the lad's dad and pulled out a wad of notes. You could buy a good secondhand car in those days for that. Down went the money and my dad nodded me outside into the yard. We shaped up. I let fly with half a dozen machine-gun punches and laid the lad out right there in the yard – he barely had time to throw a punch. We had no need to go hawking that day.

I was gathering a new gang around me. One was a young Uttoxeter lad called Dave Russell, who we called 'Old Soldier' because he had been in the army for a bit. He was in his late teens and was unhappy at home: his father was very hard on him and Dave couldn't take it any more. One night he had been fighting in town and came home with blood on his collar. 'So you think you can fight?' said his dad, and thumped him. For the first time, Dave hit him back, and that was pretty much the end of their relationship.

Dave was working in a biscuit factory carrying hundred-weight bags of flour and emptying them into a sieve. He had no mask to wear and was covered in muck all the time. I pulled up there to see him one day and he looked ill.

'How much are you getting for working in there?' I asked.

'Three pounds a week.'

'You can sit in my van, I'll give you three pounds a week for nothing.'

I got Dave an old trailer to live in next to us. He found my dad as strict as his but fair with it, and my mam kept him fed. He became a sparring partner for Sam and me. Dave could take no end of punishment without complaining. We were always doing trials of strength. I would ask Dave to hit me in the stomach as hard as he could and try to take it without flinching. Sam and I also would get a wooden ladder, lay it across two boxes and ask people to lie on it, then we would lift them above our heads, using them as human barbells. They were frightened that we'd drop them but we never did.

Every morning at five o'clock we'd be up for a run. Then we would wash in cold water. Soldier Dave was used to his hot baths and my dad would bellow at him, 'What are you, a man or a mouse? Get your clothes off and get washed.' He used to inspect Dave, checking behind his ears.

The good food and outdoor life certainly seemed to do the trick. Our Sam grew into a living giant. He eventually topped six feet one, weighed eighteen stone and had an eighty-four-inch reach and nineteen-inch biceps. His fists were massive, sixteen inches around. He'd sit in the pub and put them on the table and people couldn't help but look at them. Sam was also the toughest traveller I ever knew – I believe he was a better fighter than me, but he stood back because I was the oldest. In the boxing ring he would face his opponent square on, with his knees slightly bent, and nobody could move him back. Even I couldn't take punishment like Sam. But he wasn't a troublemaker, more a gentle giant.

We ate like horses; I think we were the butchers' best friends. We'd see my dad walking down the road and he'd say, 'Look what I've got for dinner today,' and it would be a huge lump of beef wrapped up. My mother was a wonderful cook. Her pies were perfection. We ate plenty of fresh food and could live off the land like natives, though we were never into the traditional Romany fare of hedgehogs, or *hotchy witchie*. I would wade waist-deep into rivers to 'tickle' trout with my hands and could have half a dozen hanging from a V-shaped twig in no time, though I did it mainly for sport, as my dad made sure we never went short of food.

We hadn't been in Uttoxeter long when I had a band of men working for me: my brothers Sam and John, Gandy Hodgkinson, Colin Morfitt, a top rugby player with a twenty-six-inch neck, Paul 'Beaky' Smith, a good boxer, my best pal Alan Wilson, Caggy Barrett, Noah Lock and Johnny Wheeldon. We stuck together in a big gang – all men, no women – and I kept the lot of them. We'd be in London for a week hawking, East Anglia for a month painting barns, then maybe over to Wales, up to Manchester and Liverpool to buy scrap, further on to the little Cumbrian town of Appleby for the horse fair, then maybe to Scotland or over to Ireland for another fair. We had ten trailers (caravans) and about twenty vans and we'd pull in on a lay-by or farm we knew and look for work. I had men painting Dutch barns and repairing roofs and tarmaccing roads.

I suppose we were pretty rough. You can imagine what people thought when they saw us all pulling in somewhere. There were always scraps and arguments and often we would put on the headlights of motors at night for men to settle an argument the travellers' way. Once we were in the middle of Birmingham, having just weighed in a load of scrap, and Gandy and Colin Morfitt began arguing over a few pounds. I stopped the van and said, 'If you want to fight, fight.' They jumped out in a long line of traffic and fought in the road.

I was as wild as any of them. Once I even fought a badger and killed it and brought it back to the camp. My father went mad. 'It'll give you TB, get that away from there,' he said. My dad and I still had our fallouts: we were two strong characters who both hated to back down. I was too big now for him to hit but I would never have laid a finger back on my dad. I regret every row we had, because we did love each other and I thought he was the best father in the world.

*

MANY GYPSY FIGHTERS are happy to be kings of their own patch. They never challenge people outside their own areas. That wasn't good enough for me. It was my birthright to be champion of all of them, to do what my great-grandfather and grandfather and Hughie Burton had done.

In the mid-Sixties, I went to Norfolk with my Uncle Joe, pulling onto some common ground where other travellers were staying. We went out working and when we came back, someone had smashed the windows of our trailers. Uncle Joe warned me not to say anything because we were just two and were heavily outnumbered.

The next day, Uncle Joe was cooking a bit of tea outside when a man came across and started chatting. He seemed friendly enough. Soon a big, dark-headed fellow joined him. His name was Leefoy Price; the Prices are one of the best-known Romany breeds.

'This is the best man in Norfolk,' said the first one.

'At what?' asked Uncle Joe.

The man held up his fists. 'Using them.'

Uncle Joe could see what was coming. 'I'm afraid you are wrong, pal,' he said.

'Why?' asked the man.

'He *was* the best man in Norfolk.'

'What do you mean, was?'

'He's the best man in Norfolk now – my nephew, over there. Him with the red head.' They looked over at me.

'Well, he has to prove it,' said the first man.

That was music to my ears. I'd rather be a hammer than a nail, as Simon and Garfunkel sang at the time. We walked to the car park of a nearby pub, the entire site following us like children behind the Pied Piper, and squared off. I could tell he was a good man: he had a solid stance and he knew how to duck, sway and block. We fenced around for a few minutes, getting each other's measure, and then went at it hard. He tried his best but my arms were like pistons. I punched him all around the car park.

He went down but gamely pulled himself up and came back at me. I brushed his punches aside, cracked him on the jaw and downed him again. Once more he got up, still full of fight. I moved in close, took his hooks on my arms, then sank both fists into his rib cage. The air went out of him like bellows emptying. He crumpled at my feet, grabbing me around the knees as he went down. I tried to pull my legs free but he clung on, too beaten to rise but refusing to let go. His friends came in and carried him away and I was acknowledged as the winner. We had no more trouble on that camp.

I had fights on other stopping grounds. Most I don't even remember, but I won them all. Usually nobody wanted to mess with me: word travels very fast on the gypsy bush telegraph. Men would come up and ask who I was. 'I'm Old Bartley Gorman,' I would say, in homage to my grandfather.

My first encounter with one of the top gypsy fighters came not long after the Price fight. I was travelling in the south of England with a pal called Billy 'the Box' Vincent and we drove through the Dartford Tunnel into Kent. I saw a *tan* (stopping place) with vans parked about and a bit of a horse sale going on, and pulled in. There was a pub nearby that was so rough it was known as the 'Blood Tap'. You didn't go in there unless you wanted to fight, so I headed straight there and made it known in no uncertain manner that I was the best man in the country.

A powerful young fellow challenged me out immediately. His name was Mark Ripley and, like me, he was one of a new generation of challengers for Hughie Burton's throne.

'Come on then, I'll fight you,' I said. We went out to the car park.

'No foreigners come here and challenge it out,' he said. 'I'm the best man in Kent.' With that, he put his fist through a car headlight.

'I'm the best man in England, Scotland, Ireland and Wales,' I replied.

He came at me. Ripley was thickset – what we call *butty* – and very, very tough. We punched each other senseless. Sometimes I was very arrogant: I would go toe-to-toe just to test my opponent, throwing science out of the window. We traded blow for blow, like two bulls, virtually shoulder to shoulder. Things were just getting very interesting when it was broken up; someone said police were on the way.

We agreed to go back to the stopping ground and resume there. I had no-one with me, just Billy the Box, among a crowd of Ripley's supporters, but I was supremely confident. We found a secluded spot among the trailers and, with a circle of people around us, went at it again. I hooked him and hurt him and put him over a car bonnet but he came back with a headbutt that caught me on the cheek. He wouldn't go down, whatever I hit him with. The crowd also started to press in: there were women running around and pulling at me and hitting me. They were trying to interfere and he was still punching. He had no fear in him.

Finally it was stopped again. We faced each other, panting.

'Go back up north where you come from,' gasped Ripley.

'I go where I want,' I said.

Some of the older people in the crowd wouldn't let it go on and so we both walked back to our trailers to wash off. I deliberately stopped on the site for another three days but had no more trouble, even though the old men kept coming up to me, saying, 'Go and fetch your breed.'

'I don't need them,' I replied. 'It's just me and your man. A fair fight.'

We never came to blows again and before I left, Ripley and I shook hands, which surprised his people. But I don't want to stay enemies with any man. I later learned that he was everything he said he was – the best man in Kent and one of the most dangerous in the country. He was the kind who would stand on his own against 100 men rather than back down. We would never fight again but I would hear stories about him from time to time. Years later he was shot stone dead by his wife in a Kent pub called the Black Boy.

Through fights like this, and by talking to old-timers, I learned the secret skills of the bareknuckle fighter. Anyone can be a five-second pub brawler but to go for an hour and more against a fit, trained man requires what the old-timers called *bottom*, and an arsenal of blows that you don't learn in the gym. For example, you don't always punch with your knuckles. Sometimes it's best to use your middle knuckles – the joints where your fingers bend. Some martial artists do the same, apparently. It allows you to extend your reach and to hit sensitive targets you cannot always strike effectively with your clenched fists.

My repertoire eventually included some very nasty strikes:

Middle knuckle shot between the lip and the nose – agony
Single middle knuckle in the eye socket – causes loss of vision
Punch to the bone behind the ear – potentially fatal
Simultaneous double punch behind the ears – a jawbreaker
Rabbit punch to the kidneys – wicked with bare fists
Right to the heart – another very dangerous strike
Left or right under the armpit – excruciatingly painful
Solar plexus punch – drains your opponent's power
Hook under the floating rib – turns his lips blue
Punch to the Adam's apple – a critical blow
Bull-hammer – end of story.

The bull-hammer was my pet name for a full-blooded right smash to the temple or forehead. I named it after the poleaxe, a sledgehammer with a spike at one end: they used to kill cows or bullocks by putting a rope through an iron ring fixed to the ground to pull their heads down, then striking them between the eyes with the poleaxe. My punch had a similar effect but it didn't do my hand any good. I would break the knuckles four for five times over the years, whereas my left is fine – though I could hit as hard with either hand.

I picked up moves and tricks from all over the place. Tucker Dunn taught me the knuckle shot to the eye. Hughie Burton liked to put the knee between the legs, though that was never my style. I learned a good few moves from an old chap of six foot eight who had boxed Primo Carnera in an exhibition in Hanley in the Thirties. One thing I discovered myself is that attack *is* defence in bareknuckle fighting: your opponent can't hit you if he is covering up. The old-time pugilists would stand strong and not take a backward step, at least until the Jewish master Daniel Mendoza came along and taught footwork and clever slipping. I like to move around and showboat – I suppose it was the Ali influence – but when things got serious I would always come down off my toes and put the other man on the defensive. They usually didn't last long after that.

I like to break the mould. For example, who says you have to square off? When you square up to a man you automatically put him at the same level as you. If fighters have swallowed that over many years, that is up to them, but I do my own thing. Often I would just walk in with my hands low and explode, though you have to be tough to do it. I also liked to plant a big right out of the blue, without throwing the left first. You leave yourself open by doing it but, in a fight, who dares wins.

*

YOU WOULD NOT know it today, but in the Sixties Uttoxeter was teeming with American soldiers. There was a big US Army base nearby at Marchington and others in the surrounding area, for troops stationed here after Charles de Gaulle had said he wanted them off French soil. The Vietnam War was reaching its height and many of them were on their way to, or back from, the jungles of south-east Asia. When I wasn't travelling, my main pub was the Wheatsheaf in the centre of town, and it had a television on permanently for the Americans who wanted to follow what was happening in 'Nam. They would swagger in in their military-issue cloaks and sunglasses, swishing canes with gold handles and flashing their money. 'Hey mac, you got a sister?' they'd say. 'Bring her over and I'll sell you some leather boots.'

We got on with them well – they were always willing to sell us boots and clothing and other stores that we could make a pound on – but there were also plenty who liked to fight. The pubs and dancehalls became battlegrounds most weekends and I was usually in the thick of it.

During one punch-up at a dance at the town hall, this big Yank, the bully of the camp, made a beeline for me.

'I won't mess about with you,' I said. 'If you want to fight, we will.' I punched him once and knocked him spark out.

Word must have spread around the base about the big redheaded gypsy, because after that I was always fighting with them: blacks from Harlem, Italians like Marciano, Mid-West farmhands, Texas cowpokes, switchblade merchants from the ghettoes of Chicago and Philadelphia. Many of them boxed in the Army and some had been pros in civilian life. They loved to fight but their Military Police could be ferocious, beating them with big sticks and throwing them in the back of trucks like bags of 'taters.

I had one go with a big black, a proper pro, outside the Wheatsheaf. His name was Al, and the fight started after an English girl inside kept shouting out, 'Al's tough, Al's tough.' I decided to see how tough he was. He stripped to the waist and his torso was like black marble. We were both jabbing and hooking in an orthodox style when one of his friends flicked a cigarette at me. Somehow it went down the top of one of my Luton shoes and I felt a burning sensation in my foot. I was hopping around on one leg trying to put it out while this big boxer tried to take my head off. Finally he grabbed me in a bear hug and pinned my arms to my sides, picked me up off the floor and squeezed and squeezed with his massive arms until I could feel the breath going out of me. Somehow I managed to create enough space to tilt back my head and butted him as hard as I could right in the face. He let go and I dropped to my feet. I ducked my shoulder into his ribcage, picked him up and then shoulder-carried

King of the Gypsies: This photograph was taken in 1974, when I was thirty years old and had just challenged the Londoner Roy 'Pretty Boy' Shaw to a bareknuckle fight (which never came off).

Above: My great-grandfather Bartley Gorman the First, Irish tinker and bareknuckle champion.

Left: Jem Mace, in the middle, challenging the winner of the world title fight between Tom Sayers and John C.Heenan. Mace fought my great-grandfather on the cobbles in Dublin.

CHAMPION OF ENGLAND

MACE'S CHALLENGE TO HEENAN & SAYERS
FOR £ 1000.

My grandfather "Bulldog" Bartley Gorman the Second with his wife Caroline, in a photograph taken around 1920. Notice his three kiss-curls.

My maternal grandparents, Jack Wilson and his wife Mary. Wilson was a very wealthy horse dealer and backed Bulldog Bartley to fight any man in the world.

How they lived: That's my mother second from the right with members of her family. They were very proud travellers, always immaculately dressed, with the men in collars and ties. Notice the old cars and the lurcher dog.

My father Samuel made his living selling carpets and oil cloth (lino). He and my mother Kathryn 'Katy' Gorman, *née* Wilson, were married near Nottingham and had a big banquet in a field.

Mam with me (left) and Sam, outside our trailer. I was raised in a trailer (caravan) known as a 'tank'.

As a freckle-faced schoolboy in Bedworth. I had only a few years of schooling but did learn to read and write.

Painting barns in the hot sun: We left school to work as soon as we were old enough and painted miles of farm buildings, hay lofts and turkey sheds in East Anglia, using a long hose and a pump to spray the paint.

These two pages show some of the all-time great gypsy prize-fighters, never seen in print before. Top left is Old Bill Elliott, an unbeaten heavyweight who was the same era as my grandfather, though they never fought. Right is Riley Smith, boxer and bareknuckle man from the East Midlands and one of the top men of the 1930s.

A very rare photo of an old gypsy prize-fight: My uncle Bartley Gorman III (left) squares off against Joe Lock in Lancashire in the 1930s. Uncle Bartley was one of the best men in Wales, Cheshire and Lancashire. He won this fight.

Johnny Winters, a true fighting legend, was emulated by many travelling men in his dress and bearing.

Sam Price was a powerhouse who beat everyone he fought. He had two brutal encounters with Johnny Winters.

Benny Marshall, the master boxer from Wales who won an ABA title and became one of the best men of the 1930s.

My Uncle Ticker, booth boxer and knuckle man. He was the same height and build as me and would fight anyone.

The men take a break during a day's work: (from left) my father, cousin Kevin Gorman, my brother Sam, old John Stevens, my Uncle Bartley, John Stevens, Clarence Gorman and me. Notice my dad glaring at me to make sure I'm standing straight.

Sam lifts up our younger brother John. You can see how strong he was, even as a teenager.

Me, aged twenty, in a field in North Wales, ready to fight anyone and determined to become the gypsy champ.

him for twenty yards into a wall. He slid down it like butter off a hot knife and that was the end of Al.

Somehow I always knew I could get out of any situation. Even as a child, if a big lad had me in a headlock I would stick it out no matter how long he held me, breathing slowly and waiting until his grip relaxed slightly and I could get him. I would never give up. Watching my back against the Yanks was my cousin Joe 'Blood' Gorman, five years older than me, about five foot eight and hard as an anvil, with a stomach like a rubbing board. Joe was so ugly he was good looking. He runs a camp now at Southport, near Liverpool, and we're still the best of pals.

*

I DO NOT want to give the impression that all I did was fight. Far from it. This was after all, the Swinging Sixties, with the Beatles and Bob Dylan and the Rolling Stones dominating the charts and Flower Power on its way. We loved music, singing and dancing. My brother Sam and some friends formed a band called the Ramblers and I bought them instruments and managed them. I wore love beads around my neck and would buy shirts and rip them up the seams at either side so you could see the rippling muscles.

I also fell in love. I met Gwendoline Wheeldon, a dark-haired lass with flashing eyes around 1967, and eventually moved out of my parents' trailer to live with her. For the next three years, we travelled: around North Wales, Shropshire, Herefordshire and Gloucestershire, but mainly Norfolk. I creosoted miles and miles of turkey sheds, one after the other, for Bernard Matthews. I also bought and sold thousands of hessian sacks, making a penny profit on each. The farmers used them for their corn and meal but the trade eventually died with paper and plastic bags. Then I went into partnership scrap dealing, travelling down to London trading metal.

I got to know every inch of Norfolk, the area of Jem Mace. I befriended Allie Bailey, who ran Norwich then with his brothers and Big Leo McCarthy. We would meet in cafes and snooker halls, always doing deals. I also still boxed occasionally on amateur shows, under aliases. I'd just turn up at a show and say, 'I'm a boxer, heavyweight,' and they'd be interested. I also beat men from every major building firm in Britain. When they were laying a big pipeline through Norfolk I would go and challenge them out just for the fun of it. I remember battering one of the local toughs at a tin-hut billiard hall at Fakenham. He and his friend were looking for trouble and I was the stranger in town.

When I was twenty-four, Gwendoline said to me, 'Bartley, I'm having a baby.' We were stopping in Ringland Woods, near Norwich. A fortnight before she was due, she said she was ill. I made her Sunday dinner but she couldn't eat it. I was a bit upset because I had cooked it specially for her: you know what an idiot you can be. I took her to a doctor but he said there wasn't a problem. We didn't know then that the baby was already dead. Little Bartholomew Gorman VI was stillborn on April 19, 1969. His tiny grave is at Cottesley in Norfolk.

Gwendoline soon became pregnant again and decided that she wanted to return home. I had not seen my own parents for three years. I had made a lot of money and if we had stayed I would be a rich man today, but we went back to Uttoxeter. My son Shaun was born in Derby Hospital in 1970 and my daughter Maria arrived in 1971.

*

WHEN I RETURNED to Uttoxeter I was twenty-six and like a Hereford bull. I went to different gyms and sparred with pro fighters who didn't know me. All they wanted was a sparring partner. I liked the mystery of it all. We set up our own gym above the Black Swan Inn and named it the Uttoxeter Lads Boxing Club. My father helped to pay for everything: we had light and heavy bags, a speedball, skipping ropes, a rowing machine and a mirror for shadow boxing and Wogga Wood helped out with the training. Soon we had professionals like bantamweight Billy Williams over there and got a proper ring up.

Bobby Neill, the trainer I had written to several years earlier to ask about turning pro, was now running the British Boxing Board of Control gym in Highgate, north London. I got his phone number and arranged to meet him down there in a public house by the gym. I drove down in a mini-van and walked in with my kitbag over my shoulder. He was talking to some Americans.

'Go to the gym and tell them Bobby Neill sent you and I will be over in ten minutes,' he said. 'Strip off and get your gear on.'

I went over to the gym. There was a leather-faced old curmudgeon on the door with spectacles and an ancient coat on.

'You can't come in here,' he said. 'Who are you?'

'I'm the King of the Gypsies.'

'Yeah, and I'm the Queen of England.'

'No, I am. Bobby Neill sent me.'

He got on the phone and two minutes later let me in. I changed into my trunks and began moving around the gym, shadow boxing and warming up. Without even realising it, I took over the place. The other boxers all slowed down and were watching me out of the corners of their eyes: the big, wild-looking traveller with a mane of blood-red hair.

Bobby Neill walked in with the Americans. 'Who do you want me to spar with?' I asked.

Neill asked four heavyweights and none would spar with me. So he said, 'Go on the heavy bag and I will tell you if you can make it.'

I went on the bag for three minutes. All the gym stopped and watched me. Then Neill said quietly, 'You're one of the heaviest punchers I have ever seen in my life. And I have seen Liston, Johansson and Cooper.'

I hadn't even been hitting it as hard as I could: I had concentrated on accuracy, making sure I looked good. This sounded promising.

'Yeah, you can make it,' he said. 'Go back and have four amateur fights and I will get you a pro licence.'

'No, I'm not having amateur fights. I'm the champion of the gypsies, no-one can beat me right now.'

'You have to, you can't get a licence otherwise.'

He was adamant and, because of that, I never returned. I was in my mid-twenties by this time and had realised how good I was. I would have felt I was taking advantage by going back among amateurs. So I decided that if I couldn't make it inside the system, I'd do it outside.

CHAPTER 6

Unlicensed

ONE DAY IN 1970, I was thinking about boxing and how I couldn't fit in with the authorities. I was an outsider. And it dawned on me that the sport was not really *controlled* by anyone. World title fights were sanctioned by two rival bodies, the World Boxing Association and the World Boxing Council. In the UK, the professional game was run by the British Boxing Board of Control (BBBC), which licensed fighters, ringside officials, managers, matchmakers, trainers and promoters. It seemed to me that the BBBC did not have the sole right to authorise bouts: after all, fairground boxing booths had been going for decades, perfectly legally, outside the Board's remit. I listened to the pirate station Radio Caroline at the time – it was broadcast from a ship in the Irish Sea – and suddenly had a brainwave. What was to stop me from putting on pirate boxing shows?

I decided to promote an unauthorised event. I knew all the boxers – and the streetfighters – in the area and had no trouble getting enough of them for a show, which I staged at the weightlifting club in Rocester, Staffs. Top of the bill was a four-round no-decision exhibition bout between our Sam and a boxer called Don Halden, known as the 'Blond Bomber'. They were a nice contrast: Halden came in the ring immaculate, with his carefully styled blond hair and a spotless white towelling robe, while Sam had an old hessian sack over his shoulders with 'Gypsy' written on it. The referee was Guy Harrison, who used to work the cargo ships to the USA and fought bootleg fights in every port. The place was packed to the rafters, and I knew I was on to something. I was young and ambitious. I decided I could go bigger than Jack Solomons and Harry Levene, the two top licensed promoters at the time. And that was how I became the father of pirate boxing in Britain.

Getting Don Halden was a coup. He was a young pro heavyweight from Rugeley who had been on the fringes of the British top ten. He was also managed by wily old George Biddles, who had trained world champion Hogan Bassey. Don had been a sparring partner to British champ Jack Bodell. We had trained together as amateurs in Wogga Wood's gym and I had kept tabs on his pro career through the *Boxing News* while on my travels around East Anglia and Scotland. Halden was a real kayo artist. If you left a gap against him with your left, you'd be in serious trouble.

He was also a terror outside the ropes. I saw how he could fight one day in a pub called the Bell Inn, the drinking den of large numbers of Geordies who had come down to work in the pits and power stations around Rugeley. They were barbed-wire characters. We had been told that two men in the Bell wanted to fight Halden and me, the boxer and the prize-fighter, so we went in one afternoon with our friend Mick Mould, a very dangerous man who looked like Ronnie Kray. Mould and I went into one part of the pub while Halden went into another. We heard a commotion and when we got to the other bar Halden was smothered in blood, fighting with four men. Someone had glassed him with a beer mug.

I tried to stop it but someone took a swing at me and at it we went. It was a terrible brawl, with bottles and glasses and chairs flying all over the place. The Bell was virtually demolished. We were heavily outnumbered but more than held our own. No-one could stop it until about thirty police arrived and we were all arrested. Mould, who had cut a man's throat with a knife, hid it down his sock.

We were charged with affray and ended up at Stafford

Crown Court. They fetched us up from the old dungeons there and we had to stand with our hands up while we were searched, to impress the judge. We were all going to plead not guilty but my QC had a word with the judge in chambers, who agreed that if I pleaded guilty I wouldn't go to prison. I talked Halden and Mould into accepting and they were both given suspended jail sentences. I was fined £30.

Halden was dynamite in the ring but loved to look his best before a fight and hated anyone messing up his blond hair. I once went to see him fight while he was still licensed and walked into the dressing room.

'Bartley's here to see you, Don,' said George Biddles.

I mussed his hair.

'Don't do that, don't touch my hair,' he said.

I didn't care if they put a sack on me. I wanted to be rough and rugged like Jack Dempsey, get them down and out. I think I knew after that incident that one day Halden and I would get down to it. Anyway, he retired from licensed boxing at just twenty-three and joined my unlicensed stable.

Apart from Halden, my main attraction was my brother Sam. We called him 'the Rhino'. No-one would mess with Sam; not even me. I saw men move in and smash it out with him but they always backed off first. You couldn't push him over. He fought flatfooted and was no fancy dan but he could take hooks, jabs, crosses, anything, and just smash and batter back like a big Marciano. He was awesome. Joe Phillips, whose yard we lived in, had his own taxi service with a contract to transport prisoners around the country. Sometimes he would pay Sam to drive the men because they would never try to escape with him in the car.

Most of my fighters were from Staffordshire and many I knew well, like Johnny Wheeldon, who was my girlfriend's twin brother, and Colin 'Mighty Moff' Morfitt. There were some tasty boxers, like Billy Williams, the 'Cannock Ball of Fire', a former ABA finalist and National Coal Board champion who fought Ken Buchanan as a pro, and Tommy Beardsmore, who was Territorial Army champion for eight years and beat Alan Rudkin as an amateur. Tommy was never counted out. I trained all these men at several different gyms. One was the Wheatsheaf, one at the Black Swan, one in an old scout hut. This was my world, of sweat and liniment, of skipping ropes and medicine balls and leather bag mitts.

Through friends and contacts, I assembled a syndicate to finance the shows. It included respectable men: one who is now on the bench in Lincolnshire, a doctor, a lawyer and a millionaire. I knew the Boxing Board would go nuts about my unlicensed shows and I wanted these men backing me in case it went to law. At the other end of the spectrum was Mick Mould. He owned a chain of fish and chip shops and was basically a gangster, dressing in a different suit every day and driving a new car every year.

We booked the Victoria Hall in Hanley for a show in December 1971. The BBBC soon got wind of it and weren't happy; they didn't mind scrappy shows in small venues but the Victoria Hall was well known and too big for their liking. We even paid to have twenty policemen on duty at £2 each. A Mr Johnson from Stoke-on-Trent council requested my presence at a meeting at the town hall. They wanted to ban the show. Harold Groombridge, my main partner at the time, and I went along and were ushered into a boardroom dominated by a huge, polished wooden table.

'Mr Gorman,' said Johnson, 'I have arranged for you to meet the Lord Mayor. Now I don't want you to get nervous.' He must have been trying to rattle me.

'I wouldn't get nervous if it was the Duke of Edinburgh,' I replied

'Do you have the receipt for the venue booking, Mr Gorman?'

I took it from my pocket and placed it on the table. He inspected it.

'You definitely have paid for it, haven't you?'

'Yes.'

I reached over and slid the receipt back to my side of the table. His eyes narrowed.

'Mr Gorman, I don't think you trust me.'

'Oh, I wouldn't say that, Mr Johnson, you look like a real gentleman to me.'

'Well, you have pulled the receipt away from me.'

'Well, it is my receipt.'

He tried to tell me that my tournament was illegal but I knew it wasn't. They were boxing with gloves, under rules, with officials. It was certainly more organised than the booths.

He got up and went in to see the Mayor. A cup of tea was fetched. When Johnson returned, he still seemed unhappy but he realised there was little he could do.

'I tell you what I'll do, Mr Johnson,' I said. 'I'll make sure you are in the front row.'

His eyes lit up. 'And the family, Mr Gorman?'

'Yes. There'll be six seats for you.'

'You are a gentleman.'

Top of the bill was Don Halden against Chuck Bodell, half-brother of Jack Bodell, the former British and Empire heavyweight champion. Chuck was a streetfighter from Swadlincote, a colliers' area, and was a fearsome sight, with a bald head and a bear-like body covered in black hair: he looked like a granite gorilla. Blue-eyed Halden was just the opposite, clean-shaven and with a hairless chest. They weighed-in at a hotel and Halden couldn't help looking at Bodell through the corner of his eye. He knew he was in for a tussle. We billed it for the Heavyweight Championship of the Midlands and it turned out to be one of the toughest fights I have seen in my life. It was a good sales gimmick having Jack Bodell's half-brother and once again the venue was packed.

I loved gimmicks, anything for a few newspaper column inches to sell a show. We matched eighteen-stone John Peaty and twenty-three-stone Zue Shaw and billed it as the greatest combined poundage in ring history. Another bout on the bill featured Barry Fradley, who was six foot eight, and Peter Bartram, who was six foot four. They were both like rakes and we billed them as the two tallest middle-weights ever to fight, which was probably true. Fradley had been due to fight Bartram before but had pulled out without explanation. This time he came to me and said, 'Can I have a private word with you?'

'Sure.'

'The reason I won't fight is because I'm ashamed of my body,' he said. 'I'm that thin. If you let me go in with a vest on, I'll fight him at the Victoria Hall.'

'No problem. But I want a guarantee you'll fight this time.'

On the night of the show, I sat at ringside in dinner suit and bow tie, smoking a cigar. The two beanpoles came into the ring, Fradley with his vest on. I leapt to my feet.

'Hold it. Hold everything.'

The MC looked at me.

'Doesn't that man know this is a professional tournament? Tell him to take that vest off.'

If looks could kill. Fradley was furious, and took it out on his opponent. Bartram knocked Fradley down four times but Fradley knocked him down five times, and won on points. Oh, and I forgot all about the tickets for poor old Mr Johnson from the council, and he was stuck right at the back. I waved to him from my front-row seat.

The response from the BBBC was terrible. They sent detectives and were threatening the boxers that if they fought on my shows they would never be allowed to appear again in the licensed ring. Some had to box under assumed names. I told the MC to announce, 'Bartley Gorman has given instructions that all members of the British Boxing Board must stay out of the fighters' dressing rooms, please.' They hated me even more for that.

Once we realised how popular our shows were, we changed our name to the Anglo-American Boxing Federation, to give ourselves an international flavour. In a further snub to the Board, we adopted a different rule system. I wrote to the well-known promoter Chris Dundee, whose brother Angelo trained Muhammad Ali. He wished me well and sent me the eighty-eight-page rulebook of the New York State Athletic Commission. It stipulated that decisions should be rendered by the referee and two judges, rather than just by the referee as in England.

I didn't box on my own shows because I was too busy. I tried to run it properly but there were all sorts of shenanigans. For one show, Sam was due to fight a coloured fellow, but two days before the event his opponent was nowhere to be seen. I jumped in the motor and started touring around. You'd be amazed what you can find if you just keep your eyes open. Driving past a roadway construction gang, I saw a large black man wielding a pickaxe. He looked the part. I pulled up and shouted to him.

'Can you fight?'

He put down his pick. 'I'll fight anybody,' he said.

I told him what it was all about, agreed a purse with him and two days later he was boxing as 'Alanzer Jansen', allegedly a top heavyweight from the United States (the name was copied from Alonzo Johnson, a decent boxer of the time). He did his best but Sam made short work of him.

I devoted myself to promoting full-time. My headquarters was the Wheatsheaf, just around the corner from our campsite in Uttoxeter. I was a heavy drinker, like John L. Sullivan – I loved Bass beer with brandy and port chasers – and smoked cigars. 'I smoke and drink to give the other man a chance,' I used to brag.

In February 1972, we staged a show at the Elite Cinema in Uttoxeter. It featured Halden against Rocky Davies for the unlicensed Heavyweight Championship of the Midlands, but the drama was on the undercard. 'Big Hearted' Artie Meadows – whose son Shane is now a film director – kayoed a vicar's son, Dave Smash, in ten seconds, knocking out his front teeth. Smash was unconscious on the ring floor and his leg started twitching. Officials from the BBBC were in the crowd – and we didn't have a doctor. I could sense a tragedy.

I got someone to rush me round to the local physician, Dr Penty. I begged him to come immediately and, if anyone asked, to say he had been there all night.

'I can't come,' he said.

'I need you badly, Doc,' I said, and pushed £25 into his hand. He was out of the door before he even had his coat on. It was a good job his house was only 500 yards away. He got an ambulance to take Smash to hospital, still unconscious. He came round after half an hour. It taught me a lesson to always have a doctor. Amazingly, the BBBC never caught on.

But whenever things are going well, fate has kicked me in the teeth. I'm almost like an undertaker, the people I've carried to their graves. First my dear Aunt Rose died, then my father fell terminally ill with cancer. He was taken into hospital at Burton-upon-Trent, where he lingered for six weeks. Though he had encouraged me to box when I was younger, my father had never really wanted me to be a fighter. Yet secretly he was proud of me. He was heavily sedated on morphine, but one day they took him off it and when I arrived to visit him, he told the nurses, 'This is my son. He's the heavyweight champion of Ireland.'

I would sit with him for hours. One day near the end, when I was leaving after a visit, he feebly waved me over to his bedside and spoke in a hoarse whisper. 'Test them all, son,' he said. 'Test them all.' He was only fifty-five when he died. I will never forget him lying in the casket of Japanese oak, the hardest wood in the world, with more than twenty silver crucifixes made into the handles. He was laid out in the trailer with yellow candles around the casket and white sheets around the walls and on the ceiling, pinned with purple bows. It was beautiful but horrible at the same time: what a taste of sorrow. I sat up with him every night until the funeral. I can still see him now with his big gold ring on, the diamond catching the light of the death candles, all the weight gone off his body but still with his head of black hair – a hard, strict, old-fashioned man with strong values, who beat me and loved me at the same time.

The hospital was full of travellers every night, great friends of my father like American Billy Finney, perhaps the richest man among all travellers (he once offered to back me against the London fighter Roy 'Pretty Boy' Shaw for a £100,000 straight bet), who came every day in his Rolls-Royce, and my aunt Sibby Deadman, a true Romany, who was ninety years old and would weep as she held my father's great hands, looking for all the world like Queen Victoria, with the Salvation Army Band playing outside the window. The funeral cortege was a mile long.

Shortly after my father was buried, I was summoned to a meeting with Rabbi Boswell. He had been a close friend of my father and was a very wealthy, influential travelling man. He had been to a couple of my boxing shows in his Roller, but now he wanted it to end. 'I want you to stop doing this and start earning a living,' he said. Rabbi thought I was getting too famous. He wanted me to keep a lower profile and to live a simple gypsy life, following in my father's footsteps hawking and selling carpets. He was an utter gentleman and spoke what he thought was for our own good. I listened respectfully to his words but was set on my own course. I continued promoting and Rabbi never came to another show.

One day I rang up Bramcote Barracks and arranged for an Army boxing team to take on my fighters in a tournament. They thought it was sanctioned by the Amateur Boxing Association (I wonder where they got that idea) but, come the night of the tournament, they found out the truth. The sergeant-major came to see me. He had two Dalmatian dogs on leashes.

'It has come to my attention that your fighters are all unlicensed,' he said. 'My men can't possibly box on your show.'

How was I going to get out of this one? I had a full house.

'You are the British Army, aren't you,' I said. 'You can fight in the Congo and in the jungle and in Belize?'

'That's correct.'

'And yet you are telling me that you can't fight in a boxing tournament in Staffordshire?'

That clinched it. He immediately gave permission for his six boxers to fight my men.

Another night we had a packed house and were five minutes away from the 8pm start when I realised we had no gloves. I briefly debated whether to let them fight bareknuckle – my boxers would have done whatever I asked them – but again there were busybodies from the BBBC in attendance. Wogga Wood's gym was about fifteen miles away, so instead I jumped into a friend's E-type Jag and it almost left the ground, the speed we went. I found Wogga in the pub, got him to open up and we grabbed all the gloves we could.

I made sure my boxers were always evenly matched and value for money. I wanted them all to be tested. As a result, we had queues for every show, and every pub for miles would have posters. Some of the businessmen backing me wanted me to apply for a proper promoter's licence and go legit but as a traveller I didn't want to be part of the establishment. The Boxing Board were threatening to take us to court and I wasn't having that. I wanted to do it my own way and intended throwing them all over – Mickey Duff, Solomons, Levene, the lot. Frank Warren was unheard of then, though he would later rise to success by the same route of unlicensed fighting. I was going to be the biggest in the world. The *Boxing News* wouldn't report my fights, which annoyed me, but they couldn't black out the whole of the media and we were getting good coverage. I was on the verge of national attention and I was planning to hire Earl's Court in London. We almost got the former British heavyweight champ Joe Erskine to come out of retirement to fight our Sam. Erskine wanted £500, I got him to accept £250, but the minute he told his manager, he wouldn't let him box for any money. I always rated Erskine highly – a very clever boxer. I even thought about staging bouts in a marquee at Appleby Horse Fair but there would have been murders in the crowd.

I was determined to go worldwide. We took an office in Stoke and finally named ourselves the International Boxing Federation (not related to the later IBF based in America, though I believe they got the name from us). We couldn't accommodate all the people at our shows and made a fortune on fight nights but we had terrible arguments in the syndicate. At meetings there would be people shouting and banging on the table and tea cups flying. Most of the rows were over money. I drove a very hard bargain.

One day Colin Morfitt had a terrible hard fight. He won and came for his prize and as he picked up the trophy, part of it broke off. He pushed me over some chairs and stormed off in a huff. Colin, who was known as 'Mighty Moff', comes from a very old Romany family called Grapes. He became a very good rugby player and is a successful business-man. I taught him how to fight and he later beat a 6ft 8in American soldier in a cobblestone fight in Rio de Janeiro, Brazil. These were the kind of men I had around me. Of course, they wanted paying good money for their boxing matches but I knew if they won I could pay them less because they'd be in a good mood and I'd get the reporters to interview them even if they weren't going to publish it. I always knocked them down.

Sometimes, however, the disputes took a far nastier turn.

*

AFTER MY DAD died, my two brothers and I used to take turns staying with my mam in her big Morecambe trailer at Phillips' Yard. If John and Sam fancied a drink, I'd stop in with her while they went out, and *vice versa*. On this particular night we had all stopped in and gone to bed. Mam was in the bedroom, Sam and John were in the side beds and I slept on the floor in the living room because I was training at the time and wanted to be tough like Jack Dempsey. I was twenty-eight, Sam twenty-seven and John sixteen.

At two o'clock in the dead of night, two cars pulled into the yard and four men got out. Sam was woken by a loud rapping on the trailer and got up in his underpants to see who it was. The instant he opened the door, a huge fist crashed into his mouth and sent him back into the trailer. In stormed Don Halden. Behind him was Mick Mould, my partner on the syndicate, and a garage owner called Brian Perrin, 6ft 2in and 18st. Outside was the fourth man, Paul 'Beaky' Smith, one of my boxers.

I woke with a start to see Sam and Halden slugging it out in the kitchen part of the trailer, with Mould and Perrin coming in behind. Pots and pans were falling all over the floor and making a terrible racket. I leapt up and punched both Mould and Perrin straight back out through the door. Then Sam and Halden fell out over the step, still struggling.

Our John and my mother came out to see what was happening. By now I was outside, at it with Mould again. It was vicious street stuff. 'Stop it, stop it,' shouted my mam. She hitched up her nightie and ran around to the Wheatsheaf, where she knew the landlord and landlady, Steve and Sue Whitehead, yelling, 'Help, help.'

I smashed Mould down to the ground and he scrambled up and ran off into the darkness. It was hard to make out what was happening in the commotion, as the only light was that showing through the open door of the trailer and a glow from behind the curtained windows. I saw Sam now fighting with Perrin after Perrin had set about our John.

I knew the mind Mould had and reckoned he might have gone for a weapon, so I ran back into the trailer to the wardrobe where my dad had kept his twelve-bore, double-barrelled shotgun for shooting rabbits and vermin. I hate guns – absolutely detest them – but I thought my family might be in mortal danger and knew that if Mould came back with a shooter then even Sam and I couldn't fight him with fists. I found the shotgun and shoved my hands into the Crown Derby bowls to find the cartridges. Fortunately they had been thrown out; otherwise someone might have died that night.

I ran back out with the gun, saw Halden, and put the butt of it right over his head, then rammed the barrel into his belly half a dozen times. That wrote him off. Then I ran into the town centre to find Mould. He was outside the police station with some officers. As I approached I could hear him claiming that we had attacked him. I grabbed him and threw him against a wall.

'He attacked us with my mother in the trailer,' I said. 'Don't believe a word he says.'

The police knew me and knew I didn't lie. They arrested Mould. I set off back to the yard and came across Halden looking the worse for wear in the middle of Bridge Street.

'I'm going to kill you stone dead,' I said.

'Don't look at me with those wild eyes,' he said. 'It doesn't worry me. I've fought the toughest men in England.'

I set about him and it took five police to drag me off. By the time order was restored, officers had arrived from as far as Stafford, Derby and Stoke. In the car they found the watches, jewellery and coats that Mould and his men had taken off, proving that they had come to attack us. They charged Mould for fighting with me, Halden for fighting with Sam and said Perrin was on the fringe of it.

While they were waiting for trial, Mould came round to see my mother. 'Mrs Gorman, help us,' he said. 'I'm very sorry, we did wrong. But can you help us get off?' She spoke up for them but the police were determined to press charges. They ended up pleading guilty at Birmingham Crown Court. Mould got nine months and Halden six. Perrin got a suspended prison sentence. 'Three brothers attacked at night,' it said in the paper.

We found out later what it was about. Someone had been making anonymous, abusive phone calls to Mould's chip shops. Mould had told me about it one day but I thought nothing of it. Then one night when they had been drinking, another one of these calls came in. Mould passed the phone to Halden, who listened and said, 'It's Sam Gorman.' Of course, it wasn't – it later turned out to be the husband of a woman who worked for Mould – but off they set to do us damage. That is the kind of hair-trigger men they were: violent, quick to anger and slow to ask questions. I became friends with them again afterwards but it was never the same.

Of the four men who came that night, three are dead now, all to do with motor cars. Mick Mould had a heart attack and died behind the wheel of his car, Beaky Smith was run over and Perrin also died in his motor. Twenty years after the incident, workmen took some guttering down from the

Wheatsheaf pub. They found a rusty handgun lodged in one of the pipes. Mould and his mob must have thrown it there before the police came.

With the success of the promoting, I had pushed the bareknuckle fighting to one side. But I still had cause to raise my hands from time to time. There was a group of hulking brothers called the Uptons who came from the neighbouring town of Cheadle and were known as the Cheadle Cowboys. They actually would dress like cowboys and march through the town. One night in the Wheatsheaf, my friend Mick Harper had a row with a man trying to tap up his girlfriend. One of the Uptons, known as 'Mad Dog', stepped in and threatened Mick, so someone fetched me from another part of the pub and I came through and knocked Mad Dog out with one punch. A lump rose up on his forehead like a mushroom as I looked down at him.

The next day he decided I'd caught him with a lucky punch and challenged me to a bareknuckle fight. We met in a field midway between Uttoxeter and Cheadle and fifty people made a makeshift ring. It was a summer's evening in August 1971. People were betting on how many seconds it would last, not how many rounds, and it didn't go much longer than in the pub; he never had a chance to land a punch. I hit him three or four times and it was over. I regarded men like that as ten a penny. They were no match for the true gypsy fighters, though I must say Mad Dog was not the best of the Uptons; that would be his brother, Big Jim, who was always friendly with me and whom I never did fight.

*

I WAS IN my pomp. When I walked into the Wheatsheaf seven or eight men would hold out their empty jars for me to fill. I always sat on the same stool, commanding the bar, a cigar clamped between my teeth and with queues of people waiting to see me about a dozen different bits of business. And I had money to burn – literally. I once lent a man a fiver when he claimed he was skint, only to see him a few minutes later with a wad of notes. I took my money off him, put it in an ashtray and burned it – and a fiver was worth something in those days. I planned to take my pirate boxing to America and was regularly making trans-Atlantic calls. I reckoned I could take the States by storm. Yet for all my ambition, there was still something missing . . . something nagging. I had not yet been given the credit I deserved as a fighter in my own right.

One Friday in August 1972, I was flicking through the *Boxing News* when my eyes fell on a story about a tournament for heavyweight boxers:

EDDIE SEEKS HIS HEAVY HOPE

Eddie Thomas, the Welsh manager whose fighters have already brought two world titles to Britain, is setting out to fulfil one more ambition.

His hope is to find a heavyweight with potential enough to become British champion and make a formidable challenge to any in the world.

The hunt will begin with a competition he plans to stage in Wales itself during September or October.

'In past years such competitions in London produced Joe Erskine, Jack Gardner and, of course, [Danny] McAlinden, which is why I plan to try one myself,' said Thomas. 'If there is any youngster now working in a coal pit or making furniture who thinks he can fight I'll be willing to decide his worth somehow. If I can find the youngster I want, I'll willingly spend £5,000 to £10,000 developing his potential.'

The tournament was to be at the Double Diamond Club in Caerphilly. There were to be eight fighters, with two reserves, and a top prize of £500. It was supposed to feature the debut of Tim Wood, the reigning ABA heavyweight champ, and other entrants included a Nottinghamshire miner, a scaffolder, a seventeen-and-a-half-stone Liverpudlian and a handful of fledgling pros. The search for a star was a big thing at the time and a lot of promoters and managers were looking for the next world-beater.

Thomas said he planned to have the winner working and living in the Welsh mountains for six months, chopping trees and running through the snow and rain. This sounded like the thing for me. It was how fighters should be. And Thomas was a top man, having taken Howard Winstone and Ken Buchanan to world titles. He said he wanted to get some of the men down to his gym to try them out before the competition to see if they were fit to enter it.

Imagine if I could be both bareknuckle champion and heavyweight boxing champion at the same time. No-one from the past could have claimed such a thing, not even my grandfather. And I truly felt I could beat any man alive.

So without even considering it, I jumped straight in the car with Alan Wilson and set off for South Wales. Alan, who was only nine stone soaking wet, was my best friend and trainer. He had tattoos over his knuckles: 'Irish Tinker' on one hand and 'Romany Gypsy' on the other. We turned up unannounced in Merthyr Tydfil and asked directions to Eddie Thomas. We found him and he took me to his house. He said he knew a lot of Irish travellers. Thomas showed me Aberfan out of the window; I later learned he had been one of the first on the scene at the terrible disaster there and had carried many of the children's bodies away.

He wanted me to show what I could do, so we climbed these rickety stairs to his gym in Merthyr. The walls were peeling and you could see through the rafters. I had on jeans and a pair of boxing boots, my red, thick-soled size tens that my dad had made for me. I warmed up with a bit of moving and slipping, then in walked a tall heavyweight with head-guard on, trunks, gloves, boots and gumshield, ready to go. He was Roger Barlow, from Coventry. He had boxed for England as an amateur and would later be rated in the top ten as a pro, though I didn't know him from Ali at the time.

'How shall we go?' I asked Barlow.

'Let it go its own way,' he said.

I didn't even have a gumshield. I gloved up, climbed into the ring and we went straight at it. Boxing is a different game from bareknuckle: you get 'set' for it, taking a stance and a guard, whereas in a prize-fight you can do your own thing. Barlow was the up-and-coming man at the time but I never missed one left on him. I must have hit him with 100 idle jabs in the first round. In the second, because I was messing with him, he clipped me with a beautiful right cross. It was the most perfect shot I have ever taken. I went back on my heels all the way across the ring and into the ropes, like a stone skipping across water. I wasn't hurt, more dumbfounded, and I admired him for it. Then I went into him throwing five or six jabs so fast they were like one punch, hooking off the jab, rattling a tattoo on his stomach with left and rights, then rubbed the laces of my glove hard up his nostrils on the sly. Thomas wouldn't let me go out for a third round. 'You have got the best left jab I've ever seen,' he said. 'I'll enter you for the tournament and you'll take the £500.'

I went back home determined to stay off the beer and get myself ready. I had no doubts I was going to win. But when I told the Braddocks, they didn't want me to enter. They thought that boxing in a novices' tournament was just messing about. I even got a phone call from Big Just. 'Bartley, what do you think you're doing?' he said. 'You can't go and fight with those novices, man. Don't dishonour yourself.' They all put so much pressure on me that in the end I decided it wasn't worth it. I never turned up, and my chance of being a boxing champion disappeared.

As one door closed, another one unexpectedly opened. Joe Phillips's secretary at the garage next to our yard took a phone message and came over with a scrap of paper. She said a man had called and said, 'Tell Bartley Gorman that Hughie Burton is ready to fight him for the title at Doncaster Races.' He had left a phone number in Manchester. This was it. Big Just was finally going to defend his title against me. I got Joe's secretary to ring back and say, in her poshest voice, 'The coat is the same colour.' Meaning the challenge was accepted.

How I had waited for this moment. I was in prime condition, yet I knew Big Just would be the hardest fight I could ever have. His pride was insane: he refused to be beaten. A rich traveller called William Lee, who was great pals with Burton, told me how he would take your guts, liver and lights out, and was an animal unleashed. 'He is the dirtiest fighter in the world,' said Lee. 'Beat him to death. Do not let him get going or you will never stop him.' And this was his best friend!

The challenge was arranged for the Saturday of the St Leger race meeting at Doncaster racecourse. Burton had run Doncaster for years. It was the big meeting for all the rich, flash travellers, who would compete to see who had the best 'turnout' of motor and trailer. Everyone would be there. Where better to fight for the title? The whole gypsy world was agog. In the Blackie Boy pub in Newcastle-upon-Tyne, a group of influential travelling men gathered. There were Lees and Welches and Francises: ten men in all, and each one agreed to put up £2,000 to back me against Burton, a total of £20,000. They refused to have a drink until the business had been concluded; this was a very serious affair, backing someone against Burton, and they wouldn't discuss it in drink. That came later. Someone took a photograph of this historic meeting (see photo section).

Come the day, we set off from Uttoxeter in a convoy of half a dozen motors: it is always wise to have enough men to ensure fair play. At the head of the column was my red TR4 with chrome wheels and my left-hand-drive American Galaxy, red and white, with tinted windows and lights like dustbin lids. Only the bravest of my men were there: our Sam – who had been hit by a car and had his leg in plaster – Don Halden, Mick Mould, my Uncle Joe, Soldier Dave, Gandy Hodgkinson, Colin Morfitt, Alan Wilson, Caggy Barrett. I was in the back of the Galaxy with Morfitt driving. As ever before a knuckle fight, I felt no fear. I was twenty-eight years of age, six foot one and fifteen-and-a-half stone, fit, trained and ready. I had grown a chocolate-red quarter-beard and looked like a Viking.

When we reached Doncaster we drove straight to the Park Royal Hotel, where the tough travelling men drank. There was no point in hanging about. 'Pull up here,' I said when we reached the pub.

Sam marched through the doors swinging his plastered leg, hammered on the bar with a walking stick until everyone fell silent and announced loudly, 'My brother has come to fight Burton today – or any other man.'

The bar was jammed with hundreds of gypsy men yet you could hear a feather fall. Then I walked in, bellowing, 'I can beat any gypsy man in England, Ireland, Scotland, Wales and Europe. I am here to fight Uriah Burton right now on the racecourse.'

In seconds, the pub emptied. To challenge out Doncaster was almost unheard of. Day and night these people would talk about fights and the great fighters, but rarely would they ever get to see them because they were so secretive. To actually turn up amidst a huge gathering and challenge Big Just caused bedlam. Everyone wanted to see this one. They ran out to their cars, trucks and vans and jammed the roads down to the racecourse. I stood on the back of my cousin Pickwick Fury's transit truck so everyone could see me.

We made our way down to the field. Word had spread like a raging fire and thousands were gathering to see the fight – men, women and children running across the grass to get a good vantage point. There must have been 2000 motors and trailers. The plan was to back four lorries together and tie each corner with rope to make the ring forty feet square. I climbed onto the roof of my dead father's old A60 van and bawled out my challenge. 'Burton's a lemon and I can beat him drunk,' I shouted. I didn't mean it – I had too much respect for Big Just for that – but I knew how to drum up interest in a fight. My shirt was off and I had this chocolate stubble and red hair on my chest: the Irish were calling me 'Thom Gael', which means Big Red. I shadow-boxed, punching like a robot, my hands electric. Then I began a war dance on the roof of the van, my boots banging on the metal like a giant drum. By the time I had finished the old van was squashed to half its height.

Yet there was no sign of Burton. My people went out

searching for him while I continued to shout. They came back and reported that he wasn't there. He must have been feeling me out to see if I would turn up. I glared into the crowd with eyes like lightning. 'Bring on Muhammad Ali,' I shouted. 'I'm the only white man on earth who can beat Ali.'

When it was obvious Burton wasn't coming, I challenged everyone out. The best travelling men in England were there but no-one would fight me. For an hour I went berserk. The gypsy world had never seen anything like it.

Burton never arrived. He was testing my mettle and once he learned that I had passed the test, he knew his reign was over. It meant his title was now vacant, and all I needed to cement my succession was to beat another top man. There were no takers that day, and eventually we drove back home. We finally pulled into Phillips's Yard as it was dark. As Mick Mould left, he put his thumb up to me.

'I'll see you, champ,' he said.

CHAPTER 7

King of the Gypsies

MY FIGHT FOR THE title was arranged by two of the most notorious gypsies who ever lived. Will and Bob Braddock were living outlaws: cattle rustlers, horse dealers, fighters and drinkers, pure-born gypsies who lived on hedgehogs and duck eggs and ate tripe green. They could earn money like water yet would give you their last farthing; lived by their own code and feared no one. They were my type of men.

'Look out for the man with a straight finger,' my dad used to tell me. I never knew what he meant until one day our Sam came to me in Uttoxeter and said, 'I have met this man and once you see him you will never leave him while he lives.' It was Will Braddock. He came to one of my boxing shows and I saw that he had a straight finger: Will claimed he had been bitten by a stallion and had been unable to bend it ever since, though I later learned it was his brother Bob who bit him. He also claimed they were related to James Braddock, former heavyweight champion of the world. My dad had known I would find these men one day.

Will wore cream-coloured breeches and Luton shoes – yellow leather riding boots with elastic down the sides – and carried a cane. He was the greatest dealer you ever saw and used to shout 'Hellfire, pops-a-lary' when he was excited. Bob was six foot four, wore a watch and chain, a suit with big checks and a bowler hat. He had more cuts and scars than any man I had ever seen and had twice fought the great Atom Bomb, Tom Lee. Bob could eat for three hours: he would put out a market stall, lay it with a table cloth and then cover it with boiling hens, ham hocks, salted beef, boiled pigs' tails, cows' udders and sheep's *panshers*, washed down with bottles of Newcastle Brown Ale.

They lived their own way. For all his rough edges, Will never swore or cursed in his life, and they had a skewed sense of propriety. Once all four Braddock brothers – the other two were Jack and Isaac – decided to visit the Queen. They drove down to Buckingham Palace in an American sedan, arrived at the gates and demanded to see 'their' monarch. They thought they could just walk in and have a visit with Her Majesty and were very disappointed when the police arrived and escorted them away.

Will had bought a smallholding near what is now Alton Towers amusement park, not far from where I lived, and his base was the Raddle, a country pub with horse brasses and framed prints that overlooks the ancient Croxden Abbey and Hollington quarry, from where red stone has been cut for centuries to build churches and stately homes. The quarrymen would drink in the pub and that's where it gets its name – the red clay on their boots would stain the floor, and 'to raddle' means to make red. It had been a notorious pub but had quietened down until Will came on the scene.

We drank in there all night. There was singing, shouting, wenching, brawling and dealing, always dealing. Will and Bob were never happier than when buying and selling and both carried enough folding money to choke a horse. Hands were always being slapped to close deals, and they were shrewd. They could make a man bid twice what he wanted just by psychology.

We also had a tarmaccing team. 'Cowboy' Jessie Evans had black catgut around his eyes where he had stitched his own cuts after fights. He could lay tarmac as thin as a razor blade and was known as 'Skimmer'. Reg Martin, another one of the band, was the biggest conman in the country. He once had a fight with Hans Strieger, the all-in wrestler, at

Longnor Races and was thrown all over the place; I was then going to fight Strieger but it never came off. There was also Black Nelson Boswell. I found him parked at the side of a country lane in a three-wheeler Reliant Robin with a trailer behind it and chickens, greyhounds and ducks in little cages. He had on a great trilby hat and a handkerchief round his neck with a wedding ring through it, and his eyes were that dark he looked like Herman Munster. He was so big I couldn't believe he could fit in the bubble car.

'Can you find me somewhere to stop, brother?' he asked.

'There's a good tan down the road.' *Tan* means a stopping place in Romany; *gratch* is the equivalent in Cant. He moved onto Will Braddock's smallholding and became part of our group. We travelled in cattle boxes to tarmaccing jobs and at the end of each job, when we were paid, we'd have what Braddock called 'the big bust-up', an all-night drinking and singing session.

After Hughie Burton had failed to turn up Doncaster Races, I had challenged out every site in the British Isles but no-one would fight me. So Will contacted travellers, horse dealers and scrap metal merchants around the country to find the best fighter willing to take me on. Will also wanted to make a bit of money by betting on me. At that time there were a lot of trailers housing men working at the JCB plant at Rocester, not far from the Raddle pub. Some were relatives of a top fighter called Jack Fletcher, from London way. He was contacted – unbeknown to me – and said he would be happy to fight me.

We were tarmaccing the Raddle's car park and on this particular day I barrowed twenty-eight tons of tarmac single-handed: two men shovelled it in and I pushed it. The landlord paid us and it was time for the big bust-up. Yet for some reason, Will didn't want me to drink. Everybody was on the beer except me and I was a bit put out by it.

'If you drink, owd lad, I'm going from here,' said Will. 'You are supposed to be getting fit.'

I listened to him because I respected him, but I was upset. I also couldn't figure out why the phone kept ringing for him, and he kept getting up to make calls himself, because he was never a phone man. The later it got, the more fed up I became – I'd only had a couple of barley wines – and was about to go when Bob ordered some dinner to get me to stay.

I should have realised something was afoot. Will used to tell me, 'They will only come for you when you are drunk, owd lad.' (His prediction about them coming for me when drunk would come true when I met a fighter called Henry Francis – but that comes later.) He was keeping me sober for a reason. He knew that I only wanted to fight Big Just; anything less did not mean much to me. If he had told me about Fletcher I would have rowed with him and gone home, but he knew that once the man arrived I would not back down.

It was closing time when the door opened and a large crowd of travelling men came in. This was very unusual in such a remote place. They included Nunns, Webbs, Kidds and Fletchers, all gypsy breeds. The Kidds and Nunns in particular were wealthy men, dressed to the nines in suits and ties. 'Big Daddy' Walter Harrison from Cheshire arrived, a twenty-stone giant and one of the great gypsy fighters. I couldn't understand what they were all doing there.

'Hey, there's a man here to fight you, owd lad,' shouted Will Braddock.

The newcomers had brought Jack Fletcher with them and he was outside in a motor home. Fletcher had a reputation: he had beaten some good men in Ireland and Scotland, including Lander Scarrott, and had drawn with Levi Silks, a hard man from East Anglia. I had heard of him but thought he was just on the verge of past it, aged about thirty-seven. He wasn't a full-bred gypsy but three-quarter-bred, I believe, and worked as a roadway contractor. They called him 'Ganger Jack'.

'Where is this man, then?' I asked.

Will beckoned me outside and we went, followed by the rest of the pub. There was this big motor home, like a converted bus, and Fletcher was inside it, lying on a bed.

Will knocked on the door and Fletcher opened it. I was taken aback: he looked just like Hughie Burton, the exact size and build – shorter than me but heavier. His eyes were narrow and close set, he had a drooping blond moustache and wore a white shirt and Luton shoes laced at the front. I was fit back then, like two Jack Johnsons, but this man looked a handful. Everyone was looking at the two of us but saying nothing. It was up to us.

'Have you come to fight me?' I asked.

'I haven't come for a picnic,' said Fletcher. 'We're going to fight for Burton's vacant crown.'

To be honest, I didn't really feel up for it; I was stiff from moving all that tarmac. But I was showered, shaved and sober and had no excuses. There's no putting a fight off for a day with travellers: when you're challenged, you fight. With Will and Bob leading the way, we all set off to walk the few hundred yards down a gravel track that cut through fields into Hollington quarry. The moonlight was so bright you could pick up a pin. The quarry was a levelled area a few hundred yards across, enclosed by cut walls of stone: a natural amphitheatre. In the middle was a building with a large spotlight on the side. Someone switched it on and the yard was bathed in a yellow glow. You could make out the big saws and lumps of stone lying all around, spindles and broken church crosses and puddles of water in the reddish mud where lorries had driven through.

The men formed a loose circle around us and Fletcher took off his shirt, his braces still dangling from his waist. He was *butty* and solid and even in the half-light I could see his skin had a sheen; he wasn't some drinking man just pretending to be fit. He was in prime condition. Good. That was what I wanted. Fletcher had been building up to a big title affair and I hadn't: in a way it felt like just another street fight to me and I didn't have a nerve in my body.

There was a brief but lively argument over having Nelson Boswell as referee. The Kidds claimed he wasn't independent but in the end accepted him. Nelson had seen a lot of fights and knew what to do. I stripped off, ready to go in jeans and

American shoes, though I would have liked my handkerchief to tie around my waist, like the old pugilists used to.

Bob Braddock stepped forward, his bowler hat held high in his hand. 'This fight is for the championship of the gypsies of England, Ireland, Scotland and Wales,' he declared. 'Whoever witnesses it here tonight must go forth and tell it how it was, and if they do not, then they will answer to me.'

Then Nelson took off his shirt, revealing a big white belly and dark-tanned arms. He told everyone to keep back and motioned us together. There were to be no rounds, no kicking and no hitting a man on the deck.

'He's going to test you out, owd lad,' whispered Will Braddock into my ear. 'You had better win this one because I've got an acre of land on you.'

And so, heel-deep in red clay mud under the glare of the quarry spotlight, we fought to be King of the Gypsies.

*

WITH A SHARP JAB flush on my nose, Fletcher drew first blood. I was too confident, with my hands too low. *They haven't fetched a mug here*, I thought. I unleashed some power on him and he fell back against the door of a corrugated shed. He let go a right and it missed but as he came back he hit me with an elbow below the eye and put pins and needles in my head.

The boundaries of a prize-fight are fluid; there are no fixed ropes to keep you in. You can cover a lot of ground, moving, jumping, tripping over things, banging up against buildings, with the crowd all the time melting and re-assembling around you in a swarm. We scuffled around, the mud up to our ankles, as the Kidds shouted, 'Muller him,' which means 'kill him' in Romany, and our Sam shouted, 'Carib,' which means the same in Irish Cant.

Fletcher pulled me in. He had the grip of a wrestler and nearly threw me with a cross-buttock. I ripped myself free and after that there was no need for Nelson Boswell or anyone else. I unloaded with both hands and demolished Fletcher. He floundered, ducking down to avoid my blows and I knew he was finished. He caught me with a desperate body shot but I smacked an almighty left hook into his jaw and he fell in the clay.

'Count,' I ordered Nelson. I was always a man for the count – it means there can be no argument afterwards. Nelson tolled off the seconds up to 'ten', but there was no way Fletcher was getting up.

My friends came around me, our Sam slapping me on the back, the others shaking my hands. 'We have a new champion now,' declared Bob Braddock. I raised one bloodied fist aloft. I had done it. I had fulfilled my destiny. I was King of the Gypsies, bareknuckle champion, the toughest unarmed man in the country. Little did I know that my trials were just beginning.

Fletcher's friends helped him up. He and I had nothing more to say: I rarely talk to my opponents afterwards and anyway, he didn't seem too friendly. We went back in the pub and the celebrations began. By 5am I had drunk twenty-eight bottles of Newcastle Brown, and the party went on nonstop for three nights and days. The Nunns disappeared back to the flatlands of Norfolk but other travellers arrived at the Raddle from Ireland, Wales and Cornwall, pulling their trailers onto the car park and the surrounding fields: Prices, Lees, Hearns, Finneys, Calladines, Rileys and many others. We sang all the old songs: *The Wild Rover*, *The Black Velvet Band*, *The Shade of the Old Apple Tree* and Will's favourite, *The Man You Don't Meet Every Day*. Though thousands of pounds had changed hands in wagers, I never got two shillings out of it. All I wanted was the title – I had considered myself the best man for years, and now it was 'official'.

I later found out that they took Fletcher to his relations on the JCB site and in the middle of the night he got up spewing blood. He was taken to Burton Hospital and kept in for nearly a week with two broken ribs. I hadn't come out unscathed either; I had a black eye and a bloody nose. I never saw Fletcher again, but a year ago someone told me about him and said, 'He will never forget the fight he had with you, Bartley.' I won't forget it either.

Within twenty-four hours, every gypsy in the country knew I had won Burton's crown. Hughie himself even sent me a telegram of congratulations. He could still call himself a King of the Gypsies – once you have held the title, you are King until you die – but I was now the champion. I think he was glad to be rid of the most dangerous title on earth.

There was also a police enquiry after the fight and both Braddocks were hauled in for questioning. 'Never again, owd lad,' Will said to me.

*

THE BAREKNUCKLE WORLD was now where I belonged and, as champion, I could expect the challenges to come – and come they did. The first was in a pub in Buxton, Derbyshire, one quiet afternoon. Alan Wilson was there with his girlfriend, whom we called the 'Black Widow', young Geoff Barnett and a couple of others. It was a real pub – sawdust on a worn pine floor, old wooden stools, hand-pulled beers – and we'd had a few drinks when in walked a dozen men.

They wore big, dirty coats with the waists tied up, string tied around their breeches, and clogs. I knew there was going to be bother the minute they walked in; I always know. They had ferrets with them, terrier dogs, greyhounds and lurchers, and steam was coming off them. They were carrying dead rabbits, hares and pheasants, and stank of dead animals. They were hunters. Killers.

There was nobody else in the pub except an old man in the corner smoking a pipe. They came and sat around us. I was in the prime of my life then. If I had a new shirt I'd rip it up the seams and roll the sleeves up to my shoulders. We were drinking heavy beer – even the women were drinking pints – and we got talking to these men. One introduced the leader of them. 'This is Henry Quentin, gypsy man.'

I'd heard of him. He lived in a wagon in a wood on a

hillside in Derbyshire. He had shot his own half-brother dead and done ten years for it. He was taller than me, a big, fine-looking man with jet-black hair and wore an old soldier's coat with brass buttons, the sleeves pulled up to his elbows. The others were a mix of gypsy men, half-bred gypsy men and non-gypsy men: a band of what we call *slinks* – troublemakers, for want of a better definition. Their grey-hounds were slobbering and panting all around me in the sawdust.

'How much do you want for a couple of rabbits,' I asked Quentin.

'A pound for two.'

'I'll have two then.'

The rabbits were still warm. Quentin took a peg knife from his pocket, held up one of the rabbits and stuck the blade in. He cut the sinews of one back leg and pushed the other through it, then stretched the rabbit so it stayed stiff when cold and could be hung by the crossed legs. Then he stuck the knife in its stomach, slit it open and pulled out its guts. He held the bloody mess in his hand – guts, kidneys, liver, shitbag, the lot – lifted it to his throat and swallowed it whole. Then he got his pint of beer and swilled it down. He got the other rabbit and did the same again. I'm rough, but I had never seen anything like this. It nearly put me off buying them.

I have always been one to get my round, even for people across the other side of the pub who are part of our group but not sitting with us. I wouldn't go in a bar if I couldn't buy my round. So after I bought the rabbits, I got up and bought drinks for everyone. There was only one of Quentin's band, a little fellow in a Robin Hood hat sitting with a bottle of Guinness, who refused a drink. There's always a screw that you can't unscrew and always some man that's going to cause trouble, and he was it. A couple of times I got up to fetch trays of drinks and both times he declined.

Everything was going okay, the jukebox was playing, I was talking about hare coursing and they were on about badger baiting and cockfighting and fox killing. Then this little feller put his hand on me and said, 'I tell you something. I'll never drink with you again.'

'Why not?'

'You bought everyone a drink that's around this table but you never bought me one.'

'I asked you two or three times.'

'No you didn't.'

'I did.'

'Well,' he says, 'I'll never drink with you again.'

He caused everything to go quiet in the room. I knew this was trouble. I had been there a thousand times before.

'Right,' I said, 'I'll get you a drink now. And you'll drink it.'

'I won't.'

I went to the bar, bought a bottle of Guinness and put it in front of him.

'I won't drink it,' he said.

'If you don't drink it, I'm going to push it right down your throat. Now drink it.' So he did.

Slowly, Henry Quentin got up. He was a tall man. He turned towards the jukebox, took a running kick at it and smashed it. Then he kicked two or three tables over. This was all for my benefit. The poor barman didn't say boo. I knew Quentin could fight but I didn't know he was a prize-fighter. I later found out he'd had about ten prize-fights and lost only once.

'Do you want that man out?' I asked the barman.

He didn't answer. He was frozen with fear.

'Hold it,' said Quentin. 'Who's going to put me out? You?'

We were now facing each other at the bar.

'Listen,' he said, 'before we go any further, do you know who I am? I'm a gypsy man.'

'Yeah? Do you know who I am?'

'No.'

'I'm the king of them.'

As I said it, he threw a right cross at me. 'Hang on, hang on,' I said. I wanted a prize-fight, not a bar-room brawl. He stopped.

'So you're the King of the Gypsies?' he said. 'So if I beat you then I'm king of them?'

'Yeah.'

So they pulled the chairs back and a title fight began there and then. That's the way it is.

Quentin put up a good fight. He backed me into the wall, knocked a picture frame down and caught me with a few because he hadn't long been in and I'd had a few drinks. He was determined to beat me and all his men were shouting, 'Go on, give it him!' The Black Widow jumped on the bar screaming, 'Go on, Bartley, beat him,' and Alan Wilson was yelling too. I accidentally trod on one of the dogs and made it yelp, and as I looked down at it, Quentin almost broke my jaw with a right. Someone else threw a dead rabbit at me, hitting me on the side of the face.

I backed Quentin along the bar but he kicked me in the shins with his clogs: hard wood on bone. I drew back and bull-hammered him so hard that he flew through the swinging doors of the pub. Outside, on the pavement at the crossroads in the middle of Buxton, were some railings and somehow his head jammed in them. That brought a hush down in the pub.

'Is there any of you other men wants a fight with me now?'

I glared at the rest of them. You have to – you can't sit back down drinking once the ball's gone up. A blond-haired man with a flattened nose looked a tough one and I thought he was going to fight me, but he shook his head. We drank our beer – I never, ever, leave the beer – then left. As we walked off down the street they were still trying to pull Quentin's head from the railings.

We split up and I went with young Geoff Barnett to a place at the top of the square where they sold takeaway food. We heard a fire engine heading down towards the pub to cut Quentin out. I jumped in the Mini with Geoff and we sat eating our chicken and roast 'taters when who should come along but the man in the Robin Hood hat. I gestured him over.

'Come here.'

He stopped.

'Let me tell you something,' I said. 'Never, ever, ever, cause anything like that in a public house with me again, for no reason. Else I'll break your nose.'

He was too mean to be afraid. He stared back at me with his beady eyes. 'If you touch me, I'll blow your head off,' he said. He meant it.

'You'll blow my head off? Well, if you're going to do that, I'd better give you a reason to do it.'

I grabbed him by the shoulders through the open window, pulled him into the Mini and headbutted him half a dozen times, then threw him out and threw his hat on top of him. We left him there in a heap and went into the Eagles pub, stopping for half an hour before we headed home.

Five minutes after we had left the Eagles, the little man came in looking for me with a twelve-bore gun. When he saw I wasn't there, he had a row with another man and blasted him stone dead in the bar. It was in *News of World* the next day. The landlord and customers identified him and he got fifteen years. I later heard he killed another man in prison.

This was the kind of danger that now lurked all around me.

CHAPTER 8

Streetfighting Man

IF YOU HAVE a tongue in your mouth and a brain in your head you can earn money. I loved hawking. I would buy anything, sell anything and trade anything. Money came, money went. Despite the success of my boxing promotions, they took a back seat once I met the Braddock brothers. They got me into horse dealing; it was their life. They always had more than 100 horses, ponies, mules and donkeys at any one time and would *puv* them – get permission off a farmer to put them on his land (*puv* is the Romany word for field) then later sneak them all out, owing the farmer a lot of money. Will and Bob would also rustle cattle. I was forever getting them out of scrapes in the middle of the night, horses or cows all over the road, trying to get them into horseboxes with policemen everywhere.

I never stole but sometimes did the odd bit of poaching; well, no-one owns the animals of the earth, do they? Once we were near Rugeley, wheeling and dealing, and pulled up in the countryside in a bullnosed Bedford dormobile. There was a bit of a reservoir and then a hill with a herd of sheep on it. Gandy Hodgkinson said, 'We'll rustle a sheep.'

'Okay then.'

So four of us got out and ran up the hill into the field. The sheep took some catching but eventually we grabbed one and I gave it a bull-hammer straight between the eyes. We got the stunned beast in the back of the dormobile and took it to Gandy's house, where Soldier Dave killed, skinned and gutted it in the bath with a carving knife. We decided to have a big roast the next day and invite lots of people. The sheep was left in the bath to go cold and eventually we all went to bed.

An eighty-year-old ex-soldier called Alfie rented one of the rooms in Gandy's house. We were awoken in the middle of the night to hear Alfie wailing, 'Gandy's dead, Gandy's dead.'

Alfie used to get up in the night to go to the loo, but instead of using the toilet he would piss in the sink. After doing his business he had stumbled over the side of the bath in the dark, fallen on the sheep and thought it was Gandy. We couldn't eat the sheep knowing that Alfie had urinated on it, so in the morning Dave and Colin Morfitt washed it, cut it up into chops and gave them out to all the people in the road. They thought Christmas had come early. I asked one of them later what his chop was like. 'It was nice,' he said, 'but a bit salty.'

Our travels took us all over the country, living by our wits. Once I was with Soldier Dave coming back from Manchester and had no money and hardly any petrol. We got as far as Macclesfield when the fuel gauge hit empty. So we called at a couple of farms, scrounged some plastic bags and filled them with cow muck, then went round a couple of nice housing estates selling the bags at five bob a time as best horse manure. We got back home with a full tank of petrol and enough for a meal and few pints that night. We did it regularly after that. We'd get paid off the farmers for clearing their cowsheds of muck and then paid by the householders to put it on their roses. We couldn't lose. Scrap metal was another regular earner. We would get dynamos, break off the casing and get all the strands of copper inside. Used batteries were also valuable. You could go out in a mini-van and make a week's wage in a few hours.

By now I was practised at handling people from all walks of life. I once bought 200 bars of blue steel, each twelve feet long, off a scrap man for a quid each. I put them on a lorry and hawked them round factories for two or three quid each. I went into one big factory with my last fifty bars and the foreman took me up a flight of stairs to see the boss, a self-important little man sitting behind a huge desk. I told him how good this steel was, no rust on it. He came out, had a look, and said, 'How much?'

'Three quid each.'

'I'll have all of them,' he said. 'Take them over there and count them out,' he ordered his foreman. The foreman counted them and said there were fifty.

'When will you pay me?' I asked. This was a Friday and I wanted some cash.

'I'll pay you at four o'clock and I'll pay you by cheque,' said the little Hitler.

I went back at four and he was in his office, chewing a fat cigar and paying out his men for the week. They were all around him like lapdogs.

'I've got a question to ask you,' he said, showing his men how tough he was. 'Where did you get this stuff from?'

He was clearly implying it was stolen. I looked at him and said, 'Do you think I'm going to tell you where I got this from? What a fool do you think I am? For you to go and buy it at the same price as me? Come on, give me my cheque or I'll take it away.'

He squirmed down in his seat like a little weed. That man was so pleased to be talked down to for once, instead of all the men lapping up to him. 'Bring him his cheque,' he ordered.

We would buy anything, often just for a lark. I once acquired a broken-down piano and left it on the lawn of my friend Manchester Ken. His missus went berserk. Ken had the last laugh. He sold it on to someone after showing them how it worked by playing a tune on it; they didn't know that only eight keys functioned on it and Ken had memorised which ones they were.

I spent a lot of time in Liverpool, a place my family knew well. My grandfather's brother, Jimmy Gorman was a 'tatter', a rag-and-bone man, all around Merseyside, and is buried in Birkenhead. Many a time I went down by the docks to do deals, buying metal and broken anchors and drinking in pubs so rough the police wouldn't go there. I had fights in back streets I wouldn't want to walk down now, and brawls with men on club doors – I always went round with my shirt ripped up the sides and the sleeves rolled up, and they'd try to stop me going in by saying I had to wear a tie. Once inside I used to take off my shirt and dance near the band. They must have thought I was a caveman. Danger was all around me but I couldn't see it. I thought I was immune to it, because of the way I had been brought up. I was arrogant; there is no point in denying it. For all I know I might have been in the Cavern Club dancing to the Beatles in the early Sixties. The names of the bands meant nothing to me then. I didn't take any notice of the pop charts. I just liked good rock 'n' roll.

I was in one dockside pub in Liverpool with a London traveller called Joe Lock, who had four tits, and an Irish tinker called Jackson Delaney. We were talking about fighting.

'There is no question about it,' Jackson said to me, 'I could beat you if I was a bit bigger.' He was a very good welterweight.

'Well, I bet you could give me a good fight anyway, Jackson,' I said. 'But you ain't big enough. You know Joe here? He's your weight. If you're so good, fight him.'

Joe was straight up for it. He got his shirt off in the pub, his four nipples showing.

'No, I won't fight you,' said Jackson.

I goaded him. 'Come on, you are making an idiot of yourself.'

Eventually they went out into the yard. It was dark but there were lights in the yard. I was referee: I had to break them and count if one went down. Another man fetched a water bucket. They were both skilful and fought for thirty minutes. Jackson split Joe Lock's lip so badly that I stopped it. They shook hands afterwards and Joe went to get his lip stitched.

I was often called upon to referee fights because men knew I would see fair play. I even refereed a fight between two women in Moss Side, Manchester, at a pub crowded with gypsies. One was a black-haired Ward, the other a redhead, and they'd had a row. They stripped off to their bras and Dave put the headlights on the motor outside to give them some light. It was a vicious fight, too. There was blood running down between their breasts. A policeman came by, one of the travellers slipped him some money and he just kept on walking, looking the other way. The pub was so rough that every night the police had to come in to call time.

Moss Side was one of my regular haunts. In the Seventies it was a demolition zone: many of the rows of terraced slums were being pulled down to make way for high-rise flats and there were derelict buildings and rubble everywhere. It was full of travellers, especially Irish, who would pull their trailers onto the demolition sites and could easily find casual building work. I went all around there doing deals. You could sell anything in the pubs – antiques, furniture, tools, clocks, you name it. I always made out I only had one of a particular item, even if I had another ten on the motor outside. It made it more desirable.

In recent years Moss Side has become infamous for gang wars and drugs but it was plenty rough in the Seventies too, I can tell you. Imagine a place full of black immigrants off the plantations of the West Indies, mixed with Irish navvies and the local Mancunians, most of them poor. There were boxing gyms and illegal drinking dens and illicit gambling dives, open all hours. If you wanted a fight you could find one in an instant.

One dark night I had come out of the pub and was standing in a shop doorway eating some takeaway food when two black men approached. They both pulled out knives. Without even thinking, I kicked my heel through the shop window behind me and picked up the biggest shard of glass. The two would-be muggers looked at me, looked at the spear of glass, looked at each other and walked off, as coolly as they could. Sensible men.

A man with a bit of a reputation mouthed off at me in the pub one day. I walked outside with Soldier Dave to have a word with him and he jumped in his mini-van and locked the doors.

'If you want to fight, fight me man,' I shouted. 'Get out the van.'

He wouldn't get out. Dave said, 'Leave it, he's a waste of time, all mouth.'

I was still mad. 'I'll show him,' I said, and lifted up the front of his van. That's how strong I was. He started the van and the wheels were spinning but he couldn't get away. But neither could I now – if I dropped it he'd run straight into me and kill me! Eventually he cut the motor and I let him go.

Spending so much time in places like Moss Side and the Dingle in Liverpool, I developed a sixth sense for danger. Everywhere I went I was ready for trouble. I needed to be.

*

ONE CHRISTMAS, JOHNNY Wheeldon and I went to Manchester in an A60 van to earn a bit of dough. Johnny, the brother of my girlfriend Gwendoline, had been one of my boxers and could look after himself in a brawl. On the first day I bought a load of copper for £40 and sold it for £150. We went on the beer and were driving back through Moss Side to our digs at the end of the evening when we saw a man lying in the gutter, surrounded by police and flashing lights.

'Pull over. Travellers,' I said to Johnny.

The man in the gutter was in a blue serge suit, face down in his own blood on the concrete. He looked dead. It was drizzling with rain and the wet road shone under the streetlight.

'What's happened to him?' I asked the nearest policeman. 'Was he hit by a car?'

'No. His son did it.'

He nodded towards a big, blond-headed man being restrained by four policemen. I got out of the car, my sleeves rolled up to the top of my biceps.

'Have you just done that to your own father?'

The blond man stopped struggling with the officers and looked at me like dirt. He was as big as me and as strong as a bull but was drunk.

'Yes, and I'll do worse to you,' he slurred.

Whether the police let him go, or he broke loose, I don't know, but anyway he came at me like a madman. I waited for his rush and then bull-hammered him straight to the face. As he began to crumble, I hit him with five or six more full-blooded shots. The policemen watched as he collapsed in a heap.

'He deserved that,' I said. Then I got back in the car and we drove away.

A few days later we were still hawking round terraced houses, up entries and in factories, and a man asked me for a feather bed. I went to an antique place, got a mattress for £1, put it in the motor and ran it round to the address he had given me. It was a boarded-up townhouse that looked half derelict. I knocked on the door and they said, 'Come in.' Johnny and I took the bed in.

Moss Side is a dismal place in December. It was freezing in this flophouse but there were people living there, with a fire on and a Christmas tree and holy pictures on the wall. Some men were drinking hard liquor. I gave them the bed for nothing, a present for Christmas, and while Johnny was taking it upstairs I crouched in front of the hearth in the living room to warm myself. I happened to look up at a man in an armchair and saw that he had black stitches all over his face. It was the father who had been lying in the gutter a few nights before. He still had on the same blue serge suit. I was startled for a moment and he caught my eye.

'Hey, you,' he said, in an evil rasp. 'You were just looking at me.'

'No I wasn't.'

I was thinking, *the son must be here, the one I beat up. There's going to be a riot.*

'I seen you looking at my face,' he rasped. 'I'm asking you

121

a straight question, you with the red hair. Do you think you can do better?'

There's gratitude for you.

'Yeah, I could. A lot better.' I stood up.

Suddenly the house came alive. Men appeared in the gloom out of different rooms. This was a death trap. Fortunately Johnny had come down the stairs and quickly weighed up the situation. He pulled a huge knife out of the back of his trousers, held it in front of him and grabbed me by the shoulder. We backed out of the house and got away.

The next day, we went to a demolition site and I asked the foreman if he had any old metal.

'I'll sell you the iron,' he said.

'Okay.'

'Come back at one o'clock.'

Now we needed a truck to transport the iron. 'Let's go and get some travellers and I'll take them in on the deal,' I said to Johnny. We went to a demolition site where forty trailers were parked and the first man I saw was an Irishman called Paddy Doran. I didn't know him then, but Paddy would later become my best drinking pal. If he saw a butterfly kill an elephant he wouldn't turn a hair, he has seen that many things.

'Hey pal, has anyone got a big truck?'

'My friend Felix has,' he replied.

Felix Rooney was about fourteen years older than me and one of the best fighters in Ireland. We had met years before when I was a teenager hare coursing in Wales but I barely remembered him.

'Come in,' said Felix.

We went in to his trailer and they made us breakfast while we explained the situation. Felix had a twenty-ton tarmac-laying lorry and said he would rent it to us. Then Felix, who was very much the main man on the camp, said, 'Shall we go to the pub?'

This is typical of the Irish travellers. It was still only mid-morning.

'Okay, but I'll only have a half,' I said, fool that I was.

Felix, Johnny and I went into the heart of Moss Side. By the time we'd visited two or three pubs, we were well into the drinking, with the festive atmosphere and more travellers joining us all the time, in big old pubs full of blacks and Irish. Of course, that was the end of going back for the metal at one o'clock. We decided we'd see the foreman the next day.

Johnny ended up having a row with a man in a pub. They went outside and a few of us were watching them fight when the police arrived, arrested us and took us in. They took our names down and did a check to see if we were wanted for anything. 'Not wanted at the present time,' it came back. They let us go but warned us, 'Don't drive that motor for two hours because you've been drinking.'

We walked around for a bit and went into a butcher's shop with a lot of sheep hanging up with muslin over them. I bought a complete Canterbury sheep for thirty shillings and put it in the back of Johnny's van. We couldn't wait two hours so after fifteen minutes we jumped in the van and headed to a pub with a huge, dingy cellar, like a dungeon. There were white prostitutes in there and a full-size photo of Muhammad Ali on the wall. The black man behind the bar was draped in a fake tiger skin. 'I'm a witch doctor,' he said. It was one of the roughest pubs in Manchester.

Felix Rooney was by now quite loud and attracting attention. I got drinking with a little black guy called Bobby, who wore a pork pie hat. He was telling me all about Moss Side when suddenly he paused. 'Don't look now,' he said, 'but they're going to roll you on the stairs when you go out.'

I leaned back in my chair and casually looked through the corner of my eye. Three or four evil-looking men were leaning on the winding staircase. We were like varmints in a trap. It didn't look good, especially as they would almost certainly have weapons.

Loudly enough so that they could hear, I shouted to the barman, 'I'm starving for something to eat. Is there anywhere I can eat?'

'My brother has got a restaurant up above,' said the barman.

'How long is this place open for?'

'All night.'

'Then get some more drinks in for everyone, we'll get something to eat off your brother and we'll be back down.'

So he gave them the nod on the stairs and they moved, leaving it for later. I got Johnny and Felix and dragged them out. We jumped in the van and were gone.

The evening should have ended there but the real drama had not even begun. We next went to see Felix Doran, who was Felix Rooney's father-in-law and one of the biggest tarmaccers in Manchester at the time. He was playing the pipes. Old Felix is famed as the best uilleann pipe player in Ireland. By now we were almost legless and after a couple more it was time to go. 'I'll leave you now Felix and see you tomorrow,' I said.

One of the women in the pub, some relation to Felix, stood up and said, 'You fetched him with you, you take him back home.'

So we put him in the motor and went drinking again. We drank until the pubs shut, singing and carousing. Then Felix said, 'Let's go back to my place and have a takeaway,' by which he meant a crate of beer each. So we did.

I said, 'Felix, I don't want to go back to your camp with all the children asleep, we'll go to some boarding house.'

'I know a place then,' he said, 'not far from the trailers.'

It was a three-storey Victorian house, the only building standing on a crossroads surrounded by rubble and swan-necked lamps. We took the crates up to the top floor. There were rows of beds and two Irishmen in there. We gave them a drink. One had a melodeon with button keys and he played it while Johnny and Felix play-wrestled on the bed, drunk.

I asked the men if there was anything to eat. By now it was one o'clock, too late to buy anything, and they had only bread. Then I remembered the sheep: we could cut it up and fry some chops. I went down the stairs and out into the foggy night. As I got to the van, I found a man in the back taking the sheep out . . . it was the man in the blue serge suit with the stitches in his face. He looked at me, then ran away with the sheep on his back. 'Come back with my sheep,' I shouted. It was farcical. I chased him but he went up some alleyway and I lost him in the fog.

There was nothing I could do but trudge back up the stairs. Eventually Felix decided to go back to his camp, which was less than half a mile away. We'd see about the scrap metal the next day. I lay on a bed and threw an old coat over me and was just drifting off when I heard a terrible commotion outside, shouting and barking. I went to the window and saw Felix in the middle of the road, under the streetlight, with his fists up, roaring, 'I'm the best man in the thirty-two counties of Ireland.'

There was a mob of men, women and children facing him in a very angry mood. At the head of them was the man who had stolen my sheep.

'Felix is going to be killed,' I shouted to John.

We ran down. As we got out, there must have been sixty people attacking Felix. I said to Johnny, 'Get the motor, quick.' There was no point running in; there were far too many of them. We got the van and drove into them. They smashed the van to scrap with iron bars and bricks. Felix was on his knees in a mask of blood. I thought he was going to die. I couldn't even get out of the van, there were that many bricks bouncing off it. Johnny drove off, then turned and came back at speed. We drove at them three or four times to get them away from Felix, with our heads down. The windows were all broken.

On one foray, I shouted, 'Get under the Morris 1000 van, Felix.' He managed to crawl under it and the mob never had enough brains to tip it over to get him. Now somehow we had to distract them. We pulled up 100 yards away and got out with the motor still running. It was brick for brick then with forty men. They were overpowering us, coming from the alleys and ginnels, like Indians calling each other in the dark. I got hit in the shoulder and then nearly had my leg broke with a brick. Johnny nearly had his head crushed and was also hit between the legs. We got them away from the Morris 1000 but we couldn't hold them off any longer.

Felix's camp was only a minute's drive away, so I sped there as quickly as I could. A passing driver had rung the police and I saw a blue light at the camp. The policemen were staring at our smashed up van as we yelled, 'Come on, they are killing a man under a Morris 1000.' Most of the men from the camp had gone to a dance but Paddy Doran came back with us as we led the police to the scene. Felix was still under the motor with the mob going mad in the streets. I jumped out of the van and shouted, 'Come up one by one and I'll fight you all.'

Four riot vans arrived and officers jumped out with their batons ready and dogs snarling at the leash. The Irishmen immediately started brawling with them. Loads were arrested. We managed to get Felix into an ambulance and then followed him to the hospital. He was in a terrible mess but at least he was alive. Johnny and I finally got to bed in another lodging house. It was horrible: you went up stairs and there were rows of damp beds with men on them. I had to sleep with a club under my pillow.

Felix recovered but was never the same man after. I didn't see him again for three years but he said he got every one of them back, one by one. That night had taught me a very important lesson: one man cannot fight a mob.

*

ONE-ON-ONE was my style but by the mid-Seventies no gypsy man wanted to fight me; they can deny it now but it was true. Others didn't know who I was and didn't care. One I encountered in the Travellers Rest pub near the Winking Eye in Derbyshire, a beauty spot from where you can see all the Cheshire plain and the North Wales mountains. I was in there with Will Braddock and a gang. Braddock was rustling cattle at the time and had some in a horsebox outside. I was lying on top of the bar against the handpumps, with a load of women around me, the gypsy fighter. That's how I was when I was younger. Some of them were pouring Guinness over me and rubbing it into my muscles; Braddock told them it helped condition me.

'I'll put an acre of land on him to fight any man in England,' Will told the pub.

'I'll fight him.'

We looked around to see who had said it. There was a big lump of a fellow sitting in a corner drinking a pint of beer, with a group of men. The locals called him 'Big John'. A lot of men would get jealous when they heard I was King of the Travellers. They'd get the hardest bloke in the pub and wind him up: 'Go on, challenge him, tell him you'll give him five hundred pounds if you lose.' I also used to have a lot of women around me and that made it worse.

'He only fights travelling men,' said Braddock

'I'll fight him,' repeated Big John. He got up, walked over and slammed his hand down on the bar. 'There's six fivers. That's all I've got.'

This is what happens. Men come from nowhere.

I said, 'No.' I didn't want to fight the guy for thirty quid.

But Big John insisted. He had dark eyes, a white face, a smashed nose and big lips. I found out later he was forty-two years old and an ex-Marine. He looked like he knew the drill. So we agreed to meet the next day on Ladybower Dam on the River Derwent.

We arrived early in the morning. Will Braddock and his men cut down two evergreens with a chainsaw, made four posts out of them, tied rope around them and put saddles on the corners to stop us hitting our heads. That was the ring. The word had spread among the local farmers and labourers and dozens came in tractors and hay carts, hanging off the sides. The one unusual thing about Big John, he never took off his long coat. It did little to protect him – he was big and strong but he couldn't fight too well and I had little trouble with him. He took some punishment before he was counted out.

In 1974, my Uncle Bartley died. He asked me to go to his deathbed but I couldn't because I knew he would ask me never to fight again and by now I couldn't stop. The main arenas for the gypsies were the pot fairs, horse fairs and race meetings. There are many of these events during the year: Appleby, Barnet, Cambridge, Coventry, Doncaster, Epsom, Horsmonden, Nottingham, Stow-in-the-Wold, St Boswells and Musselburgh in Scotland, Ballinasloe and the Puck Fair in Ireland, and so on. I challenged out many of them, with no luck. I remember strutting around Nottingham Goose Fair with our Sam and Bill Braddock and nobody would fight me, even though it was packed with travellers. Nobody would say boo. Yet there were plenty of good men in the Seventies. These were the best of them:

SAM GORMAN

Our mother had made me promise that I would never fight Sam, either in the ring or out. I'm glad, because I would not have cared to fight him: he was the best of the lot, with an eighty-four-inch reach compared to my seventy-five inches, and didn't care who he was fighting. He smashed Tim Wood, a British champion, to pieces in the gym when Wood was in his prime. He also tried to demolish me in Jack Gardner's gym at Highfields, Leicester, and I had to get on my bike and tell him to ease off.

'I could take you, boy,' I said to him later.

He came back with a line of Muhammad Ali's: 'If you even dream that, you better wake up and apologise.'

In 1971, the American heavyweight contender Jerry Quarry came to England to fight the reigning British champion, Jack Bodell. Quarry was class and was looking for top-quality sparring partners. Sam went down to the gym with his gloves and was taken on. After two days, they paid him off. Quarry couldn't do anything with him; Sam wouldn't take a backward step, not even to a world-class fighter. Quarry went on to knock out Bodell in one round, so that shows you how good he was. Sam always had the greatest respect for him and later named one of his sons Jerry.

Jack Gardner, the former British heavyweight champion, was on the lookout for a protégé and took Sam under his wing. He said Sam had the best left jab he had ever seen. He also wanted me to sign for him but I said, 'No, I'm a bareknuckle prize-fighter. I don't fight with women's powder puffs on my hands.' *I didn't really mean it.* Eventually Sam was lined up to have his pro debut on a Jack Solomons show at the Café Royal in London. A few days before the bout, Gardner called him to one side and said, 'Look Sam, I have got a lot of influential friends coming to this show. I don't want you under any circumstances to let me down.'

'I tell you what I will do Mr Gardner,' said Sam.' I'm letting you down right this minute.'

He grabbed Gardner's hand, shook it and walked out. It was gypsy pride: he wouldn't be talked to like that by anyone.

JOHN-JOHN STANLEY

The Stanleys are an old and venerable breed from the New Forest and John-John was their champion. A top fighting man, he is still respected and feared down in Berkshire and Hampshire. He would wear an old-fashioned silk around his waist and was in the papers occasionally for fighting at fairs and shows. He is also a gentleman. A newspaper once reported that he and I were going to fight at a fair but it never happened. He'd have been a handful, even for me. He fought in a low crouch and punched almost exclusively to the body: barefist blows to the ribs can be terribly effective and don't damage your hands as much as headshots.

John-John's most famous fight was against his friend 'Boxer' Tom Taylor, another name known wherever gypsy men talk fighting. John-John was the bigger man but Boxer Tom could really go: he once beat five bouncers in a fight and can still do somersaults and handstands today. They fought for fifty-five minutes in a field near Watford in 1972. At one stage they had to cut the swellings on Boxer Tom's eyes with razors so he could see but he kept going. Finally John-John unintentionally caught Tom in the eye with this thumb. His eye was pulled out from its socket and hung down on his cheek and they had to stop the fight. John-John refused to claim victory because it was impossible for Boxer Tom to carry on and they called it a draw. They are very best friends now.

MARK RIPLEY
I fought Mark Ripley down in Kent in the late Sixties. He was a few years younger than me but utterly fearless and by the Seventies was known as a man to avoid. He and I never went at it again but he'd have given me a stern test. I did hear that Ripley wanted to fight Cliff Field, an unlicensed boxer who at the time was the daddy of all them in London – what they call the 'guv'nor' down there. That never came off either. I don't know who would have won but I do know that in a streetfight Ripley would have eaten most men alive.

BOBBY and JAMESY MACPHEE
Two notorious fighting brothers from Scotland, their father, Old Bobby, had been a top man in his day and was head of the clan, descended from Celtic tinsmiths. They went on the rampage at Musselburgh one year and chopped up a load of trailers with buzzsaws, for some reason. Big Jamesy was the champion of Scotland, a mountain of a man who was said to fight in a kilt. I was willing to take him on any time but we never got to it, though I was once on the same ground. I had gone up to Musselburgh Fair, near Edinburgh, which is held every August, to fight another top Scottish knuckler called Jackie Lowe. It never happened – Lowe was warned off by the police, who also came to see me about it. I still went to the fair and that was when I saw Big Jamesy, through the crowd. He was a fierce-looking man and was definitely the Scottish champ, though Lowe disputed it. He never came to me, even though I was on his patch.

Lowe was a very good man but I later heard that he and Jamesy had a row and Jamesy picked Lowe up and put him headfirst through a one-armed bandit. I don't know if it's true because I wasn't there. Lowe was a good technician but Jamesy was an all-in merchant, a big, rough man. He would be in his late forties today and weighs in at over twenty stone. Brother Bobby was another rough diamond but became a born-again Christian, like quite a lot of former gypsy fighters.

JOHNNY FRANKHAM

The Frankhams are from the south-east of England and one of them, Eli, was chairman of the National Romany Rights Association. They also have a long fighting pedigree. Gypsy Johnny was four years younger than me and one of the best British boxers of the Seventies, a skilful light-heavyweight. He was a bit of a clown in the ring and liked a drink but he could use his fists, inside and outside the ropes. He had a couple of very tough British title fights in 1975 with Chris Finnegan, who said Frankham was 'slippery as a jellied eel'. There was a riot at the Royal Albert Hall after their first fight, when Frankham won by half a point and both sets of supporters piled into each other. Johnny used to gamble away his purse money on the dice.

I challenged Johnny a couple of times to meet me bare-knuckle at Doncaster Races but he didn't show. I would have liked to test his boxing skills against mine. I was bigger than him but he was quick and experienced. His brother Sam was another good man and one of his relatives, young Bobby Frankham, became a barefist fighter in the Eighties.

SIMON DOCHERTY

The Dochertys are a vast clan of Irish travellers living in England. They had two top fighters called Simon: one was known as Blond Simey and the other Black Simey and they never fought each other because they were cousins. Blond Simey is the son of Barney Docherty, the great Irish knuckle man who was coming to England to fight Big Just when he mysteriously died on a train. I nearly fought Blond Simey several times. I had been out drinking in Coventry with Will Braddock and my younger brother John and drove our Transit van onto an old building site where lots of English and Irish travellers were stopping. Some men came round the van and we got talking to them through the windows. The conversation turned to fighting and one of these Irishmen said, 'Simon Docherty is the best man among travellers.'

'No, my brother Bartley is,' said John.

'Is that so?' said the man. 'Well if he is that good, go down on the camp now. Simon Docherty is on it.'

I looked over and said, 'What did you say?'

'He is down there on the camp if you want to fight him.'

'Fight him?'

I set off in that Transit so fast we bounced over the foundations of demolished houses, the van going up in the air. Even Will, a hard man to unnerve, was frightened.

'We're going to get killed,' he shouted

'I'll show you who's scared,' I said.

We got down to a camp of fifty trailers. Parked in the middle were two carloads of men, talking. I spun the van around, jumped out and ripped off my shirt. They set two dogs on me: I kicked one into the air and the other ran off. It was a wicked thing to do but I was in a fury. I ran at the motors and tried to overturn one of them and the men fled. Simon wasn't there.

Three days later, a band of Irishmen came to my mother's at Hinckley. 'Is Bartley Gorman here, missus?' one asked. 'He's got a red TK and we want to buy it.'

'He hasn't got one of those,' my mother replied.

'I'll tell you the truth, missus. I've come to fight him.'

'Well he's not here.'

They left. Ten minutes later, our Sam arrived and my mother told him what had happened. He went berserk. He jumped in the motor with John and clocked up 200 miles looking for them. Fortunately for them, he never found them.

It was later arranged that Simey and I would fight for a purse of £50,000 but it never happened. It would have sparked a total war and neither family would have had any peace so we called a truce. He and Black Simey always wanted to back me after that. Blond Simey is one of the finest fighters ever to come out of Ireland and he and I are now very good friends. He has recently suffered badly from arthritis but will always be tough as teak and runs three or four camps.

BOB GASKIN

My open challenge at Doncaster in 1972 had reverberated through the illegal fighting world. It had also upset the local gypsies, chiefly a family called the Gaskins and their friends. The Gaskins are a notorious breed, the scourge of Yorkshire and the East Coast. They are blond, not dark like most gypsies, and are not tall – five foot six or eight – but solid and really fearsome people.

Their main man at the time was Bob. He was a vicious character who would fight anyone at the drop of a hat. His grandmother, Old Pol Gaskin, had been the best fighting woman among all gypsies but had a fight with my grandmother – who was pregnant with my Aunt Mary at the time – and lost. Perhaps the Gaskins carried a grudge against my family from then on. Certainly there was no love lost. Bob Gaskin had lots of fights, including three against Blond Simon Docherty. Simey lost one but won the other two.

*

ALL OF THIS time, I was letting the unlicensed boxing slide, and others came in on the act. In London, one or two promoters cottoned on that they could draw big crowds by matching brawlers together outside Boxing Board control. And so the London hardmen came on the scene.

The original was probably Donny 'the Bull' Adams. A former Barnardo's boy who graduated to Borstal and later jail, he had been around for years, fighting on motorway service stations and parking lots. He would go to fairs, place a bucket at his feet and let people have three shots at his chin for a pound. He would also pick up a 56lb weight with his teeth. He had nearly fought Hughie Burton ten years before but he was now well over the hill and going grey.

In 1975, it was announced that he was going to fight a former Essex jailbird called Roy Shaw for the title of

'Guv'nor of London'. Shaw was no spring chicken either but the papers were full of it, calling it 'the fight of the century', while Adams was billed as 'King of the Gypsies', which was bullshine, as he wasn't even a traveller. Shaw was nicknamed 'Pretty Boy'. I didn't know anything about him except what the papers said – that he was a vicious criminal who had served fifteen years for a bullion robbery and had been one of the hardest men in the prison system. The pair of them even went on a television talk show saying how they would both fight to the death.

I thought it was all hokum but our Sam and his pal Matt Lee, a London traveller, both wanted to see the fight and kept pestering me to go. So on December 1, 1975, we drove out to this Big Top in a field at a place called Winkshire in Berkshire. Every villain in London must have been there. Sam and I shouldered our way through the crowd – people tended to move out of the way when we came through – and walked down to ringside. Sam looked at me. He could read my mind. I was going to wait until the fight was over, then get in the ring and challenge whoever was still standing.

'There's going to be murder if you get in there,' he said.

'I'm going to challenge the winner,' I said.

'There'll be murders.'

He was right. The security was very heavy, with bull-necked hired men in monkey suits trying to control hundreds of loud, drunken East Enders. Once the two boxers were in the ring, a burly scrap merchant from Wisbech in Cambridgeshire suddenly jumped through the ropes to challenge them. Adams and Shaw both grabbed him and the security grappled him to the floor and threw him out. If they had done that to me there would have been major problems. After that the security was even tighter – there was no way of getting into the ring.

The fight itself was a joke. Shaw knocked Adams down with his first punch, hit him a few more times while he was on the deck and then stuck the boot in. He was pulled off by the referee and the stewards and declared the winner. It was all over in three seconds.

The papers were full of it again the next day. I don't want to put any man down but Adams looked ancient and Shaw was thirty-nine. I am sure either would have found many a traveller happy to satisfy them on Gallows Hill at Appleby Fair. What did annoy me was that the winner was described as the bareknuckle champion of England. That was my title, and I couldn't let that go. So I sent a message to Shaw through the pages of the national newspapers. This was the *Daily Mirror*:

NOW PRETTY BOY FACES A GYPSY'S CHALLENGE

A bizarre challenge has been thrown out to Roy 'Pretty Boy' Shaw, self-styled barefist boxing champion of Olde England.

A gypsy 'king' wants to fight him in an illegal barefist fight – if necessary on a ship outside British territorial waters.

Burly Bartley Gorman claims Shaw is just a brawler. He said: 'Bareknuckle fighting is a traditional and honourable way of fighting in gypsy camps. This man Shaw could not stand up to our scientific and historic way of fighting.'

Recently police stopped attempts by Shaw to fight Donny 'The Bull' Adams without gloves. Eventually the two met – with gloves on – and Shaw KO'd Adams for the title 'The Guv'nor'.

Gorman said: 'I saw that contest and he has no right to that title. I have to fight him for the honour of my people – even if it does mean on a ship outside territorial waters.'

Gorman, who lives in a gypsy camp near Leicester, claims his 'brothers' would raise £20,000 for a side stake if he fought Shaw.

Shaw said: 'I would be prepared to talk about it. He doesn't worry me.'

As I say, I don't want to do another man down. 'As a rough and tumble fighter Shaw is one of the best,' I told the reporter. 'But I think I am better. I'm a heavy puncher and a very good mover. Shaw can call himself "The Guv'nor" but if he is using the title barefist boxing champion of Olde England, he has no right to, unless he wins it from me. Someone is willing to stake me £20,000 to win but I'm not interested in the money side. I am fighting for the honour of my people.'

My challenge was serious. There was talk of us fighting at Leicester with two-ounce gloves. Our Sam, Don Halden and Chuck Bodell were going to help me prepare for it and we had a referee and timekeeper lined up. But it came to nothing. Shaw went on to beat up someone called 'Mad Dog' Mullins and then won and lost against Lennie McLean. None of these were bareknuckle fights, just unlicensed boxing shows. I had finished with boxing by then. I couldn't see the point. If you put fences and barbed wire in front of a lioness on the Serengeti Plain, how would it catch a gazelle? It is the same as putting gloves on a man to fight. Who says you have to wear gloves? Who says you have to have a ring?

They made good money and there were some reasonable men on the unlicensed boxing circuit, like Cliff Fields, who had been a half-decent licensed pro, but there was also a lot of bull talked. Shaw never fought a decent bareknuckle man in his life that I know of, while Lennie McLean would later claim to have defeated someone called 'Pablo the Gypsy'. Never heard of him – and believe me, if there had been such a traveller, I'd know. McLean, a bull of a man who looked the most intimidating of the lot, took the title of 'Guv'nor' off Shaw and it became his nickname. He and I would nearly come to it a few years down the line.

I did briefly meet Roy Shaw many years later, at the graveside of the London gangster Reggie Kray, whom I had got to know towards the end of his life. Shaw must have been in his early sixties but he looked fit and tanned and still had an aura of menace. He certainly has a fighter's eyes. As to who would have won out of the two of us, well I'll leave that to your imagination.

I will say that these unlicensed shows were nowhere near as rough and dangerous as was hyped. They built up the fighters as invincible killing machines who could knock down walls and uproot trees with their bare hands. Most of them were in fact over-the-hill ex-pros, ageing bouncers or bully-boys too unfit or unskilled to ever make it in the ring. The bouts took place in public, before big crowds, under bright lights, with a referee and cornermen and security staff and medics at ringside. Some of them were fixed – the whole purpose was to make money, so nobody really cared. No-one was going to suffer permanent damage.

Bareknuckle fights are utterly different. They are illegal. They are held in secret. There are no padded gloves, gumshields or foul protectors. No time limit. No ring. The fighting area will be surrounded by the family and friends of the two combatants. Emotions run high. Many in the crowd will be half-crazed on adrenalin and drink, and some will have concealed weapons. And there are no fixed endings – ancient family honour and pride is at stake, not just cash.

In fact the fights became too serious: a matter of life or death. Something I was about to discover in the most notorious event ever at a gypsy prize-fight.

CHAPTER 9

Massacre on St Leger Day

IT STARTED WITH a chance encounter on a country road. Not long after my father died, I was driving through Ashbourne in Derbyshire when I saw a tall man with a long nose, hair two feet long with grips in and teeth like dice. I could tell a travelling man if he was lying under a stone and this one was a dead giveaway: he looked like Buffalo Bill. I stopped and hailed him. His name was William Lee and it turned out he was the brother of my Uncle Pat's wife. The Lees are one of the biggest travelling breeds and William was one of the richest of them. His business was selling carpets and he was the greatest salesmen of them you would ever meet.

He owned a herd of 500 black and white horses – he wouldn't have a brown one – with three stallions in a field. Violet, his wife, hung in gold and jewels. He also had hundreds of English gamecocks that he paid a farmer to look after. In his caravan at night he would bring in a dozen cocks and let them fight to the death on his two-inch-thick Wilton carpet, feathers flying all over the Crown Derby and Royal Worcester. His wife would be cooking while the birds were fighting. He was clean as a new pin but he was a real sporting man. He was also the only gypsy ever to win the Waterloo Cup, the annual greyhound coursing trophy.

I got to know the Lees very well. Lord Tony Gather, who

owned an estate at Ashbourne, spent six months of every year in Africa and the Lees would rent his estate while he was away. It had a caravan site, a clubhouse and acres of fields, and they held barbecues for hundreds of people. The country house had guns from the Battle of Waterloo over the fireplace.

William Lee was mad on the bareknuckle game. 'I can't understand, your Uncle Pat never did tell me he had nephews that could fight like you and Sam,' he used to say. He was great friends with Hughie Burton and it was William who told me what a monster Burton was when I was going to fight him at Doncaster. After that he put up a gym for me – I could make the punchball hit the ground – and said, 'Bartley, you are not the best fighter among travellers. You are the best fighter in England. I will put any money on you.'

We became such friends. One day he pulled up in a new Range Rover. He'd had bother with some men in Yorkshire. 'I want you to fight someone,' he said. 'He's done a very bad trick on me Bartley. Would you fight him for me?'

I jumped straight in, with our Sam for back-up in case there was a gang. We went all the way up to North Yorkshire but the man was too scared to fight me. Afterwards William said, 'I'll give you a horse for that.'

'No, no, I don't want a horse, William.'

The next day a man arrived with a cattle box with a horse in it worth £1,000. I took it because I couldn't insult him. It was over fifteen hands, a bay mare. Lee was like that: he always wanted to buy the drink, always wanted to buy the food, he was kindness beyond all reason. But I have always said in my life that the nicest person you'll ever meet is also the nastiest. And so it would prove.

William moved away and I didn't see him for a while. Then one day I picked up the *Daily Mirror* and saw the headline, 'Gypsy Man Robbed of £150,000.' That was an awful lot of money in the early Seventies. It said the money belonged to a man called Jack Lee and had been taken from a caravan. I thought no more of it, as I didn't know who Jack Lee was.

A fortnight later I was sitting with my mother in her trailer when a knock came at the door. It was four CID from the north of England.

'Can we have a word with Bartley and Sam Gorman?'

'I'm Bartley Gorman. What's it about?'

'We've come to interview you about the theft from Lee.'

'What do you mean, Lee?'

'William Lee.'

William was Jack Lee's son and the money really belonged to him. And for some reason, they were pointing the finger at me. I hit the roof. I have never taken so much as the weight of a pin in my life, brought up by my father as a practising Catholic. I had been painting barns every day, slaving to earn a few quid, and here were these police accusing me of burglary.

'Get out of this trailer, insulting me,' I shouted. 'I've got nothing to say to you.'

I do not know what put it into Lee's mind. Apparently he had told the police that me, Sam and my cousin Matt Bryan had stolen the cash, which he kept in his trailer. Sam and Matt had been to visit Lee on the camp at Pontefract but he wasn't there. His money disappeared at about the same time and that's why they were accused. For some reason Lee had it in his head that I was involved.

The police got nowhere with it but Lee wouldn't let it drop. He quizzed people around Uttoxeter, men who used to work for me. The CID dug up a shed where I used to keep gamecocks to see if the money was underneath. They even went to Marchington Aerodrome and searched a smashed-up motorcar that belonged to Sam. It was ridiculous.

The truth was that Lee was always flashing his money about. Decimalisation had just come in, when everyone had to change their cash into new currency, and Lee had been counting his money on the floor of his trailer when a man from London walked in without knocking. I know who he was; he was staying on the site.

'Oh, sorry mate,' said the Londoner.

'Come in, it's all right,' said Lee, being flash. The man clocked his pile of notes and a week later, Lee was robbed. You didn't need to be a detective to work out what had happened. Yet for some reason we were put in the frame.

I didn't hide. I even went up to Pontefract to try to sort it out and spoke to old Jack Lee. 'They wasn't that clever, you know,' he said. 'There was another sixteen thousand under that bunk.'

I was upset by the whole thing but thought it would die down. I went over to Hinckley, in Leicestershire, where my mother lived on a site and was chatting in the trailer of Jimmy 'the Duck' Winters, an old-time prizefighter who walked like a duck, when suddenly he said, 'Shaydicks.' That means police in Cant (in Romany it's *muskras*). There was a warrant out for me at the time for having no car tax and I assumed it was over that, so I said, 'Let me get under the bed.'

Swarms of plainclothes officers came on the ground as I slid under the bunk.

'By God, if it's over the tax, it's a funny do,' said Jimmy. 'Very strange. It's full of CID.' He gave me a running commentary on what was happening. 'Your Aunt Nudi's talking to two CID with walkie-talkies. Now she's heading this way.'

I heard my aunt shout from outside, 'Come out of there, my lad, hiding over the tax. It's not tax, it's William Lee they want you for. For robbing.'

They had come to arrest me. I walked out of the trailer and stood in the middle of the ground with 100 travellers and dozens of police around me. One stone-faced officer in a suit walked up and looked me straight in the eyes. No speaking. I couldn't outstare him. He was an expert.

'I've come to talk to you about William Lee's robbery,' he finally said. 'I want to talk to you in private.'

I had a feeling this was the kind of man who could get me ten years for something I'd not done.

'Listen. Anything you have to ask me, do it now in front of all these gypsy men here. I've got nothing to hide. Ask me here, now.'

'Why, do you want a conference?'

'Yeah, if you want.'

'No, let's talk in private.'

'No, let's talk out here.'

He wouldn't. In the end I agreed to go in my mother's Morecambe trailer. As I walked in, he followed me with another seven plainclothes men.

'Hang on,' I said, 'if you want to talk to me, you talk to me. Get these others out.' I pointed to a religious picture on the wall. 'Before you go any further, that's the Sacred Heart. On the Sacred Heart, I don't know anything about this.'

He didn't take a blind bit of notice. We had a long talk. He asked me questions. I told him I was innocent. He arrested me. I was taken in an unmarked car to Pontefract. The officers kept asking me about prize-fighting. They were fascinated.

'Yeah, I prize-fight all the time, bareknuckle,' I said.

'Could you get us to see one, Bartley?'

'No, sorry. Too secret.'

At Pontefract nick they gave me a drink and locked me in a cell. I couldn't say if I was there for two days or three. CID would come in, talk to me for ten minutes, then leave. In would come another two. By the end I almost thought I had done the crime.

Finally one of them said, 'We are sending for a man and when he comes here he's got something to say to you.'

I thought, *right, when this man comes, whoever he is, I'm going to break every bone in his body*. In the event, there was no man. They had made it up. They were saying it all day long. 'Oh, he'll be here in a minute,' and so on. Psychological warfare.

After a long time, in walked this giant officer, six foot five, with black curly hair. I was sitting on the bunk. He locked the door behind him.

'So you're the King of the Gypsies.'

'Yeah, that's me.'

'Have you told any lie since you've been in here?'

During the questioning, one of the things I had denied was throwing a half-hundredweight rock through the

Training in my fighting prime in the Seventies. I used the boxing ring to prepare for bareknuckle fights.

...am knocking out 'Alanzer Jansen' ...n one of my pirate boxing shows. ...ven I had to get on my bike when ...parring with Sam.

Top fighting men of the Fifties and Sixties. Left is Sam Ward and above is Jim Crow, both from the north-east and both unbeaten. Ward punched so hard he could break a bone wherever he landed.

My uncle 'Fighting' Peter Smith, who helped save my life at Doncaster but was badly beaten and had £10,000 stolen.

Albert 'Nigger' Smith, a boxing champion and rugged bareknuckle man of the Sixties and Seventies from the east coast of England.

Big Jim Nielson, the 17-stone champion, with his wife. He lost to Uriah Burton at St Boswell's Fair when Burton bit his tit off.

Caley 'Big Chuck' Botton and my cousin Kathleen in Las Vegas. Caley was champion of Canada and a top man in the Burton era.

The one and only 'Big Just', Uriah Burton, holding an open-air court on his site near Manchester. He reigned as King of the Gypsies before me and was a brutal all-in fighter who would stop at nothing to win. He was also a man of iron principles.

Bob Braddock and (inset) his brother Will. They were my biggest backers and also two of the greatest horse dealers you could ever meet. They arranged my fight for the title against Jack Fletcher in Hollington Quarry in Staffordshire in 1972.

A historic gathering in the Blackie Boy pub in Darlington to raise money to back me against Hughie Burton. From left: Henry Nicholson, Black Wiggy Lee, Tucker Lee, Wally Francis, Jimmy Francis, Terence Lee, Chucky Francis and two men who wish to remain anonymous.

Two of my close friends and sparring partners: Siddy Smith from Leicestershire (left), posing beneath boxer Tony Sibson's Lonsdale Belt, and Tommy 'Tucker' Lee, who was always one of my biggest supporters when I was fighting.

THIS IS A CHALLENGE

I Bartley Gorman, challenge any Gypsy Man in England, Ireland, Scotland or Wales or for that matter, the World, to fight me for my title, for £1,000 or more or less per side.

The fight must take place in a 20ft. square ring, under New York State Rules, with 6oz gloves and no less than 20 rounds.

I will name the place and date of fight. The referee will be Don Haldon, Judges-Matt Hyland and Jim Holmes, Timekeeper, Fred Parker.

This challenge stands for 1 Month as from 10th September 1977.

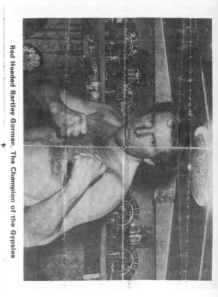

Red Headed Bartley Gorman, The Champion of the Gypsies

The challenge: These leaflets were distributed at Doncaster racecourse in 1977 to show that I was still the heavyweight champion of the gypsy world.

Boxing days: One of my unlicensed tournaments, with (left) MC Johnny Austin, Rabbi Boswell (who tried to persuade me to give up promoting) and 'Blond Bomber' Don Halden, the hard-hitting heavyweight boxer I fought outside a pub.

Martial arts expert Robert Shaw, wielding a ceremonial sword. He caused me to fight him on my land at Uttoxeter.

John-John Stanley (top) and Boxer Tom, two great fighters from the south whose contest in 1972 was one of the longest of modern times.

Two Kings: My meeting with 'The Greatest', Muhammad Ali, in Birmingham in 1983. He told me he had been champion of the world three times. I told him I was the Lord of the Lanes.

With my trainer Alan Wilson in the mid-Eighties. I loved tradition and am seen here wearing tights and an old-fashioned silk around my waist. Alan, a lovely man, was later murdered.

Chief Inspector John Kendrick is about to arrest me in a Staffordshire car park, where a huge crowd had come to see me fight Johnny Mellor in 1986. We were bound over to keep the peace.

window of a man I'd had a row with. I decided to come clean. 'Yeah, I have told a lie and the lie was in saying I never put that rock through the window. I did, but only because he insulted my father and mother. That was the only lie.'

'Before we go any further, you're the King of the Gypsies. I'm the judo champion of Yorkshire Police. If you've told another lie, I'm here to tell you now you'd better go straight from this cell and get the first plane out of England.'

I have been angry in my life but never as mad as this. Born in the heart of England, Robin Hood country, never committed no crime, and now this.

'You're telling me to get out of England?' I shouted. 'My country, where I was born? Why you . . .'

I didn't punch him. I stood up, put my hands on his shoulders and crushed him down. He folded like an accordion. Even I didn't know I had such strength. Other officers were watching through the spyhole and I could hear them outside, frantically trying to open the door. Ten CID rushed in and one put his arms around me.

'Come on Bartley, we know you're innocent now. Do you want a cup of tea?'

'No, just let me go.'

I was released but it didn't end there. The most hurtful blow of all came when William Lee rang me himself. 'Even Will Braddock thinks you've had the money, Bartley,' he said.

I couldn't believe that. Braddock was my mentor. I loved him like a brother.

'He doesn't, William. He wouldn't say that.'

Lee and his wife Violet picked me up in their Range Rover and drove Sam and me through the night to Braddock's house near Market Drayton.

'What's this, Will?' I said. 'Are you saying this about me?'

'Good Lord, I never said that, like.'

'You did say it, Will,' said Lee. Then Violet fell down on her knees in the middle of the house, her gold jewellery jangling, and clasped her hands together and wailed, 'It's cold as my brother in the clay that you said it, Will.' That was a blood oath; she had worshipped her brother, who died young. I knew that she was telling the truth. Braddock must have been after some reward. Tears came in my eyes.

'I never thought you would do something like that to me, Will,' I said as I walked out.

*

IN THE AUTUMN of 1976, I was barn-painting in the Derbyshire hills. It was a Friday and I finished late and drove back to Stoke-on-Trent, where I was living in a small terraced house with Gwendoline and our two children. I stopped on the way as I always did to buy Shaun and Maria some sweets.

As I came in the house, Gwendoline met me. She looked pale and drawn. 'Bartley, your brother John's been here. He's been battered. Bob Gaskin came up to him at Doncaster, asked where you were and hit him. His eyebrow looks like a shark's mouth.'

'What? Gaskin's hit my brother John? My baby brother? Bob Gaskin?'

'Yes, and they've got a ring up there at Doncaster and they're waiting for you to go and fight.'

I gave the children their sweets, walked back through the hallway and kicked the front door off its hinges. It was my John, whom I carried out of the hospital when he was born, carried into the world and loved like he was my own little child. I jumped in the Transit van and headed for Hinckley, where Sam lived. I went that fast that a tyre blew and the van went into a skid and nearly overturned.

Sam was in bed in his trailer. 'Sam, Bob Gaskin has put stitches in our John's eye and cut all his lips.'

He half-opened one eye. 'Let me sleep, I'll deal with him in the morning,' he mumbled, then turned over and went back to sleep. Sam would not have cared for Jack Johnson, Joe Frazier and Mike Tyson in the ring at the same time.

I made myself a cup of tea while Sam slept. An hour later, John arrived. I couldn't speak when I saw him. He had a long cut over his eye, a split lip and a busted nose. His face was bruised and swollen and his hair was matted with congealed blood. He was with a band of travellers led by Tucker Lee, a well-known Romany from up Darlington way. John had been living with Tucker's family and they had gone to Doncaster for St Leger week. He had been step-dancing on a board covered with salt to the sound of a melodeon when Bob Gaskin approached with his gang of men.

'Where's your brother?' demanded Gaskin.

'He's not here,' said John.

'Why isn't he here to defend his title? He's scared to fight me.'

'No he's not.'

Gaskin hit John several full-blooded punches to the face. I'm proud to say he didn't go down but his brow was slashed open.

The men said Gaskin had put up a ring and was waiting to fight me for £10,000 a side. I didn't have that kind of money but no matter whether it was £10,000 or ten pence, Gaskin was going to suffer for what he had done. A hired man called Danny Shenton was apparently ready to fight our Sam, and some of the others with John had brought boxing boots with them and were also expecting to fight. Tucker Lee said he could guarantee us fair play, even though it was Gaskin's backyard. 'We've got a lot of men there, Bartley, and they'll all be waiting, ready,' he said.

Because of his assurances, I didn't round up any of my own breed. Instead I stayed the night at the house of my pal Frank McAleer. Frank was a proper Irishman, drinking every day. We'd be sitting in a pub and I'd say to Frank, 'Show them what tough men is.' Then he would eat his pint glass: chew it and swallow it without cutting his lips.

I lay in the bath all night, thinking about the man I was going to fight. Gaskin was a bad man from a fighting family. He was the champion of Yorkshire and the surrounding counties and didn't care for man, woman or child; he didn't care for death. He went round with a band of notorious men, all feared; perhaps the most infamous band of gypsies that ever walked the British Isles. He had beaten a lot of men but I was the champ, the redheaded king of them all, and he wanted my title. He was also best friends with William Lee, the man who had accused me of theft. *Perhaps the two incidents were linked?*

Very early the next morning, Sam picked me up in a hired Vauxhall Ventura and we drove to the Hinckley camp. Someone threw a twelve-bore gun and a box of cartridges in the boot.

'Stop. I'm not going,' I said. 'Take them cartridges out. Out! Else I do not go, even if he has put a hundred stitches in John. No guns.' I'm not a gun man, have never messed with them in my life. So they took them out.

My uncle Peter Smith, a scrap iron dealer, said, 'I've got ten thousand pounds. I'll back you.' He had the money in a bag and jumped in the motor with his son Len. But it wasn't money I was going for. My father would not have rested in his grave if I had let the man get away with it.

We made the same procession I had taken four years earlier when I went to challenge Big Just. Then the mood had been one of high spirits, even elation; now it was grim, dark. There was little talking on the way. Everyone was sombre. We had boxing boots on and were ready to fight, one after the other.

At Doncaster, Sam pulled up on a traffic island. He wore a greatcoat and was smoking a cigar. He stood on the island shadowboxing. Doncaster was a beehive of gypsies from all over the British Isles and Europe and even America – it was *the* flash race for the flash travellers. As the Mercedes and Rolls-Royces rolled past and saw Sam, they tooted their horns. They knew what it meant.

We drove down near the racecourse. There were dozens of buses and maybe 1,200 people there. Everybody had known from the day before that it was coming off. We got out of the cars and started walking towards the ground where the trailers were, followed by hundreds of people. Coming the other way we met Hughie Burton.

'Bartley, my Bartley, don't go down there,' he said. 'There's too many of them. They'll kill you.' Hughie knew Bob Gaskin had a mob waiting. Once he wouldn't have cared but he was too old now and the Gaskins were too much for him.

'I'm going down there,' I said.

Hughie tried to get me out of the way by an old toilet block to talk me out of it but I wouldn't listen. He was older and wiser and knew how dangerous these men were but I wanted revenge. I was in a fighting trance, pacing in a circle.

'Someone will die today,' I said.

'Bartley is like our Oathy,' muttered Hughie. 'He doesn't fear anything.' He was finished as a top fighter but still, what a man: big, blond hair, ponytail. He said he was with me and we started walking again. There were thousands now sitting on top of caravans: no police or house-dwellers, *gorgi* people, just gypsies.

A nephew of Hughie's called Wick-Wack Burton, a notorious man who was friendly with the Gaskins, came up to him.

'What are you here for?' said Wick-Wack. 'You're too old.'

'Are youm with us or are youm with them?' asked Hughie. That's how they talk.

'I'm with them,' said Wick-Wack.

'You hit me then,' said Hughie.

'You hit me,' said Wick-Wack.

I was moving around, waiting for Gaskin.

'No, you hit me.'

'No, you hit me.'

You hit me. No, you hit me. Is this schoolboys here or what? I thought. 'Come out the way, Hughie,' I said. 'He said he isn't with us. Never mind "you hit me, I hit him, you hit me first." I'll hit you.'

I was stripped to the waist and ready.

'You hit me?' said Wick-Wack. 'Come on den, I fight you straight away.'

He took off the jacket of his green mohair suit, removed his shirt and put up his hands. 'You title?' he asked, meaning, is this for the title?

147

'Yeah.'

It was the quickest title fight in history. As he threw a shot, I downed him with a right cross to the eye that opened a four-inch cut on his brow and put him straight into the sludge. One punch ended the fight but broke my thumb at the same time. They took him away, his mohair trousers coated in mud.

By now there were hundreds of travellers around me, fanatical. Like a fool, I had left the car behind and jumped on the back of a flatbed truck to be driven the rest of the way to the ground. I could see what looked like thousands coming from the trailers, so many that the heat was rising from them. The grandstand wasn't far away and the Queen was in there to watch the St Leger.

When I got down to the place we were supposed to fight, Gaskin wasn't there. The first thing I looked for was the ring. No ring. There had been one but it was smashed up in a heap somewhere. And Tucker Lee had no men at all to see fair play. We were on our own. *Hmm*, I thought, *I know what this is going to be now: no fair fight here.*

They had taken Wick-Wack Burton to the Park Royal Hotel, where Gaskin had rounded up a gang of fighting men from the North. Among the Gaskins and Deers and Harkers all drinking was a stocky man in a white pullover. He was Danny Shenton, a *gorgi* and the best fighter in Yorkshire. They had offered him £1,000 to fight our Sam: £500 up front and £500 when the fight was finished. There was Peter Honeyman, another notorious fighter, Big Bocker, a horrible giant of a man from Bishop Auckland, and others. Gaskin was wealthy and had paid them.

I waited down on the site for at least an hour and was getting fed up. 'Bring the car down,' I told Colin Lee, so he fetched it. Am I glad he did. I sat inside and put on the radio: *Tie A Yellow Ribbon* was playing. *I'll stay just a couple more minutes*, I thought. What a fool to have waited with no men.

*

'THEY'RE COMING,' SOMEONE said.

I looked and could see them arriving on trucks – tip-cab
Fords and TKs, big tarmaccing lorries – and they were like
troops, soldiers. I jumped out of the car and stood there in
blue jeans and red boxing boots, a purple handkerchief tied
round my waist, my fighting colours. As they came nearer,
they started to jump from the lorries and fan out, marching
towards me in a line. They looked like something out of a
Walt Disney cartoon: they had long necks, short necks, fat
heads, long heads, fat arses like Donald Duck. That's how I
saw them and that's how they were. I'm looking *through*
them and they're still coming. They were horrible. Beast
men. They had iron bars and baseball bats in their hands
and they were going to try to kill me. But it was too late
now. This was gypsy pride at its uttermost.

I saw a crowbar on the ground, picked it up and gave it to
my brother. 'Sam, hold that and see me fair play.'

'No,' he said, and threw it down. Foolish. If I had known,
I would have kept it myself.

'Moment of truth,' I bellowed as they approached. 'I'm
the King of the Gypsies. Moment of truth.'

I was like a white Zulu with chocolate stubble, red curls
hanging down. 'Where's Bob Gaskin?' I shouted.

Ten men shouted back.

'I'm him.'

'I'm him.'

'I'm him, brother.'

The one I was certain was Gaskin, who looked the
toughest, hardest of all, walked straight towards me. He was
short and thickset. I didn't even put my hands up; I was
never going to take a fighting pose with these men. They
weren't going to stand around. There wasn't going to be any
fair play. They were intent, with a purpose. They were
coming for blood. I walked straight at him and hit him so
hard that he went up in the air and down again and landed
on his head. And that was the end of him.

Hell lit up. I was suddenly fighting four or five men at
once. I downed two of them but others took their places.

Out came the weapons. A man in a white vest went for my brother. Sam flattened him with a single blow, then kicked him in the ribs, saying, 'Git up, rabbit.' Another came out of the crowd with a long iron bar and hit Sam over the temple. Then they dragged him down and piled onto him like a rugby team. Big Bocker had brown boots on him and started kicking Sam virtually to death; booting his head with no stop.

All of our party were attacked and every single one was forced to run. They put twenty stitches in Tucker Lee's head and a dozen in my Uncle Joe's head. Tucker's son Tommy got away and some of the others escaped by the skin of their teeth. John Lee lost the roof of his mouth and ended up in Carlisle Hospital – to this day he doesn't know how. Even old Hughie Burton was attacked, though not seriously.

A man hit me and I thought it was his fist. I had never been down in my entire life but I went on one knee. *Christ*, I thought, *can that man hit*. I looked up and he had the half-shaft of a car in his hand. I carry the lump to this day on the side of my head. He hit me again and I took it on my forearm, then again and again. There were at least ten on me now. I knew I must not go down.

Danny Shenton, the hired muscle, stood there in his big white jumper, waving his arms. 'This is not my scene,' he shouted. 'I don't want this.'

'Then give us our five hundred pounds back,' retorted one of the mob.

'If you ask me one more time, I will ask you for the other five hundred,' said Shenton. 'I came for a fair fight.'

I was knocking them over like skittles when I saw Sam down. I realised I had to get to the car to get him out of there. They were hanging on to me but I was that powerful that I waded through them like Samson. My red hair marked me out: they now all knew who Bartley Gorman was and they wanted me. Wick-Wack Burton was whacking me with an iron bar. I waded twenty yards, still on my feet, dragging them along. God must have been with me.

Somehow I got to the car. I got into the Vauxhall Ventura and immediately they started smashing it to pieces. They had kettle irons and jumped onto the roof and bonnet, putting the spikes through it. Every window was broken except the front. People were screaming and crying and spewing up.

Sam struggled into the back of the car: don't ask me how, this was every man for himself. The rest had run like greyhound dogs. I was so pleased to see him. He leaned over to me.

'Are you all right, my brother.'

'Yes, Sam.'

They pulled him out of the car. I had hold of the steering wheel to stop them dragging me out too. Unbeknown to me, they put Sam's head down under the wheels, in the sludge and the dirt, holding him there for me to run over his head. Fortunately I couldn't start the car. Next they tried to tip it over. I opened the passenger door and jammed it so they couldn't. Some men leaned inside trying to rip me out. The car was an automatic and try as I might, I couldn't start it. So I put my hands on top of the door and pulled it to. They iron-barred my knuckles and fingers – they won't make a fist properly now, they click. Then they jabbed at me with bars through the other window and tried to slug me with baseball bats.

'Stop it,' I shouted. One man shattered the front wind-screen and the glass came into my eyes. My eyes cried blood.

There came a silence. Over by the gates as you come into Doncaster, where the caravans park, are lines of dustbins. I saw a tall, bald-headed cousin of Gaskin's go over to the bins and pick up a big Woodpecker cider bottle. He broke the bottle over a caravan tow bar and came back with the jagged glass towards the car.

'Don't put that bottle in me,' I said. 'I come for a fair fight.'

I thought he was going for my throat. I was still holding the buckled steering wheel, my eyes full of glass and blood. Then Bob Gaskin – I know it was him, no matter what they say – took the bottle and as he came at me I lifted my leg up to kick him away. I started kicking but they grabbed my leg and put the bottle in it and grated it against my shinbone. I screamed with the pain, I tell the truth, and my back arched in agony. I screamed like I had never screamed even as a child.

They were trying to cut off my leg. I don't know what happened next, whether somebody took the bottle off him or not, but somehow I got my leg back in. Then the beating started all over again. People were starting to go now with fright.

Our Sam, who had taken a merciless hiding, jumped in a Mercedes car. The terrified driver said, 'Get out.'

Sam just mumbled, 'Get going.'

I was the last man left. I thought I was going to die. They continued hammering me. I took more punishment in those eight minutes than any boxer in his entire career. The blue sky was now going blood red and turning round and round and I was going giddy. I wasn't even defending myself any more.

A dear little lad of no more than seven or eight ran in and cuddled me, a little Irish tinker. 'Leave him, leave him,' he said to the men. They threw him in the air like a rag doll.

I thought, the next one that hits me, I'm going unconscious. They'll surely leave me then. So the next one that did, I slumped, pretending. I was limp but still had my arm hooked around the wheel. Blood was coming out of my mouth like a faucet. It was a lack of blood that was making me lose consciousness. You would have thought they would quit then. Not a chance. Psychos. It became worse. They put an iron bar down my mouth, broke my teeth and smashed my larynx. I was gagging on the blood.

I don't know why the words came out, because they are not words I ever use, but I said, 'You are hurting me too much, my brothers.' It made no difference. They kept calling me 'redheaded bastard' all the time. They were pulling my hair out, flesh coming off the scalp, all my big bouncy curls. They were fighting each other to get at me.

My Uncle Peter was a tough man who looked like Rocky Marciano. He had already grabbed a giant off the top of Sam and thrown him ten yards. I saw him trying to get men away from the car. 'Help me, Peter,' I said.

He ran in. 'Don't, Bob, please don't do that to him,' he pleaded.

As he said it, they all stalled to look at him and I turned the key in the ignition. The engine roared into life and I did a wheel spin and took off. A hundred men later claimed they saved me but it was my Uncle Peter. They turned on him and put out every one of his teeth with iron bars. They also took his money, the whole ten grand he had brought to stake on a fair fight.

I took off in the car but couldn't get far. The St Leger race was running and if I had gone through the barrier I'd have gone straight into the middle of the race but I only made it about 150 yards before I started to weaken from the blood pumping out of me. I saw little Frank McAleer, whose house I had stayed at the night before. 'Hold my head up, Frank,' I said. I was too weak even to raise my head but Frank wouldn't come near, he was too scared. Everybody was.

A tall, dark figure lurched in front of the motor. His clothes were in shreds and he looked like a corpse dug up after a month. One eyeball was nearly out of his head. His skin was purple, a solid bruise. I had seen fighters in a mess but nothing like this.

'Who are you?' I murmured. It was Sam.

Then I looked down and the carpet of the car was soaked in blood from my leg. My jeans were rolled up and the blood was oozing thick like plastic. I found a piece of rag in the car and I tied it around my wound.

A giant policeman appeared. I found out later he was called Jess Maguire. He took his tunic off and clamped it on my shin and I held onto him. An ambulance went flying down towards the crowd with its flashers on and siren blaring. I heard later that they got guns out and held up the ambulance. A second ambulance was held up, so the third wouldn't go down. Policemen appeared everywhere with dogs. Hughie Burton came, picked me up and put me on a stretcher held by two policemen. Through the mist of my mind I could see the Gaskins standing there like grotesque cartoon characters.

I will never know how I did this, but I rolled off the stretcher, threw back my shoulders and shouted, 'Come on, one of youse now, one man.'

Not one stepped forward.

'Bartley Gorman, King of the Gypsies,' I bellowed. 'King of the Gypsies.'

Then I fell back onto the stretcher and they carried me to the ambulance.

CHAPTER 10

Bad Times

THE SCENE AT the hospital was carnage. There were doors banging, people screaming, men slumped on seats covered in blood, orderlies pushing bodies on stretchers with tubes sticking out of them, doctors and nurses running with stethoscopes flying.

As they wheeled me in, the first person I saw was Tucker Lee. His head was swathed in so many bandages it looked like a beehive. Then I saw Sam, in a terrible state, my Uncle Joe covered in blood and my Uncle Peter with his teeth smashed out, his mouth a gaping hole.

A nurse took my pulse as a doctor examined my wounds.

'Have you been drinking?' he asked.

'No,' I mumbled.

Suddenly I felt as though my stomach was coming out through my throat. I began to retch and the nurse pushed a stainless steel bowl under my chin. I must have spewed six dishes of blood. It was a thick jelly, like liver. They put me in an intensive care bed. I started to go dizzy and felt myself slipping away. I barely had strength to pull off the blanket and when I looked down, the bed was full of blood. How much blood does a man have in him? Fortunately a nurse spotted me and they all came running again. This time they rushed me into the pre-op room to prepare for surgery.

The nursing sister said, 'We are afraid gangrene might set into your leg from all the sludge.'

'Take it off then, below the knee.' I didn't want to die.

'No, no, we can't do that,' she said.

Sam appeared, like the walking dead. I grabbed his hand. I had always had a fear of being buried alive. 'Sam, if I die in this operation, don't let them bury me for two months. Make sure I am dead.'

I had never been put under before. I was on drips and tubes and needles, connected to some kind of monitor; it looked like the cockpit of a plane. They put the anaesthetic in and I immediately started to go. I looked at this beautiful nurse. 'Well I can always say the last thing I will ever see is a beautiful woman,' I told her. Then I was out.

They performed microsurgery on my leg, stitching together the muscles and tendons that had been sliced through. It took hours and while I was unconscious the hospital car park filled up with travellers' vehicles. The corridors were packed with bands of gypsies – Irish, Scottish, Londoners – and dozens of police. They couldn't control them. BBC radio was reporting that there had been 'a big disturbance just two hundred yards from the Queen.' A horse called Crow had won the St Leger.

When I came to, I had tubes everywhere: glucose going in one hand, blood in another, a tube in my stomach, another in my penis, another in my throat. They must have piled me up with sedative because there was no pain. They weren't supposed to give me a drink but I pleaded for one and the nurse let me. They put me in a room on my own. Later, people told me they were comparing me to Duncan Edwards, the Manchester United footballer who only lingered after the Munich air disaster because he was so strong and fit. Edwards died in the end and many believed I would die too. The doctors told me that even the Queen had sent for information about me; she had heard about the disturbance and wanted to know if everybody was alright. The *News of the World* carried a report saying the trouble had first flared up at Appleby Horse Fair, which was wrong, although I later found out that Bob Gaskin had fought Simon Docherty at Appleby that year and had lost. He had a grudge against the

Irish and perhaps that was another reason for what had happened.

Despite my condition, I had a constant stream of visitors. Gypsy men kept arriving and stuffing the drawers full of tenners and fivers for me. There were bottles of whisky and Guinness under the bed and hidden in the cupboard. Hundreds of boxes of chocolates, bowls of fruit and rosary beads arrived. I gave most of them away to the nurses. The phone never stopped ringing.

Tucker Lee came in. He had a sawn-off twelve-bore under his coat. I was lying in the bed, couldn't move, and looked down to see the gun pointing at me, resting on the bed.

'Don't mess with those men,' I said.

A nurse fetched in a golden basket six feet high and put it on a table. It was like something you would see at a Mafia funeral, filled with red and white flowers. There was a note with it: 'Very sorry what happened race week. Better luck next time. Will see you when you come out of hospital and give you a send-off. Keep these flowers.'

Tears came in my eyes. I knew who it was from: the Gaskins and their cronies. I took it to mean they would come after me when I came out of hospital – and to keep the flowers for my funeral. I made the nurses take it away.

For several days I was in a serious condition but eventually they moved me onto a ward. I had a plaster cast the length of my leg and later a rubber and iron calliper to hold up my foot, so it wouldn't drag. All the tendons had been sliced. At night, all you could hear on the ward were accident victims yelling, 'Help me, help me.' Like wounded soldiers. On the fourth night, a man shouted, 'God help meeeee.'

And I said, 'And me tooooo.' I couldn't help it. It was like a chorus.

I couldn't go to the toilet under my own steam for three weeks but after a fortnight I was well enough to give a couple of interviews. One newspaper had the headline: 'Gang tried to cut off gypsy fighter's leg.' It said, 'A gypsy fighter from Hinckley has claimed that he was attacked with crowbars and a broken bottle after he successfully defended his barefist heavyweight title,' and quoted me saying, 'I am lucky to be alive. They were like savages. I really believe they tried to kill me. I went to defend a challenge on my heavyweight title on St Leger Day. As far as I knew it was going to be a clean fight. If I knew it was going to turn out like it did I would not have gone.'

I sent for Jess Maguire, the policeman who had saved me, and offered him a reward but he wouldn't take it. 'It's all in the line of duty,' he said. But they did call up the special protection police from Scotland Yard, the top men. They were armed and stood behind the curtains all night with earpieces in until the day I left. They also came to interview me. They wheeled me into a quiet room in my chair and told me about Danny Shenton, the hired fighter. He washed his hands of it, like Pontius Pilate, when he saw what they were doing to me, despite the money they had offered him. He was the only man that did.

One of the CID stupidly said, 'He would have beat you fair and square anyway.'

I jumped up, ripping out the tubes. 'Put this down in your notebook,' I said. 'I'm getting these men. I'm not hiding anything. I'm going to blow them to pieces.'

I later learned that William Lee, the man who had accused me of robbing him, had paid the Gaskins £25,000 to attack me. Lee's son, young William Lee, came to see me and cried his eyes out at my bedside. His father never came near me, though I was to see him years later and he was all over me. 'I know you never done it Bartley,' he said, but I could never be the same with him. He later died of cancer after flying all around the world to seek a cure. Ironically it was Lee's sister Priscilla, my aunt, who nursed me through in hospital and fed me special gypsy foods. Will Braddock, who had missed Doncaster because he was ill, also sent me duck eggs and cured ham but I couldn't eat anything except Priscilla's food.

Hughie Burton came. He had been attacked as well and showed me a bit of a scratch on his face. Poor old Hughie: Doncaster ruined him, really. He was never the same man after it. He said the only wound he had seen as bad as my leg was on a stallion in Ireland. In his book, he would write:

> As I came on to the road, I saw Bartley Gorman in the front of his car bleeding to death from the wounds in his leg, he was lying on the floor and surrounding him was a pool of blood. Ambulance men were standing by watching, as were the police. I stopped and intervened and placed a belt round Gorman's thigh to stop the bleeding, then lifted him onto the stretcher and put him into the ambulance. I stayed with him all night and all next day, he was on the danger list for several days.

He still had enough pride to look down at me in my bed and say, 'Well Bartley, I'm the only King of Gypsies that can say now that he never was beat.'

'That's right, Hughie,' I said. But it took a small army to do it.

*

I HAD MIXED feelings about the men who had almost killed me. On the one hand, I wanted to tear them apart. But I knew that if I ever encountered them, I would not be able to control myself, and I didn't want to go to prison over scum. I also didn't want my relatives involved in what would turn into a blood feud. Many people would be maimed or worse.

On one of her visits, my mother made Sam and me swear that we would not pursue them. I could see the pain in her eyes and when my mother looked like that I couldn't refuse her. But retribution was waiting for Bob Gaskin. At my bedside one evening, my mam started crying, and said, 'Before two months today, Bartley, the man who did this shall be laying in this bed where you are.' When I came out of hospital, I think after a month, Sam rang me up and said, 'Guess who's in the same bed as you, Bartley. Bob Gaskin. He's been shot. Trying to beat up a man's fourteen-year-old lad.' Apparently Gaskin had gone round to this trailer and the man's wife threw a kettle of boiling water on him and then her husband came out and said, 'You're not going to do what you did to Bartley Gorman,' and shot him in the side with a 4.10 shotgun. Blew all his guts out. He's got a bag on his side now. I wasn't bothered about him after that because I knew he was finished. I have never seen him or the other men from that day to this.

None of the Gaskins was ever arrested: I wouldn't tell on them. I'm no informer. I did ask what would be the charge and the police said attempted murder. They would be looking at fifteen years. The only man arrested turned out to be me. There had been a warrant out on me before Doncaster for fighting with a man in Uttoxeter. So when the police there read about me in the papers, they came up to the hospital, arrested me in my wheelchair, and charged me with grievous bodily harm with intent. Yet I was completely innocent.

What happened was that a dozen southern travellers had come to Uttoxeter and pulled onto the racecourse. A man called Glyn Thorogood had stolen a vibrator machine for tarmaccing and done a deal to sell it to them. He came into the Black Swan pub where I was drinking with my friend Caggy Barrett and asked to speak to me outside. He knew I had a lorry.

'I've got a tarmaccing vibrator and I have sold it to these travellers for two hundred pounds,' he said. 'I'll give you twenty pounds if you move it down to their camp because they are waiting for it.'

Three times he asked me and three times I said no. I don't like thieves. I returned to the bar but he followed me back in, whining. I gave him the deaf ear until his girlfriend, in a loud, plummy voice, said, 'Bartholomew Gorman, why are you so ignorant when someone is talking to you?'

'Glyn, come outside,' I said. 'Now listen, I have told you I am not having anything to do with it. Get it into your head.'

I went to the toilet, which was across a cobbled entry from the pub. In the meantime, the travellers turned up. They had given £50 down for this vibrator. I could hear through the toilet window that they were having words and one of them said, 'Give me my fifty pound back.' I heard a scuffle and when I walked out Thorogood was lying on the cobbles, in a bad way. I walked into the pub and said to his missus, 'Someone has hit Glyn, come out.' They had to fetch an ambulance. So what does he go and do? Blame Caggy and me, and claim that it was us who hit him.

It was only when I was taken in my wheelchair to Doncaster police station and charged with GBH with intent that I knew Thorogood had blamed me. This was twice I'd been blamed for a crime I hadn't done, while the police didn't seem interested in the men who nearly murdered me. I had to be at Uttoxeter Magistrates Court on October 7, even though I was still in a terrible state. They wanted to put me on an identity parade but my barrister successfully argued that they wouldn't be able to find ten men with plaster casts on their legs.

I was a wreck. Before Doncaster, I was as fine a physical specimen as you could wish to see of a male in his late twenties. Afterwards, you could have blown me over. I was frail, on crutches, and went down to twelve stone. When I finally left hospital and got home, I found the boxing boots I had been wearing that day. They were full of maggots feasting on the congealed blood. Our Sam was in a similar state. It was as though he had been painted with a black brush: his whole body was a bruise. They had broken his cheekbones and smashed his teeth and he had stitches all over his head.

I still have the estimate for repairs to the Vauxhall Ventura which Sam had hired that day and which probably saved my life. Every window had gone in, the boot lid, doors and bodywork were destroyed, the front and rear seats were damaged, the carpet was covered in blood, the wing mirrors, aerial and sun visors had been ripped off and it needed a complete re-spray. The repair bill came to £637 – in 1976.

It would take me fully two years to build myself up again. In the meantime, my trial for the Thorogood assault was at Stoke-on-Trent Crown Court. I had discovered that

Thorogood had asked a man called Graham Parker if he would take the vibrator before me, so I got Parker up as a witness. The judge asked him what his occupation was.

'I'm a professional receiver of stolen property,' he said.

'And a very successful one, it seems, if you can tell a crown court judge that,' said the judge.

I could have died when he said it, but our barristers gave Thorogood a terrible time in the witness box and the jury found Caggy and me not guilty. I was very relieved: the guy up before me was on a lesser charge of GBH without intent and got five years.

Though I was at least free, these were the bad times. I could hardly do anything. I lost all my ambition. I had to claim sick pay, the only time in my life I have claimed benefit, because I couldn't work, and I never promoted another boxing show. I had also been planning to go to America to fight bareknuckle, starting in the southern states and fighting my way across the continent, challenging the toughest man in every town. That went out of the window. I lived in my mother's trailer for a while, then moved into a house with my Shaun and Maria. I was stuck inside, swallowing these strong diazepam tranquillisers, a shadow of myself. I was still on crutches, and went in an ambulance to hospital three times a week for rehabilitation.

Fate was set against me: I became embroiled in yet another court case. Our John and Austin 'Chinaman' Lee came to see me and said they'd take me out for a drive to see Mick Mould and have a drink. They had to help me into the vehicle. Mick was a very nice man but unpredictable. 'I don't like looking at my friend like this,' he said when he saw me. 'I'm going to arrange for you to fight these men fair and square.'

We were going drinking in the village of Abbots Bromley, where they still hold the medieval horn dance, and Mould said he wanted to visit a couple of his shops first to tell them he wouldn't be back that day. We pulled into the car park at the back of one of his fish and chip shops in Rugeley and there was a Tarmac lorry parked there with four men inside.

Mould told them it was a private car park and asked them to move on. They told him where to go.

They couldn't have said it to a worse man. Mould picked up a brick and threw it through the windscreen of the lorry. This is a man in a £300 suit and polished shoes, immaculate. One of the workmen got out and started fighting with our John and Austin Lee. Then two others jumped out and they all started brawling. I clambered out of the car and was propped up against a wall on my crutches, watching this ridiculous scene, when the driver of the lorry decided to suddenly reverse – towards me. I stuck the crutch out and it probably saved me, stopping the lorry for long enough for me to hop out of the way and shout, 'Whoa.'

Mould and the others won the fight and these men drove off with black eyes and bloody noses, straight to the nearest police station. We went into the chip shop and the other three put on white smocks and started frying fish, as if they worked there. I went into the toilet in the back. The next thing, the three of them were hiding in the toilet with me because they saw the police coming. They arrested all of us and locked us up. Austin and John later went on the run and were never brought to court. Mould and I were charged with causing actual bodily harm. I pleaded guilty because I was too ill to go through with a trial. I was fined £60 and the others didn't even offer to pay it.

After months of doing little more than lie on the bed, I gradually began to feel a little better. My great friend Peter Sutton, a slaughterman, built me up with fresh meat and looked after me and my children. I bought a Transit caravan that Gwendoline could drive and intended going to Norfolk to convalesce. Our John had been living with Tucker Lee's family and had had a fight with them and came to see me with his shirt ripped. I was so pleased to see him. I had been eating Valium like Smarties, dangling little kids on my knee watching television. 'You can come down to Norfolk with me,' I told John. I got him sorted out with new clothes but two days before he was due to go, the Lees came to see him and he immediately went back with them. He had been the cause of my nearly getting murdered and yet he had left me just like that. All the bottled-up shock and emotion came out, and I sat weeping on the sofa. It put the top hat on it.

I went down to Norfolk with Gwendoline and the children and stopped in a field by a farm. It was a site for strawberry pickers near Norwich and others were stopping there as well. Shaun was six and Maria five. There was a bit of a pond and I was frit of the children getting drowned, so I parked away from the others, in an isolated spot. It was the week Elvis Presley died.

One night I was in bed when I heard a Transit pull in off the road. I opened the curtains and saw this van with ten men, some on the top rack and others pouring out of the back. One was opening the gate, shouting, 'You gypsy bastard.' They must have been local men, looking to have some sport. I grabbed the sleeping children and shouted to Gwendoline, 'Let's go.' I snatched up some blankets and put the children in the Morris 1000, still on my crutches. Then, as these yobs swarmed towards us, I drove straight across the field with no lights on into a huge cornfield, the corn coming up above the roof of the car. There was nowhere else to go. Eventually I stopped and sat there, waiting and listening in the pitch dark, the children scared and bemused.

We stayed there all night. That was my lowest point. As we sat huddled in the little van in that field, in the black of night, I felt helpless and ashamed. Here I was, the toughest unarmed man in Britain, now weak as a child, unable to protect my own children, running away and hiding in long grass like Samson shorn of his strength. A gloomy depression came down over me. Part of it has never left, for I knew I could never again be the man I was.

Once dawn broke, and we could see the coast was clear, we drove back to the trailer. They had smashed it to pieces. Wrecked. I contacted friends of mine in Norwich, Allie Bailey and Big Leo McCarthy, men you don't mess with. That night we waited for them to come back, but they never returned. The next morning I packed up and left the site.

I WAS STILL in a bad way a year after Doncaster. The muscles of my leg had wasted away when they took the plaster off. I needed an iron clamp on my shin for several months and have never been able to fully raise my toes since. Yet because I had survived, my fame spread even further. I became a legend. And there was something I still had to do: I had to show that Bartley Gorman could never be beaten. Doncaster, the scene of the crime and the meeting place for the gypsy world, was the place to do it.

Will Braddock egged me on. 'I'm going to set a ring up and I want you to fight Gaskin on Hughie Burton's ground at Partington,' he said. Hughie agreed to bring in reinforcements to guarantee fair play. Though I was still in a bad physical state, I went to a printers and ordered hundreds of small, glossy leaflets. Each had a photo of me squaring up in my mother's caravan, the Crown Derby plates behind me, and read:

THIS IS A CHALLENGE

I, Bartley Gorman, challenge any Gypsy Man in England, Ireland, Scotland or Wales or for that matter, the World, to fight me for my title, for £1,000 or more or less per side.
The fight must take place in a 20ft square ring, under New York State Rules, with 6oz gloves and no less than 20 rounds.
I will name the place and date of the fight. The referee will be Don Halden, Judges Matt Hyland and Jim Holmes, Timekeeper Fred Parker.
This challenge stands for 1 Month as from 10th September 1977.

No gypsy man had ever done such a thing before. The leaflet also listed my measurements: height, 6ft 1in; weight, 15½st; reach, 75in; chest, 43in; waist, 34in; biceps, 17in; neck, 18in; fist, 12½in, and so on, and had an address for challengers to contact.

Early one morning, I was driven up to Doncaster with four blacks and two white men I knew from the Midlands.

Their leader was a fellow known as Shaft. I didn't take Sam or John or any of my blood relatives. This was something I had to do myself. My thoughts were terrible as we drove up. We didn't go to fight but to put the challenge out. The men went around every trailer at Doncaster handing out the leaflets. There were fewer travellers there than normal because of what had happened the year before and my enemies weren't there, but someone gave a leaflet to them. Even Bob Gaskin apparently said, 'That man truly was the best man among gypsies.'

I stipulated gloves because I wanted to ensure it was a fair contest: no more iron bars. When I had challenged Roy Shaw through the papers, it was a spur of the moment thing, but this was going to be organised properly. And they didn't like that. They sensed the danger of it. In the weeks that followed, the leaflets turned up all over Britain. Someone gave one to old Reilly Smith, one of the great fighters of the Twenties and Thirties. 'If we were the same age I bet we could have some fun on the front lawn for half an hour or so,' he said.

We did get some phone calls but they were mostly cranks. The only man I did come close to fighting was the new 'Guv'nor' of London, Lennie McLean. He was massive, an ogre with a huge chest and shoulders, a neck wider than his head and a face like an angry bulldog. He had beaten Roy Shaw and was always in the papers bragging about how hard he was.

A journalist who knew the Braddocks gave them the phone number of a man in London called Dave Chipping who could help sort out a fight between McLean and me. He was apparently McLean's manager. Will Braddock called the number and spoke to Chipping, who eventually said, 'I'll put up £200,000 for Lennie to fight your man.'

Will wasn't about to swallow any bull. 'Now listen, owd lad,' he told Chipping. 'There is no way you London men are going to pay us £200,000, even if our fighter knocks yours out in half a second. And there is no way any gypsies are going to give you £200,000. But I'll tell you what. Bartley will fight him for ten Park Drive cigarettes.'

The Braddocks told me that some *tike* wanted to fight me – *tike*s means paid men, hired guns. We never heard anything more about it. Many people have asked me since if I could have beaten McLean, who went on to act on television and films and became a well-known character. When his autobiography was published, just before he died a few years ago, it became a bestseller. He was undoubtedly a powerful, menacing man who didn't even have to raise his hands to terrify a lot of people into submission: one look was enough. I wouldn't argue that he was the King of the Bouncers. As to who would have won if we had fought bareknuckle, I'll leave that for others to speculate.

*

IN 1978 I BOUGHT a small house in Tean, a village near Stoke, for £1500. I had wanted to stay in a trailer in Norfolk, cooking in the open air, taking my kids to the seaside, but Gwendoline wanted them back in school. Very reluctantly, I agreed.

It wasn't long before I hooked up again with Mick Mould. As you may have gathered by now, Mould was nothing but trouble, though he was very kind. He'd sit in pub, stare at perfectly innocent men and say, 'I don't like the look of him.' On this particular day we went to a pub called the Plum Pudding near Cannock. I was playing pool when a man came behind me and punched me in the side – hard. It was Don Halden, the Blond Bomber. I hadn't seen him for three or four years. He had quit boxing now and was seventeen-and-a-half stone.

'You bastard, you.'

'How you doing, Bart?'

We started drinking. We went to a pub in Abbots Bromley and he threw a few jabs at me, joking. I punched back and accidentally caught him with a hook to the head that I meant to miss.

'Oh, I'm sorry Don.'

'You shouldn't have done that Bart.'

He must not have forgotten that hook. It rattled his head. But I didn't mean it. We went down to a country pub at Kingstone. Halden said to me – and I hate being called Bart – 'I'll tell you Bart, Hubert Klee said he'd give me a thousand pound to fight you because you've been going round all the camps challenging all gypsies.' Klee was a wealthy man in the area and heavily into fighting.

'Yeah, but that's a gypsy thing, isn't it? It's not really anything to do with you. I thought you were my friend, Don.'

'Yeah but I need the thousand quid.'

'Well, he ain't going to give you a thousand quid to fight me here now, is he?'

'No, I want to fight you.'

'Come on, then. Out in the car park.'

Out we went. There was an old wall outside and I took my shirt off and punched the wall, nearly knocking it down. 'I'm going to kill you Don. You know you definitely started this. I'm going to destroy you off the face of the earth. You shouldn't have done this, because we have been friends for a long time.'

Some men came outside. We faced off and walked around. Then Halden said, 'No, we don't fight Bartley.'

That was good enough for me. It had been nothing to do with gypsies or money, just for pride, for no reason. We went back in the pub. Then he started again.

'I'm not drinking with you Don. I'm going,' I said. I got up and left. I had come in Mould's motor and left mine at Abbots Bromley, so I started walking, by a little brook with iron railings alongside it. I heard a shout.

'Bart, come back, I want to fight you.'

'Go away Don, I want nothing to do with you.'

'You're gonna fight, there's no way out of this.'

'No, forget it.'

I'd got about 200 yards now. He was following me, his big white shirt flapping loose. Well, a man can't walk forever, can he? So I stopped. No witnesses.

'I've got to fight you Don, but I don't want to. I've told you I'll destroy you.'

I had an old yellow soldier's vest on and took it off. Just when we had squared up, he said, 'No, I ain't going to fight you.' After all that.

'Okay, but I'm going now.'

Halden had a brutal chopping right. I bent to pick up my vest and as I lifted my head up he fetched that big right into my eye. My grandfather once said he felt a particular punch till the day he died, and I can still feel that mighty right of Halden's now. It dished my face in. I had let a *gorgi* man draw the box on me. What a mug. I stood there with blood coming out of my eye. I don't know what would have happened if he had followed it up. But he didn't.

'So you want a fight, do you Don?'

I put my hands on his shoulders, pulled him to me, hit him in the chin with a short punch and he was out with the first one. His head twisted and I fetched it back the other way with a left. As he was falling, I sent one into his midriff, and down he went.

I walked off but couldn't help looking back. Halden was still lying on his back in the middle of the lane. He hadn't moved. I thought I'd killed him, so I had to go back.

'Don, Don, this is me, Bartley, come on Don, I'm your friend.'

I lifted him and carried him over and put him slumped down by the railings, so he wouldn't choke on his tongue or his vomit. I was also bleeding down my vest. I went back into the pub, the Blythe Inn, and said, 'Go and pick your big champ up.' They went out and saw him propped there while I told the landlord to order a taxi.

They took Halden to the hospital, while I went to Hinckley. I felt okay, but the next morning my face felt like it had turned inside out. I was up for the next two nights, pacing up and down, unable to sleep, breathing heavily with the pain. My aunt gave me painkillers but it made no difference. Sam's wife took me to the hospital at Leicester. They X-rayed me and found the bone between my top teeth and my nose was broken, the bridge of my mouth was cracked and my nose was also broken. That's how hard

Halden could hit. They put a plastic shield inside my mouth, needles in it and in the bone of my nose. I was still in pain a fortnight later.

If that was how I felt, how was Halden? I rang up Stafford Hospital. With those few short punches, I had fractured his skull and broken two of his ribs. They had just let him out.

CHAPTER 11

The Battle of Longrake Mine

'I'LL TELL YOU something, Bartley. If you had been fighting me at Doncaster instead of Bob Gaskin, that would never have happened.'

So said Big Johnny Webb as we sat drinking in a crowded public house in Coventry. It was late afternoon and the light was fading. Dozens of travelling men stood in groups by the long bar or sat at tables scattered around a spacious wooden dance floor. Webb was holding court, a huge man of six foot three and twenty-one stone, with black hair, a big belly and braces. He was a well-known pugilist, said to be the best fighter in the West Country, home of some of the best bareknuckle men. There had been talk of us fighting once but it came to nothing. Now he was acting friendly enough but there was an undertone to his conversation that I didn't like.

I had gone for a lunchtime drink with John and Elias Taylor. John was the champion of the Fens, while Elias is the best middleweight gypsy in England; that's what he says, anyway. We ended up in this drinking den – I think it was the Port of Calls in Earlsdon. Then in came Johnny Webb with his brothers, all big men. They were staying nearby on a gig site.

The minute Webb walked in, John Taylor said, 'I don't like this man and I never liked him.'

'That's your business,' I said. John was always saying things like that.

Webb and his brothers joined us and eventually he fetched up about Doncaster. 'Tell me about it,' he said.

'I don't want to talk about it Johnny. Everybody knows, anyway.'

Webb ignored me. He criticised Bob Gaskin and gave me credit for the punishment I withstood. 'But I'll tell you straight that it definitely wouldn't have happened if you had been fighting me,' he said. He meant I would have got fair play. He said it four or five times, to make sure everybody knew it.

'Do you know, Johnny, I like a man like you,' I said. 'You are my kind of man. You would fight me fair and square would you?'

He nodded.

'Then let's fight now.'

'No, I won't fight you.'

That threw me: he had been dropping enough hints, and a notorious fighter like Webb wouldn't normally refuse a direct challenge. Then one of his brothers jumped up. He was even taller than Johnny, lean and fit and aged about thirty, with a bushy Afro hairstyle and a thick, black, bandit moustache. They called him Mexicana.

'I'll fight you,' he said. 'Why fight the worse man?'

It was a set-up. This Mexicana was even better than his brother, though I didn't know at the time. I stood up and we glared at each other but Johnny Webb intervened. 'You're not fighting for nothing. Title at stake?'

John Taylor immediately replied, 'Yes.'

We stripped off. I judged him to be 6ft 4in and about 14½st, not an ounce of fat on him. He was the one gunning for me, not his fat brother. This is where the challenges come from, not where you expect – the long, tall, lithe, fully trained man. His stomach was like a rubbing board. The other men in the bar cleared the wide wooden floor. They were standing on tables and stools to get a good view.

'Everything is at stake?' shouted Johnny Webb, one more time.

'If the man beats me he is the best man in England,' I said.

Mexicana fought square-on with his fists cocked, swaying his body from side to side at the hips like a cat. I had never seen a style like it. I was doing my Jack Johnson thing, left foot forward, palms open to catch his punches. He rushed into me, pushed me against the wall and tried to butt me. I hit him, hard, three or four times against the side of the head and the serious fighting began. Mexicana came in close again and bear-hugged me, trapping my arms. They pulled us apart and before I could take a stance he was on me again with a hard shot to the neck. He followed it with a flurry of good punches, roughing me up. I liked it. I came down on flat feet and started punching it out with him, sending him backwards.

The landlord picked up a telephone behind the bar to call the police but someone grabbed his arm and warned him off. Webb swayed back towards me like a cobra.

'I'll show you about fighting,' he said. '*I'm* the champion of the gypsies.'

'I told you it wouldn't be a Doncaster job,' called his brother.

They were getting over-confident. Time to end it. I waited for Mexicana to come in again and as he did, I faked a bull-hammer right and let go a tremendous left hook. If it had landed he would have been out for a week, but he ducked and it scythed through his frizzy black hair.

I felt a jolt in my shoulder. A wave of agony stabbed through me. The force of the swing had ripped my left arm out of its socket. I stepped back, clamping my jaw against the pain, and turned southpaw, my right fist forward, my now-useless left swinging like a colt's leg. I glanced at the eager faces in a circle around us: no one had spotted my injury.

My system was in shock with the pain. I have never given best in my life, but if a child had pulled my arm then I'd have had to quit. And I knew that if Mexicana found out, he would wrench my arm clean off. I narrowed my eyes and tried to keep my face inscrutable, though my breath was whistling through clenched teeth. It was pride that took me on: the bruised ghosts of my forebears, of Boxing Bartley and Bulldog Bartley and fearless old Ticker. I could not surrender. Never. They'd have to carry me out.

As Webb came at me I stepped in and punched with my right: bam, bam, bam. I marched forward, hitting without stop with the same hand, ignoring his blows, blanking out the agony. I was almost blinded by the pain banging in my brain, oblivious now, determined only to punch, pound, pulverise. I drove him the length of the bar, glasses and bottles tumbling off it, his legs sagging, his eyeballs rolling in their sockets and his head bouncing back like a speedball.

'Enough!'

I don't know if it was Mexicana or his brother Johnny that cried out, but I almost collapsed with relief. I put my good arm around him. 'I tell you something, you're a good fighter,' I gasped. 'I have got to give you credit. You can always say you fought for the title.'

I just wanted to get out of there but I had to finish the show. 'Drinks all round,' I shouted. I dropped some money on the bar, shook hands with Webb and his brothers, and left. John Taylor tried to insist that we go on the car park and fight again. I think he wanted to try out Johnny Webb. He still didn't know about my arm.

Through gritted teeth, I hissed, 'The man has just given in. Leave it.'

We got in John's Volvo. I nearly fainted.

'Get me to the hospital, quick as you can.'

'What is it, what's the matter?'

I told them about my shoulder as we drove. Elias Taylor whistled. 'When I saw your big left hanging at your side, Bartley. I thought, what a style that is!'

I got through the hospital door crouched over with the pain. A foreign doctor came and examined me.

'How did you do this?'

'I was in a bit of a scuffle.'

'Hmm. It must have been some scuffle. Your arms are as big as my thighs.'

They put an oxygen mask on me and tried to force the dislocated shoulder back in its socket, but couldn't. The pain was unbearable. After a while they said they'd have to give me an anaesthetic. I had to sign a pink consent form and then they put me under. In the meantime, John Taylor had set off to my mother's to tell her I was in hospital, only to be stopped on the way by police for drunk-driving – typical.

When I awoke, my arm was back in. I asked the doctor how he had done it and he said they had used a wooden mallet to knock it in. It was in a sling for weeks, but it has never come out since. They said Sonny Liston never really hurt his shoulder when he quit in his first fight against Ali; well I believe he did, because I suffered the same in that fight, and I can vouch that the pain was too much. As for the Webbs, I never saw them again, though I heard Mexicana later fought a good man called Cooper to a draw in the New Forest.

*

MY ARM WAS barely out of the sling when I was back in action, and this time the Braddocks were the cause. I was drinking in the Raddle with the usual crowd: Bob and Will and Reg Martin, and Bob was moaning.

'There's a man from Ripley and he won't give me back my horse skin.'

They used the skins for floor or wall coverings. This man from Derbyshire had taken one from Bob but wouldn't pay him. It was the sort of petty dispute that dealing men are always getting embroiled in.

'We'll get it,' said Will. 'Let's take boyo.' Meaning me.

What the hell. I knew it would end in a drink and a sing-song and that was all I wanted. So the four of us set off, me not knowing or caring who the man was. I wasn't to know he was the best fighter in Ripley. We arrived on a housing estate and I waited in Will's Vauxhall Zodiac while Reg and Bob went to get the skin. They came back without it. The man had three or four friends with him and had told them to clear off. One of them had pushed Reg.

'Come with me,' said Bob.

I went to the house with him and did the talking. 'This man wants his horse skin. Will you give it him, mate?'

'If you don't go now, I am going to give it you like you've never had it before,' was his reply. And he looked good.

'Give him his rug.'

'I've told you what I'll do to you.'

'Come on then.'

We went onto a green opposite his house, both in our shirtsleeves, and without more ado we started fighting. I'll give him his due: he didn't know who I was and he didn't care either. There is no respect in this game. A farmyard cock will fight a champion fighting cock to the death and it's the same with streetfighters. But I cut him to pieces. He fell to his knees and I went down on my knees with him so I could still punch him. Bob and Will had to pull me off.

Slowly, the man regained his feet. He staggered into his house, came out with the rug and gave it to Bob. We went down into town for a drink and at about 10pm they insisted on going to the roughest pub in Ripley. Sure enough, there was the man I had fought, with a large group of friends. I thought this was going to end in trouble – a lock-up job for certain – but the man walked straight to me and shook my hand.

'You're the only man that has ever beaten me and the best I have ever fought,' he said. 'I'll buy you a drink.'

'No, I'll buy you one.' I was that relieved that it wasn't going to be another Doncaster job.

I think the fight was just a test by Bob to see if my arm was okay, because a few days later he presented me with a far more serious proposition. This time we were in the Horseshoe at Longnor, near Buxton. He fixed me with his dark stare, his face criss-crossed with scars: a butcher's block, was Bob.

'You're a correr mush, an't ya?' he said. A fighting man.

'Yeah, a bit of one.'

'Well, I've got a man fer you, boyo.'

He had been down to the Rhondda Valley in South Wales buying pit ponies and had come across some fighting men. Bob had put up money for me to fight their best man: £1,000 against forty ponies at £25 per pony. Bob said I could have ten ponies if I won the fight. I had two young children and knew they'd love a pony each. I'd sell the others. 'It's arranged, boyo,' said Bob. 'You're to fight him down in South Wales where the ponies are.'

That was all right with me. My grandfather had been the scourge of South Wales.

'Oh,' said Bob, almost as an afterthought, 'and you'll be fighting him underground. Down a mineshaft.'

'Hang on, hang on. I'm not fighting down any pit.' Gypsies don't like going underground and I'm no exception.

'That's where he wants to fight you. If you are the man they say you are.'

This was several years after Doncaster but I was still wary about where I went. No way was I going down some dark hole in the ground in some lost Welsh valley. But Bob and Will loved the idea: after my title fight with Fletcher they'd been hauled in by the police and had vowed they would never put on a fight in such an open place again. Having it underground would be a good way of avoiding the law – and would also be a good *craic*.

I still refused but Will wouldn't give up. He knew a man that worked at Longrake mine, near Youlgreave in Derbyshire, and came to some arrangement with him. A week later, he said to me, 'If you won't fight down in Wales, will you fight this man up here in a mine?'

'This man must badly want to fight me, then.'

In the end they talked me round: they said the mine would be just a bit of a tunnel that you walked down. And it would be unusual: the first gypsy champion to fight down a pit shaft. But I wanted twenty ponies and I wanted my pick.

'No,' said Bob, 'there is other men in this as well as you and they're putting up the money.' They wanted to cut it four ways: Bob, Will, Reg Martin and me.

'I'm going to take the punishment and only get a quarter? No way.'

In the end they agreed to let me have a dozen ponies. They called the men in Wales and the fight was arranged for the following weekend. I knew nothing about my opponent except that his name was Jack Grant and he was supposed to be the best man among all the miners of South Wales. So I knew he'd be tough.

Ten of us made the trip: me, Bob and Will, Reg Martin, Old Roly Mare, a horse drover who always wore a smock, Caggy Barrett, Alan 'Twilly' Wilson, Freddie Wuthard, Ezzy Taylor and Nelson Boswell. Caggy and Twilly were my cheerleaders, like Bundini Brown for Muhammad Ali. It was a winter's day and the surrounding hills were white with snow. The mine was closed but Frank, the foreman, let us in on the sly. He must have been bunged a few quid. As we hung around, I was thinking about my ponies. I wanted to see them.

'You hadna won the fight yet,' cautioned Bob.

We waited a good while, getting colder and colder. Frank made us tea in a wooden hut. Then three or four cars drove into the compound and a large number of men got out. One of them, in a suit, looked very tough and I figured he would be my opponent.

'Don't tell him I'm Bartley Gorman,' I said to the others. 'Say I'm called Nathan Appleyard.' I didn't want the police onto me again.

Frank fetched us yellow pit helmets with lights on. The Welshmen had brought their own, far superior to ours. We were led to what was basically a large iron bucket, big enough to hold three men. It hung from a thick steel cable that went up to a wheel on a large crane operated by a man sitting in a cabin. This was to take us down into the bowels of the earth. Bob stepped into the bucket first and went down with a couple of the others. Then it fetched up again. I waited to go down with Frank, the top man: I figured he'd know what to do if anything went wrong. We had to step over a gap and the man said it was 200 feet down and then another 100 feet of water. Slowly we were lowered down the shaft. What little light there was soon receded, to be replaced by the glow from our helmet lamps. The dank rock walls were just a few feet from our faces. The crane rumbled and cranked and water ran down the green rock. As we sank, it got darker and darker and quieter and quieter.

I don't know how far we descended but it seemed like miles. At the bottom it was pitch black and silent. We walked along the shaft for a few yards. The roof was very low and underfoot were rail tracks for the coal trucks. There were no lights down there at all. Bob was talking to the Welshmen. It wasn't the man in the suit I was going to fight but another fellow who looked in his late thirties, though it was hard to tell. He was stripped off and looked the part, about five foot ten and thickset with bony elbows. His head was bald, his nose was flat and his two top front teeth were missing. He had cords of muscle and a big tattoo. I thought, *what am I doing here?* I was there because of my friendship with these people and because they would think it was good and exciting, but I was fighting a miner in his own environment. A gypsy man should have been fighting in a green lane.

I was wearing Doc Marten boots and fought in a vest for the first time since I had been an amateur boxer. It was so cold I didn't want to take it off. Bob walked with me and put his hand on my shoulder and in the half-lights I could see my opponent had no front teeth and eyes like glass. His bald dome gleamed under the lamps and I could see shadows on his face. I know they breed them tough in South Wales but it never crossed my mind that I might lose.

'The pub'll be open soon,' said Bob, 'so let's get it over with.'

The others stepped back but there still wasn't much room, which was another mistake for me, because I'm a mover. I was trying to get them to pull girders and timber out of the way while Bob started introducing the fight.

'Never mind about all that crap,' said Grant.

We started and I knew straight away he could fight. I had no space to manoeuvre and within seconds he'd grabbed me by the belt with his left hand and put his head into my chest and hit me a dozen times in the side with his right. It hurt. I got my hand around his head but most of my punches hit him on the forehead. The man was a powerhouse but so was I; it was like putting two gorillas in a phone box. We went up against the rock and some iron girders. The shouts soon went from, 'Come on, Nathan Appleyard,' to 'Come on, Bartley.' I hit him as hard as I could behind the neck with rabbit punches. He lashed back at me with knuckles, forearms and elbows. I couldn't see properly with the torches in my face. It was a nightmare.

We got tangled in a clinch. They pulled us apart and sluiced the blood off us: they had two plastic buckets of water and sponges. Then we started again. I cut my knuckles on his teeth and it became very brutal, a feel-your-way fight. Grant hit my head and it banged against the rock. All the lights on the helmets seemed to go into a chain. I hit back, throwing wild because I couldn't see. I put my arm behind his neck again, pulled his head towards me and butted him flush on his flattened nose. I'm sure I broke it. Then I held him tight in a headlock. Some of the Welshmen intervened again and dragged us apart. One of them pushed me very hard under the chin to get me off Grant, so I started rowing with him. I said there wasn't enough room to have a clean fight.

'Look, what do you want, mate?' he replied. 'The man has come into your backyard.'

'Hang on,' I said. 'I'm in his backyard, an alien environment.' Caggy Barrett started a shoving match with one of them and Will and Bob had to stop it.

It was do or die now. We were smothered in gore but we still went at each other like pitbulls. He was trying to keep as close to me as possible, to rough me up on the inside and not give me room to punch. So I pushed him back and, as he came flying back in, caught him with the hardest left hook I ever threw. For a second he seemed frozen, then he pitched face-forward onto the tracks. He was sparked out completely. We all thought he was gone, his white body pale as death in the lamplight. His men slapped his face and put water on him but he didn't come round. Everyone was getting very anxious. What would we do if he was dead?

There was a phone down there and it rang. It was the man at the top who operated the crane. He was frit that it was going on too long and said he'd have to call the police. We had fought for twenty minutes.

'I'm going up,' said Frank.

We put Grant in the bucket and took him back up, carried him to the hut and tried again to revive him. By now I was very, very worried. I never intended to hurt someone that much. I told Bob Braddock he could keep his ponies; nothing was worth this. Finally, after more than half an hour, the man came round. He was groggy at first and didn't know where he was. Then he recognised me. 'You can fight, you ginger-haired bugger,' he said.

We took the Welshmen for a drink to a pub called the Jug and Glass. I was singing and they joined in with Welsh songs. They asked me where I was from and I said, 'Ireland. I'm a gypsy man.' I don't like to talk to opponents afterwards too much, otherwise you end up fighting again, but Grant kept coming to me and saying, 'You are a professional boxer, aren't you?' I could see all the blue on his face where he had been down the mines and that he was scarred as badly as Bob Braddock. Grant said he'd had a lot of fights. His real name, it turned out, was James Preece: he had been fighting under an alias as well. He bought me a pint and I bought him one.

'You ought to fight for the championship of the world,' he said.

'You're a tough man yourself,' I said.

'They breed them tough where I come from,' he said.

He didn't have to tell me that.

*

ANOTHER WELSHMAN THAT the Braddocks tried to fix me up to fight was David Pearce, the British heavyweight champion from Newport. He was fifteen years younger than me but had failed an eye test and was being forced to retire from pro boxing. Will Braddock got on the phone to his managers and offered him £20,000 to fight me with gloves for the unlicensed British title. I even spoke to Pearce myself on the phone. At first he accepted but then he declined. I would have gone for the heavyweight championship of the world if I had won that. I would have moved into the *gorgi* circles.

Instead I fought a man bareknuckle in a stone barn used for cockfighting in the Peak District. It had straw on the floor and a corrugated iron roof. This man was a powerful fellow with curly blond hair, the spitting image of Joe Bugner, and many of the people there were convinced he *was* Bugner. We did nothing to dissuade them and it later became something of a legend around that part of the country. In fact I believe the man was a Polish farm worker. There were very few people there, it was so hush-hush, but he had a circle of backers and there was a lot of gambling money riding on it. The atmosphere was tense and I thought something might go off because of the money.

He caught me with a good shot in the first few seconds but after that he had shot his bolt: he must have been gambling on catching me cold. I toyed with him for ten minutes until he was exhausted, then finished him with two or three good punches. He went down but needn't have; he just didn't want to go on.

Though there was a lot gambled on fights like these, I never earned any money from fighting. Anything I did make came from dealing. In 1980 I sold my little house in Tean and bought a one-and-a-half-acre plot at Wood Lane, near Uttoxeter racecourse, for £5,550. Its previous owner had lived there in a caravan but had hanged himself. It was in a prime site, surrounded by green belt and across the road from the town golf course. I was immediately offered twice what I had paid for it, but refused. I had prayed for a place like it for my kids. I moved onto it in a trailer with Gwendoline and the children and named the site Fort Woodfield.

I bought it lock, stock and barrel. There were saw benches and vices and log splitters and machines up there. I opened the previous owner's old trailer and had started clearing out cups, saucers and blankets when I found some papers. One said, '£700 in sweet jar under slab.' I pulled up some two-by-two slabs outside and sure enough I found several jars full of money: half crowns, florins, white fivers and old John Bradbury pound notes. It came to £5,000. It also said there was a jar full of sovereigns, but that I never found.

What I didn't know was that the permission for a caravan on the land was only for the lifetime of the previous owner. I put down a drive and a parking area and had my trailer connected to water and electricity but, within a year, East Staffordshire District Council refused to renew the caravan licence and issued an enforcement notice ordering me to move.

I started a long-running fight with the council. I fought an appeal against the decision and then it went to a public inquiry. I told them I had had enough of travelling and just wanted to live peacefully in my trailer. Shaun and Maria, then eleven and ten, were both at local schools and I wanted to give them a stable upbringing. It wasn't as if we were knocking on our neighbours' doors asking them to buy clothes pegs or lucky heather. But the neighbours didn't want me, though they dressed it up by saying they were 'concerned about future residential development' on the site.

My appeal was quashed by a Department of Environment inspector. My barrister said that, as a gypsy, I should be treated exceptionally in accordance with current government policy and anyway the caravan was unobtrusive but the female inspector said the very fact that I wanted to settle there meant I was 'not a travelling gypsy'. I was in a Catch-22 situation. She also said that 'the caravan undoubtedly detracts from the rural character of the area', which was rubbish, as you could barely see it. I was supported by the National Gypsy Council and still had the right of appeal to the High Court.

In 1983 I reapplied for temporary permission and the council said I could have it for three years if I agreed to sign certain conditions. Again I refused. I even wrote a letter to the Queen. A second public inquiry was held in March 1984. I told them, 'I want my children to get a proper education and not keep moving from school to school.' I eventually won my appeal and got permission to live there for another three years. For the first time in my life I had somewhere of my own that was worth having.

*

IT HAD BEEN more than twenty years since I had watched a newsreel of the young Cassius Clay on top of the Empire State Building, proclaiming that he was going to be champion of the world. I had honestly felt then that one day we would fight. He was only two years older than me and I was as confident as he that I would be a champion boxer. But of course, it had never happened.

Our lives followed very different paths yet there were always parallels. He had chased Sonny Liston, the brooding champion they said was unbeatable; I had pursued Uriah Burton, feared among all travellers. Clay – or Ali, as he became – had to contend with racism and opposition to his religious faith; I, with being a gypsy. We had both become champions. We had both been more flamboyant, more outrageous, than anyone before us, pushing back the boundaries. And we had both paid a price – a terrible price. We had overstepped the mark. I bore the scars, physical and mental, of the knuckle world. And by 1983, Ali was also showing signs of the damage he had suffered from too many brutal encounters in the ring. There were reports that his fingers shook, his speech was slurred, his face was puffy and his movements slow. But he was still The Greatest.

In August of that year, he came on a visit to England to open a mosque in the Midlands. He stayed at the Albany Hotel in Birmingham, and an acquaintance of mine who had got to know Ali well over the years invited me to go and meet him. Apparently Ali was quite keen to meet the King of the Gypsies, so I went along with my brother Sam. As we walked to the hotel, we saw a yellow Rolls-Royce with 'Float like a Butterfly, Sting like a Bee' on it. That could only belong to one person. We were taken up to his room on the eighth floor. The door was opened by one of several huge bodyguards festooned in gold rings and bracelets and so tall they made even Ali look small. My first impression was what a handsome man he was. He was talking to some Muslim lawyers and doctors and looked bored. Then I was introduced to him as the champion of the gypsies, and a light appeared in his eyes.

'You gypsies are real good at making money,' he said.

'Not as good as you,' I said. 'Half a million in a minute.'

I told Ali about watching him as a brash young man and how it had inspired me. He took me away from the other people and over to the window, with its view over the city.

'You see out there is the wide world?' he said. 'And I was the champion of the whole world three times. *Three* times.'

'Yes, and down there are lanes,' I said. 'And in those lanes live gypsies. And I'm the champion of all of them.'

He looked at me, widening his eyes in mock surprise. 'You must be *reeeal* good.'

Someone asked us to pose together for photographs. We squared off in the room but he wouldn't put his hands up in a fighting pose, so neither would I. I threw a couple of jabs into his palm for the photographer and pretended to clip him on the jaw. He was a gentleman and our sparring was never more than a bit of play-acting but, I have to be honest, I thought I could take him.

Every couple of minutes the phone would ring. Calls were coming in from all over the world. Ali, ever the joker, picked up the phone and pretended to be a woman, talking in a high-pitched voice. I sat down on the pile carpet but Ali got up and gave me his chair. He fetched another for himself and pulled it over right in front of me, blocking me in. Suddenly he was serious, talking about his religion and beliefs. He could change mood in an instant.

There was a knock on the door. It was the police. Earlier that day, somebody had apparently made a threat on Ali's life and they had come to check he was okay.

'What's going on?' he said.

'Somebody wants to kill you,' I said. 'But don't worry, I'll look after you.'

Ali pointed at me and did his eyes-wide-open routine. 'You! You look after me! Tell them to come here.'

The cops came over. They were uniformed men and women with walkie-talkies. I don't think the threat was genuine: I think they had really come because they wanted to meet The Greatest.

'I don't need no protection,' said Ali. 'I come from the toughest country in the world. I'm not scared of death. I believe in Allah the Almighty. I don't care if I die of cancer of the throat. I'm ready to meet my maker.'

He goofed around with the police for a while. Then we talked some more. Eventually Sam and I got up to leave. After a lot of handshakes and goodbyes, Ali followed us to the door and watched us walk down the hotel corridor. I looked back and he was standing to his full height in the doorway, pulling a proper fighting pose. I looked him over and the real Ali did stand up. That was when I admired him most.

CHAPTER 12

Suicide Fighters

THE GYPSIES WERE fanatical over me when I was fighting. No matter where I went, men would study me from yards away. If I went into a pub they would all crowd in. Most just wanted to be in the company of the champion fighter but there were others whose intentions were less friendly.

They lurked in corners, in pubs and clubs, at fairs and on campsites, and would stand and stare, trying to catch my eye, itching for trouble. Many were wild, unknown men. I called them Suicide Fighters. As I got older, I could sense more and more of them coming out of the woodwork and could spot them a mile away. They would rarely walk up and challenge me to my face. They liked to study me and pick their moment. 'They will come for you when you are drunk, my lad,' Will Braddock would warn.

I was at Newcastle Fair with Tucker Lee when half a dozen Suicide Fighters came into the pub in turn and challenged it out. I was sitting with a crowd of Lees and Prices, watching as each of these roughnecks came in and declared, 'I'm the best man in Wales,' or, 'I'm the best man in Staffordshire.' This was for my benefit, though not one said anything directly to me. I let them blow off: when I didn't take them up, they had to fight each other. 'There was that many fights that if a man had gone round afterwards with a ragbag collecting the clothes off the floor they would have had a good weigh-in,' Tommy Lee said later.

In the end Will Braddock stood up and announced, 'I will put an acre of land on this man.' Then he turned to me. 'You had better say something here.' So I stood on the table among the beer glasses, ripped off my shirt and challenged out every man in the pub. Suddenly nobody wanted to fight. I sat down again. Beside me were Ivan Botton, the champion of Nottinghamshire, and Pete Tansey, a bodybuilder who was one of my sparring partners. It would take a brave man to push his luck with them – but there were those willing to do it. An eighteen-stone, dark-haired man – not a traveller – walked in. He was Micky Leek, said to be the toughest man in the Potteries. He came straight to our table and, in a stiff, formal manner, said to me, 'I hereby challenge you out to a fight. I am not a gypsy but we will call it the Heavyweight Championship of the Midlands.' He put both his hands on the table and leaned towards me as he said it.

I was a bit taken by surprise. 'Will you?' was the best I could manage.

'Yes.'

He was calling my bluff. Then I got my bearings. 'I've no need to fight for the championship of the Midlands when I'm the champion of the country.' I stood up. 'Come on then, let's get it on.'

'No, no, no. I mean in six months' time when I've done my training.'

He had thought I would duck out. I insisted that we fight there and then but he backed down.

It was no good relying on the Queensberry Rules. You had to be ready for anything: wrestlers, streetfighters, headbutters, martial artists. One of the latter was Robert 'Rodey' Shaw. He had been one of my young unlicensed boxers a decade earlier but after Doncaster I had lost interest in promoting and hadn't seen Rodey in years. Then one afternoon I was sitting in the long grass at Fort Woodfield having a little picnic of ham, tomatoes, spring onions and a glass of beer. Enjoying myself. Up came a man on a motorbike. It was Rodey. He had to introduce himself because he was a big man now – 5ft 10in and 15st – and I didn't recognise him. He had made himself like a rock, really fit, a scary man with black curly hair and eyes that met in the middle.

We shared some food and drink and he told me that for ten years he had been studying the martial arts and had become a fifth dan. He had been to China and Japan, wore black shoes like slippers and could walk without making a sound. He later fetched me books and photos of him training with monks. He had also been in the Army, in the SAS or some such: he could hide in the grass and ten men couldn't find him, until all of a sudden he'd leap up in front of you. He had some moves. He could grab you by your nipples, pull you to him and butt you. Rodey took to hanging around my site, prowling about practising his martial arts in his black outfit and belt, showing off these lethal moves. A lot of men visited and they were all wary of him; they thought he was a madman. I laid down one rule to him: 'Rodey, when any travelling men come around here, don't start showing moves in front of me. You can show anyone else but don't bother with me.'

One day I was lying on the floor in the mobile home watching a wildlife documentary on the TV. Outside was a group around a fire, talking. I was building on the site at the time and had five or six tons of concrete blocks lying around. Rodey would smash them, breaking the blocks with his fists, his feet, even his forehead. Sometimes he'd have you hold a block up and he'd sidekick it and break it in two. I was always telling him to stop or I'd have no blocks left. He wanted these men to hold one for him but none had the nerve to do it. I was watching this thing about wildebeest on the African plain when I heard a shout.

'Bartley, will you come and hold this block?'

I'm thinking, *I wish he'd stop breaking these blocks*. 'Hold it yourself.'

They all came to the door and started nagging. I got up, looked out and there was another load of blocks broken.

'Give it here,' I said. I held a block and Rodey kicked it in half straight into my chest.

'There you are. Now, you broke a hundred blocks, just pack them up and let me watch this programme.'

I went to walk back into the mobile home. Rodey blocked my path. He sank into a stance and threw a lightning volley of punches and kicks an inch from my face while growling and making animal noises.

'Excuse me Robert, I want to watch the television.'

He wouldn't let me pass. Now I was really annoyed. He'd broken my blocks, stopped me watching the documentary and done what I told him never to do, bother with me in front of other men.

When you are messing with a boxer in the ring, you don't play him at his game. Otherwise he's onto a winner; it's like trying to sing against Tom Jones. My motto with a boxer is attack and never finish until he falls at your feet: don't give him a chance to do his moves. It was the same with this man: give him time and space to do his thing and he could take your Adam's apple out with a kick. I'm a bareknuckle prize-fighter: rabbit punch, the lot. The fifth dan is going to do the same. So my thinking is to move in on him and put him on the defence all the time. Otherwise he would destroy me. He wasn't there to play games.

So I walked straight at him and unloaded the heavy artillery. He staggered but didn't fall; instead he tried to grab my hands to get me in an armlock. I blasted him back and he ripped his teeth across the edge of one of my hands: I found out later they call it the 'tiger's teeth'. But I was too fast and punched too hard for him. I backed him up against the side of the trailer and would have slaughtered him if the other men hadn't restrained me.

'Rodey, I did warn you.' I was annoyed, blood on my hands.

He went to swill his face off with water. 'We must never do this again Bartley,' he said, cleaning away the blood.

'No-one was doing anything, only you.'

Rodey eventually lost it mentally. He had done too much fighting. He came to see me one day after an argument with his wife and asked for a piece of string: he wanted to hide

With my children Maria and Shaun. We never actually lived in a wooden trailer like this but it made for a nice photograph!

Marcko 'Hangallis' Small, the gypsy ringmaster (referee) who was behind plans for me to fight the American Jade Johson.

Joe-Boy Botton, from Hemel Hempstead, who once told me he would fight any other 50-year-old in England for £10,000.

With my girlfriend Ann Shenton at the funeral of antiques dealer Les Oakes. The man with his arm around Ann is Billy the Black, who I once fought, and on the right is Malcolm Barrett, an old friend and very successful business man.

Two of the most feared gypsy fighters of the past thirty years. Henry Francis (above) is as deadly with his head as he is with his fists. Our brawl in a car park in Nottinghamshire was stopped by the police.
Henry Arab (left), from the north-east of England, has knocked out so many teeth he is known as the 'Dental Surgeon'.

Newspaper reports of the Irish fighting scene.

Left, the mighty Joe 'the Hulk' Joyce a real rough-and-tumble brawler.

SUNDAY WORLD, December 3rd

FISTS OF FURY!

By KAREN BERGEN

Big Joe <u>punches his way to</u> 'King <u>of the</u> Travellers'

THIS is Big Joe Joyce.

He can put a man in hospital with his bare fists.

And that's exactly what he did this week when he fought another traveller bare-knuckled for over an hour and a quarter in a ritual battle for the coveted title of King of the Travellers.

When the dust cleared, a battered but victorious Joe boasted to SUNDAY WORLD: 'There's not a man in the country I can't fight.'

More than 150 travellers from all over the country had watched silently and respectfully as Big Joe and the other man, Anthony O'Donnelly, stepped to the waist and hurled punches.

• Bruised and bleeding, bare-knuckled Big Joe Joyce squares up after winning the title and dispatching his opponent to hospital.

Right, the famous contest between Ernie McGinley (left) and Dan Rooney at Crossmaglen in 1990.

allenger, during a fight for the crown at Cossma

£80,000 at stake as family fighters BARE-KNUCKLE BLOODBATH

SLUGGING IT OUT: James McDonagh (left) and David Nevin

BLOODIED: Ollie Nevin refused to give in despite his injuries

Left, coverage of a series of fights between the Nevin and McDonagh families. The irish are more open about knuckle fights and many are now filmed on video.

Bernie Ward (left) and friends in a field in Ireland. Bernie was called the 'King of the Travellers' in a court case, though he denied it.

Jimmy Quinn-McDonagh beating Paddy 'the Lurch' Joyce near Drogheda, Ireland, in November 1997. McDonagh won and allegedly collected a purse of £20,000.

Lewis Welch from Darlington, an ex-boxer and one of the best current bareknuckle men.

Big John Fury in boxing pose. He is 6ft 4in and weighs around 18st when not trained down.

Terry Ward, 'the JCB' from Darlington. Terry had one of his biceps nearly chewed off in a fight.

Ivan Botton, who stands 6ft 2in and is the champion of Nottinghamshire.

Charlie Moore, another top young gypsy fighter from the north-east who won a string of amateur boxing titles but gave the game up.

My son Shaun playing rugby for Uttoxeter. He's not a fighter, fortunately, but on the sports field he takes a lot of stopping.

In my fifties and still throwing the bull-hammer into my big heavy bag. I had my last fight in 1997 and then turned my back on the bareknuckle arena.

My three dear grandsons: Bartholomew Gabriel, aged four, with his mother Maria, and on the right Nathan William, aged seven, and Joseph Samuel, aged four. I wouldn't swap one of their smiles for all the gold in the world.

Returning to Hollington Quarry, the place where I won the title in 1972. We had to fight among the cut stone and junk.

out in the woods and was going to use it for snares to catch animals. I told him to go home to his family. That was the last time I saw him. Not long afterwards he was driving to Burton upon Trent and crashed into a lorry and died. The strange thing was that the lorry had 'Robert Shaw' on the side, which was his name. He was only thirty-eight. I was very upset because he was a very kind man and even though he was only a labourer he left £10,000 to the Freemasons and a lot of money to children's charities.

*

LIAM GALLORAN WAS built the same as Rodey Shaw: a short block of a man with mixed Irish and traveller blood. He had seen the inside of a few jails and was a notorious prison fighter; he had once knocked out a warder and had a run-in with Paul Sykes, a former heavyweight title challenger from Yorkshire who was one of the most feared men in the prison system. He also went to Ireland for prize-fights.

I once went into a bar with Liam and he called for two pints. For some reason – perhaps Liam was barred – the landlord refused him. Liam smashed the entire bar to smithereens in less than ten seconds. I stood there with my mouth hanging open while he wrecked all of the fixtures and fittings with a chair. I knew this was a police job for sure so I left sharpish and drove off in my Transit van. I don't mind admitting I wanted to get away from the scene of the crime. I didn't know that Liam had followed me out and jumped onto the roof rack. When I finally pulled up I opened the door and this grinning head looked down from the roof and said, 'Are you all right, Bartley?'

Though he lived in Manchester, Liam used to hang around in Stoke-on-Trent with some Irishmen, a couple of whom had been slung out of America for prize-fighting. I sometimes went for a drink and a song with them. On this particular day we were in the Five Towns pub in Hanley and these men were saying they had tried to get Liam a prize-fight in Boston but it had fallen through when they were deported.

One of them said, 'Well, why go to America when you can have a fight here?' and indicated me. We were all drinking, my sleeves were rolled up and the pub was full. 'You ain't got the money for him to fight me,' I replied. I had no intention of fighting Liam; he was a friend.

Liam said nothing at first, then piped up, 'You don't have to have money if you are a travelling man. I'll fight you for nothing as long as we remain friends after.'

'Let's go out on the car park,' I said.

'No,' said Liam, 'where the argument starts, I settle it.'

He ripped his shirt off in the pub and we fought. I shouldered him over towards the doorway and threw a thunderous bull-hammer right. Liam ducked, I hit the door frame, the brickwork gave way and the wall collapsed. It was like something out of a film. I knew I could hit hard but this was ridiculous – there were bricks and dust everywhere. Liam took one look at me and that stopped the fight. We had to go because the pub was wrecked. It was only an old rotten bit of wall, dangerous really, but I still demolished it. Liam talks about it to this day.

I have cleared many a barroom and I agree with my grandfather that a bareknuckle fighter should be a drinker as well. I don't know much about football but I was in a pub in Uttoxeter in the Seventies when five Derby County soccer hooligans picked on a friend of mine, whom they accused of being a Stoke City fan. I got so annoyed I ripped the pub door off its hinges and all five of them fled.

Another time I was in the King's Head at Newcastle-under-Lyme with Will Braddock and loads of travellers, all wearing a load of gammy gold rings I had sold them, when one man there made a remark about me and when I pulled him over it, he shoved me away. I knocked him out. The landlord was a big Italian, about forty-five years old in white silk shirt and gold chain, and everyone was scared to death of him. He came around the bar and grabbed me with his forearm around my neck. I pushed him back onto the bar and hit him. He was nearly breaking my neck. I hit him in the ribs and he went down like a burst balloon.

His hysterical wife, a blonde all in gold, came charging round the bar with a huge ornamental sword. She slashed at me four or five times as all the travellers jumped back. She was mad as hell. Braddock got behind her and took the sword off her but she was cutting curtains and everything. I left – again.

*

FIGHTING WOMEN WITH swords is not advisable, nor is taking on a gang of men on your own, no matter how tough you are. 'Two can worry a bull,' is an old gypsy saying, and it's true.

It happened to me twice, not including Doncaster. The first time, I was jumped by four men outside a pub. I actually knew them: Billy the Black, Paul 'Beaky' Smith, Colin McVeetch and Keith Tompkinson. I had been dealing scrap with a friend called Ken Cooper and whatever we earned, we drank. We would have a weigh-in, get the money and go straight to the pub. We were drinking this afternoon in Uttoxeter with Billy the Black – an Irish-Scot brought up by travellers – and some Scotsmen. An argument started, I think over a game of brag, and someone pushed Ken, who was terrible for starting fights.

'Don't push him,' I said.

I had no sooner said it than one of them down-charged Ken and he was out for a few seconds. I went to get hold of the man and Tompkinson and Billy the Black interfered and kicked the table over. There was a bit of a commotion and the landlord threw these other men out.

Ken and I stayed drinking for another hour. When we left, four men came out of the bushes and trees at us; they had been waiting all that time. At least they didn't have weapons. The first to run at me was Beaky Smith, who had been one of my boxers. I knocked him down with one punch. Billy the Black, a pretty big fellow, jumped on my back and tried to pull me to the ground with his hands around my throat while McVeetch and Tompkinson punched me. I ran backwards into the wall three or four times and knocked the stuffing out of Billy, forcing him to let go, then set about the other two and beat them. They were scattered among the bushes and elder trees, scratched and torn. Billy the Black jumped in a van. I gave chase while he shouted abuse out of the window. The van was only running on two cylinders and had no acceleration but just as I would catch him he would manage to put on a spurt and get away.

I walked to another pub, the Three Tuns, and saw Ken Cooper standing by a wall.

'You're a handy man, Ken. You ran off and left me.'

'I never ran away from anyone.'

'Yes you did. I've two minds to break your jaw, Ken.'

'If I ran away, hit me,' said Ken. So I knocked him straight over a privet hedge. He came round and said, 'If you feel that bad, hit me again,' so I knocked him over it again. This time he didn't come back.

Then who comes walking up the street but Beaky. I collared him and he said, 'Listen, you couldn't beat Chuck Bodell in a million years.' I don't know why he said it.

'I can beat Chuck Bodell any time, my friend,' I said.

Beaky said, 'Look, if I hit you I can knock you out.'

'I know you can't. I'll give you a shot then.'

'If I don't knock you out, though, you'll hit me back.'

'Why are you worried about that? You just said you would knock me out.' But I swore I wouldn't hit him back.

I stood with my hands down and said, 'Hit me.' What an idiot. He was a very good middleweight boxer. He spat on his hand, clenched his fist and wound it up. I expected him to aim for the point of the jaw or the temple, just as I had taught him. Instead he hit me flush in the mouth and bust open my lip.

I said, 'You're a disgrace. You hit a man in the mouth to knock him out?' I never hit him back but said to him, 'If you ever tell anyone that you hit me and I didn't hit you back, I'm going to break your jaw.'

'Fair enough,' he said and we shook hands.

The next day my lip came out like an orange. I walked

into the Black Swan and Beaky was playing cards with a load of men. 'What happened to you?' one of them asked. I claimed that I had run into a door. Beaky was laughing into his beer but daren't say what had happened. He never did tell anyone. He told me later that in all the boxing he did, no one had ever decked him until I knocked him down.

The other time that I fought a group was against some bouncers, and is described later in this chapter. There was also an occasion when I fought two Irish travellers at once. It started, as so often, in a pub, when my pal Alan Wilson called me from the Black Swan in Uttoxeter and said this pair had come from London to see me. I was getting ready to go somewhere else and was determined to have just a quick shandy with them but once I got there and found out they were Irish, that meant goodnight to whatever I had planned. 'Flash' Gerry Doran and Lee Harbour were womanisers, gypsy playboys, but fighters too. I had known Lee when I was a teenager in Wales and we'd nearly had a fight with some men in Newtown. He had come after all these years to see what sort of man I really was. I ignored it when he said, 'You don't seem the man that we've been hearing about.'

Ann Shenton, my girlfriend (Gwendoline and I had split up) was driving us so we went to Derby drinking, then to Nottingham, then to Burton, then back to Uttoxeter. All the time they kept muttering to each other, 'I don't think this man can fight,' and all this. Eventually I'd had enough of it – it was clear what they were after – and challenged them to a fight. I took off my shirt and went into the car park of the White Horse in Uttoxeter.

Neither of them came out. Apparently they were arguing over who was going to go out first. I went back in and they said, 'Which one do you want to fight?'

'I've had enough of this. I'll fight the two of you now. Come on.'

They both pulled off their shirts. Harbour had on a vest. I hit him a shot and he sucked his stomach in that much his trousers fell down before he hit the deck. Doran squared up to me with his friend on the floor and I tripped over Harbour's body as I tried to get him. I swung at Doran, hit the bar and broke the two last fingers of my right hand. The landlord ran around to break it up just as I stepped back, and my heel broke his toes. It was like a Popeye cartoon. Eventually I put Doran out of action as well and left the pair of them in a heap. The landlord ushered me out. The next day I sent Alan Wilson down to see the landlord and he had a block tied to his broken toes. He had been going to send for an ambulance because they couldn't bring the two of them round but in the end they got them awake and into a motor: they are tough nuts, those Irish.

A week later they were with some friends of mine in a pub in Hemel Hempstead. Harbour had a broken jaw and was supping Guinness through a straw with his mouth wired up. He had little pliers in his pocket so he could cut the wires if he was going to spew up. Doran could still speak but had a ruptured spleen. 'Bartley is as good as they say,' said Doran. He was telling the whole pub what had happened – exaggerating his own fighting abilities a bit – while Harbour had to listen, mute. Then Doran got up to go to the toilet and groaned with pain. Harbour pointed at him and tried to laugh, which only made his jaw hurt even more, and he started moaning too. Everyone cracked up at them.

*

USUALLY MY FIGHTS were man against man. Caggy Barrett told me that there was a hard Scotsman on the Springfield estate, a very rough area near Cannock, who wanted to challenge me. I wasn't interested because he wasn't a traveller but Caggy said, 'He'll fight you whether you are a gypsy or not.' Another Suicide Fighter. Shaft and Wilf, two of the men who came with me when I handed out the leaflets at Doncaster, knew this Scotsman and met us in the Globe in Rugeley. They said he was from up in the Scottish Highlands and had come down to join his relations working in the local coal pits. A couple of his pals were in the pub and said they could take us right to him.

We drove to a pub with bouncers on the door on the Springfield estate. I waited in the car park. He came out and he was a big fellow with a flat nose, just a beer-bellied Suicide Fighter. We stripped off and I knocked him on his arse straight away. He didn't want to know after that. I made Caggy count to ten just to make sure.

We went back to the Globe and got drinking. That day I had bought a Rover car for £10. A ginger-haired man bought it off me for £20. We went back to someone's house, taking three two-gallon plastic containers of cider. In the early hours, I said, 'Take us back.' Ginger who had bought the car drove us. I was in the front with him and Caggy was in the back.

The minute we got into Uttoxeter, a blue police light came on. Ginger, who was legless, wouldn't stop. So the police passed us with the siren on and pulled up in front of us. We just drove on straight past them. I climbed into the back seat with Caggy and said to the driver, 'This is your motor now, I want nothing to do with this.' A big drum of cider spilt all over us. The chase was on. The police car passed us three or four times and each time we got away. We got onto a dual carriageway, took a bend and the police car spun round to block our way. The doors flew open and uniformed bobbies jumped out. I said, 'It's up to you Ginger,' opened the door, jumped straight through a hedge, through barbed wire and ran, ripping off nearly all of my clothes. The others did a bunk as well. I went through another hedge and looked behind me and someone was running over the fields after me. We took hedges and ditches, even a tennis court. I was pulling thorns out of me a month later. When I got into the town I was virtually naked.

Now, everyone in Uttoxeter knows Bartley Gorman and so this was a rather embarrassing situation. I was going to ask the first person I saw if they could put me up. I saw a man and I beckoned him, trying to hide my nakedness, but he wouldn't come. Instead he was beckoning me. It turned out to be Caggy: he had been chasing me, not a policeman.

That's cider for you. We made it back to his place and got away but they arrested Ginger and he got a few months inside.

*

THE WILDEST SUICIDE Fighter I ever met was the Staffordshire Wolfman. This was another attack that came out of the blue, at a Bonfire Night party at the bungalow of Peter Sellars, a wealthy travelling man. Peter had put up a marquee with a band and scores of travellers were there. I was talking inside the bungalow when this big farmer hit a woman and cut her lip. I can't abide that sort of thing so I asked no questions but moved straight in on him and slaughtered him against the Welsh dresser. There were broken plates and dishes everywhere.

The man's best friend, a scrap dealer called Johnny Mellor, interfered. Johnny was ten years younger than me, a stocky lad and a reasonable fighter. He used to take the stance of a fighting cock. His father, old Johnny Mellor, had been the greatest horseman at Appleby Fair. He said something about me hitting his friend so I said, 'Well, I'll fight you then.'

'All right. This Sunday morning.'

'Let's fight now.'

'No, I'll fight you for five thousand pounds, Sunday morning.'

'Okay.'

Jimmy Braddock, Will's son, shouted, 'I'll have another five grand on Bartley.'

With the fight arranged, Mellor left. The music was on and everyone was enjoying themselves. I went outside with Pat Finney and Maria Maguire, the wives of two friends of mine, and was walking arm in arm with them along the driveway when someone took a running kick at me and tried to break my leg.

It was the Staffordshire Wolfman. His real name was John and he was known and feared throughout the county: he would fight a badger barehanded, go down a hole with men holding him by his feet. He was a proper hunting man, kind of a wild man. He once lost his licence for drink-driving and so used to come down the high street in a pony and trap, go to the pub, have ten pints and go home in the trap.

Immediately he kicked me, the band stopped playing and the crowd ran over to watch. We were at the end of the drive near the road.

'So you want to fight, do you?' I said.

I hit him, bull-hammer straight to the head, and down he went. Instead of leaving him there, I bent down to pick him up and he wrapped his arms and legs around me, digging his fingers into the veins of my neck, and sunk his teeth into my face. The harder I tried to push him away, the deeper he bit. He wouldn't let go. I couldn't shake him off and ended up on the floor with him. I'm not used to that kind of fighting. There was only one thing for it: if he wanted to fight like an animal, we'd both fight like animals. So for the first time in all my life, I bit a man back. It could be no other way: this was gutter combat. I got his nose in my mouth and chomped so hard my teeth were nearly meeting.

I thought, *if you take this man's nose off, God will never forgive you.* Also, he stank. So I let him go. He was calling me 'w****r' without stop. I straddled him, put his head on the pavement and every time he said it, I punched him. His mouth and nose were bleeding but he never stopped saying it until a police car came and I got up off him. There were so many crowded around that the police didn't know who to arrest, so they left me alone. Later Peter Sellars got a hosepipe to wash the blood off the road.

I was in court several days later for a motoring fine and there was the Wolfman with two big plasters over his nose. 'You are mental,' I told him, 'to cause that trouble. Why did you do it?'

He said he'd recently had a fight with Colin Morfitt, one of the toughest men in the area. 'I wanted to see who was hardest, you or Morfitt,' he said.

I still had the business of the fight I'd arranged with Johnny Mellor. This would be totally different: not an all-in brawl but a properly organised prize-fight, to take place shortly after dawn on the car park of the Little Chef restaurant at Uttoxeter. Mellor was a heavyweight and had fought Billy the Black forty minutes to a draw, so he was no slouch. Word spread like wildfire. I was a legend among travellers but the vast majority had never seen me fight. Now was their chance. Within four days there were 1,500 of them in town. They came from all over Great Britain and Ireland and as far afield as France and Spain. My place at Fort Woodfield was thick with gypsies and there were campfires burning all night. I woke up one morning and fetched a pint of milk to make tea, only to find out there were 500 people wanting some.

On the morning of the fight, Rodey Shaw came up on a motorbike and changed into his karate gear. He was stalking around outside while the travellers eyed him warily. He did look dangerous. There were gypsy fighters everywhere, old veterans and young up-and-comers like Henry Francis, 'the Outlaw'. One man had a false eye made of gold with a diamond in it.

I was driven to the car park in the back of an Escort van. Half the town was waiting – and a line of police riot vans. Too bad, I wasn't going to stop now for anyone. We pulled through the crowd and I jumped out of the back of the van right among the crowd with my fighting gear on, shouting, 'Where is he?' Sam and John joined me, both stripped to the waist, and we prowled through the crowd, a Beatles tape blaring out from a ghettoblaster. But it was clear that Mellor wasn't there. Someone had tipped off the police and he had been arrested leaving his father's farm.

The officer in charge, in a peaked cap, came over and told me to go.

'I'm going to make a speech,' I said.

'If you do, I will arrest you,' he said.

I went to make my speech, saying I was the King of the Gypsies, and he did arrest me. They put me in the back of a riot van, right behind the driver, who turned round and said, 'I'm not driving this motor an inch until you move him from behind me.' But I was quiet as a lamb: I was brought up never to put my hand on the Queen's uniform.

They convened a special Sunday court for Mellor and me and we were charged with disturbing the peace. I was asked my occupation and replied, 'Beggar,' because I was so annoyed. Mellor said he was a contractor. They fined us £250 each and bound us over to keep the peace for two years in the sum of £1,200. 'Police KO gypsy bare-fist fight' was the headline in the next day's *Daily Mirror*. Mellor and I later had a big drinking session to bury the hatchet and that was the end of the matter.

Another fight that never came off was between me and Bobby Frankham, a young relative of Johnny Frankham. In January 1988, the *Daily Mirror* published a double-page spread on me after I challenged Frankham – who had recently been barred from boxing after attacking the referee in the ring – for '£1 million a side'. It was a load of hokum about how I dined on hedgehog stew, rubbing the grease into my skin to toughen and keep it supple, and how I soaked my fists in petrol. At the end of the piece the journalist, William Marshall, wrote, 'To all concerned: If you have a million nicker and your friends quite like your face the way it is, stay out of a fight with the red-haired bloke smelling like a pitstop and spitting lumps of hedgehog . . .'

Sound advice, and Bobby Frankham took it. Years later, he was asked to advise the actor Brad Pitt on bareknuckle fighting for a movie. Pitt visited him at his site in Watford and Bobby told reporters, 'I was once offered a million pounds for an illegal fight in the hold of a container ship in the North Sea but I decided against it on the advice of my dad.'

In September that year several doormen didn't take heed. I went with my friend John Taylor to watch my cousin John Fury boxing at a sporting club dinner at the Grand Hotel in Leicester. It was a black tie do and we were in a posh motor and both in new suits but they wouldn't let us in. I offered them £100 just to let us stand by the curtains to see John fight but these men had heard of me and wouldn't have it. I guess they wanted to show their authority.

I was okay until I was manhandled. Two of them grabbed me by the arms. I decked one, then the other. John Taylor put another one over the bonnet of his Bentley. We beat up four of them altogether. They weren't worth a carrot anyway; just bouncers – I had no respect for them. All they do is hit little kids and drunks. We had to disappear after that because I was still bound over to keep the peace over the Mellor fight but somehow the newspapers got hold of it. 'PRIZEFIGHT GYPSY KO'S SIX BOUNCERS' was the headline in the *Daily Mirror*. Some onlooker told them, 'The first two bouncers were big, beefy guys, well over six foot, but he poleaxed them.' That bit was true but I don't think there were six of them.

I don't want you to get the impression that I was fighting every day – far from it – but I did have to be watchful all the time with these Suicide Fighters; you just never knew where the next one would come from. You could be out having a perfectly pleasant time – as I was one day in Coventry with a gang of Irish, Welsh and Scottish travellers – when something would happen. On this day we'd all had a drink and were driving back to the Aston Firs site at Hinckley in four cars. It was only when we were halfway there that one of the men in my car said we were going to the camp because there was a man who wanted to fight me. He was known as 'Ginger' or 'Red' Bob McGowan and was a very tough Irishman who was in Coventry labouring.

When the cars arrived, the camp was pretty empty. Jimmy the Duck was sitting in the doorway of his trailer drinking cider, his shirt off, braces hanging down, round white belly. We pulled up at the bottom of the camp and got out. Red Bob was waiting.

'Do you want to fight me?' I asked.

'Yes,' he said.

'You will get severely hurt if you do.'

'No, it will be the opposite way around.'

'We'll fight then. Up there on the green.' I pointed to the top of the camp.

'All right then.'

We took our shirts off and started to walk up side by side, the others following behind, like in a Spaghetti Western. We passed Jimmy the Duck sitting on his step. 'Do you want to see a man knocked out, Jimmy?' I said. 'Well, you are just about to see one.'

Then I passed my Aunt Nudi's trailer. 'Nudi, watch this man get knocked out.'

I could hear the others laughing behind me because they knew Red Bob was a hard case and reckoned I was in for it. I knocked him straight out with the first blow. Unconscious. As he lay there, our Sam drove up. He had been out painting a barn and had paint all over his face. He saw the crowd and ran up, raging at the men for fighting on the camp where he lived. He challenged them all out but none would fight him. Then he picked up Red Bob, slung him in the back of a car and told them all to clear off.

*

IT WAS NOT long after my fight with Red Bob that Uriah Burton died. He'd have been sixty-one or sixty-two years old, and to the last was a demon with his fists. He fought Edmon Evans from North Wales the year before he died, in a stables behind closed doors on his site near Manchester. It was a terrible fight and people could hear the noise inside, like a horse was kicking the sides. The best man walked out: I won't say who but let's say that Big Just went to his grave undefeated.

He had devoted the last few years of his life to various causes: he was always a man of principle. Hughie walked from Dublin to Belfast to promote peace in Ireland and offered to do it again accompanied by religious leaders, though none of them took him up on it. He even said he would hire out the King's Hall in Belfast 'when I will meet anyone who objects to my ideas, if they wish to be physically aggressive, I will engage them in a boxing ring, but will not attack, only defend myself.' He called for one world government and the abolition of armies, advocated a single world language like Esperanto and thought prisons should be demolished and miscreants made to do community service or, if serious offenders, sent to isolated islands to provide for themselves.

His death was a shock to me, for I had always admired him. They laid him out on a board in his trailer, with a melodeon on his left and a wreath from me on his right. My message read:

> To my gypsy brother Big Just
> King of the Gypsies
> I know we will meet again.

Traditionally, prominent gypsies were burned in wooden trailers with their belongings, and there was a big debate about having a funeral pyre for Big Just, but the authorities would not allow it. Had it been me, I would have done it and to hell with them. He was cremated and his ashes were scattered in Wales near the monument he had erected to his father.

Bob Braddock died too – indestructible old Bob – and his death was linked to Hughie. Bob and I had been drinking one night when he said, 'Let's go over to see Big Just in Manchester.' He wanted to arrange a fight or something. This was typical of him: drink all evening, then drive 200 miles to see someone on a whim. We stopped at an all-night garage in the Potteries and as we pulled in there was a robbery in progress. Bob leapt out of the car while it was still moving and ran to help the poor woman cashier, who was terrified. I turned off the engine and jumped out and saw some men fleeing. I gave chase and had a scuffle with a couple of them but they managed to get in their car and escape.

When I came back, Bob was lying in a pool of blood. They had hit him over the head with an iron bar. I got a bucket of water and threw it over him and it sluiced the blood all over the forecourt. The police arrived and he was taken away in an ambulance. He never fully recovered and died not long after of a brain tumour.

His brother Will died too. He went blind towards the end. I went to see him and his last words to me were, 'Take care of yourself.' The Braddocks were my biggest backers when I was at my fighting peak. They were throwbacks to a different era. They'll never make men like them and Hughie Burton again.

CHAPTER 13

Fight at Sam's Funeral

IN THE SUMMER of 1990, the Irish travelling community was alive with talk of the biggest fight for years. Dan Rooney and Ernie McGinley had agreed to meet for the bareknuckle championship of All-Ireland at Crossmaglen, on the border between North and South, the region they call Bandit Country. They made quite a contrast. Ernie (whose real name is Denis) was a stocky bulldog of a fighter with cropped hair and a stubbly goatee. Dan was a giant, tall, heavy and handsome, with thick black hair. Both were top fighting men, brave, hard and experienced and more than ten years younger than me. I had met a couple of McGinleys before and was quite friendly with them. I also got on well with the Rooneys, though we'd had the odd fall out. It was Dan's uncle, Felix Rooney, who had been attacked by the mob on that terrible night in Moss Side nearly twenty years earlier (see Chapter Eight), and one or two of the family still blamed me for it.

Big Dan was one of a large number of brothers and was said to be the champion of his breed. He had first claimed the Irish title after beating the ferocious Joe Joyce, who was known as 'The Hulk' and who had been the top man in Ireland in the Eighties. I had been due to fight The Hulk once and went to Liverpool with my cousin John to catch the ferry to Ireland but the fight was cancelled. Joyce later told everybody I fought him but I never did. His contest with

Dan was brutal. Joe apparently had Dan over but Dan got up and knocked Joe down. Joe broke his ankle as he fell and couldn't continue.

Dan and I had never got to it but I had fought his brother – another Felix – in the Eighties. A large number of Irishmen had been staying around Uttoxeter and, as usual, we had all gone drinking. Felix was one of the group and made some remark that I had left his uncle to get a beating that night in Manchester.

'I don't leave any man, friend,' I said. 'Let me tell you the story.'

I told him what had happened and it was dropped. We ended up at Peter Sellars's house – the place I had fought the Staffordshire Wolfman – enjoying ourselves, with music on, but Felix started again. I was sick of it.

'Do you know who I am?' I asked him.

'I don't care who you are,' he said.

'I'm Bartley Gorman, the king of every gypsy man.'

'I don't care for Jack Johnson, never mind you.'

There was uproar, with people holding each other back and tables and chairs and best china going over. I didn't want to fight Felix because I was a guest in Peter's house and also I didn't want to fall out with all the Irishmen, many of whom were my friends. It causes bad blood.

'I'm going for a drink,' I said, and left in my blue Transit van. As I pulled away, Paddy Doran, my best drinking partner, jumped in and for some reason sat on the dashboard. I was flying along, drunk, looked in the mirror and saw twenty cars chasing me: Volvos and Transits with beds, baths and antiques on top. The Irish thought I had taken Paddy to beat him up. They didn't know we were best friends.

Eventually I pulled up in the middle of Cheadle, thinking, *this is no good, I will have to fight him*. The convoy screeched to a halt and blocked off the road. I jumped out and stripped off and so did Felix and we went straight at it among rows of empty market stalls. I jabbed him and he flew back straight into a wall, but he came back at me shouting, 'I don't value anybody.'

We started punching, really fighting, with the Irish all round us yelling and pushing each other back to make room for us. Five minutes in, I'm boxing and playing with him and he's flustered and going mad trying to punch me. Froth was coming out of his mouth. The more he did it, the more I was taunting him. I didn't realise we were next to the police station. They must have called for reinforcements because suddenly ten officers came running with batons drawn. They broke up the fight and told us to get in our motors and go. I went to Will Braddock's and said, 'Felix Rooney wants to fight me for as much as I want.' That night we went looking for him but in the end it was called off. There'd have been too much bother over it.

Because of all this, Dan Rooney had it in his mind to fight me. A pal of mine, Alec Goram, was in a pub in Soho, London, with some Irish travellers when this black-haired giant came in.

'Where are you from?' he asked Alec.

'I'm with the lads,' said Alec.

'Where are you from originally?'

'Uttoxeter.'

'You'll be a mate of that Gorman's then?'

'Yes.'

'A mate of Gorman's isn't a mate of mine. Do you know who I am?'

'No, and I couldn't care less,' said Alec.

'I'm Danny Rooney.'

'So what?'

Dan picked up Alec by his collar and threw him over the bar.

I had more immediate concerns. That summer my mother died, at the age of seventy-nine. For many years she had lived at the Aston Firs site in Leicestershire, on the same plot as her brother Joe, and we took her body back there for the vigil. They buried her in blue because she was a child of Mary. I remember kissing her in the coffin and a tear fell out of my eye onto the shroud and left two little stains. I couldn't leave my mam's coffin; I even jumped in

208

the hearse with her. There were eight Rolls-Royces in the funeral cortege through Hinckley, with truckloads of flowers. Her niece Maria Wilson sang a beautiful solo at the funeral. It broke my heart.

Afterwards, my brother Sam went into training to fight the winner of McGinley and Rooney. 'I'm going to show these men what a real fighter is,' he said. He declared he would take them on one after the other, and he would have. It is hard to describe what a powerhouse Sam was: a heavyweight Roberto Duran. He had his own gym and trained a lot of men there but never had many knuckle fights because nobody would face him. People looked at him in awe because they knew he wasn't some built-up bodybuilder; his size and strength were natural. I was definition but our Sam was mass. He had a weights bench specially made because his arms were so long that he couldn't use a conventional one.

He was a great boxing fan and was in Leicester for one show when Frank Bruno baulked his way at the side of the ring. 'I didn't know whether to blast him out of the way or not,' said Sam; he said it so simple, as if Bruno was just anyone. I used to point to Sam and say to men, 'See that man there? I can beat him with one hand behind my back. If you can beat him first, I will fight you.' Sam would be scowling at me. Yet he was not at all a violent man. He loved his music and even cut a demo disc in a studio in Derby with his friend Rockin' Johnny Austin (now an MBE for his charity work) under the name 'the Rocksam Duo'.

The Rooney–McGinley fight went ahead in August 1990. Hundreds of travellers descended on Crossmaglen, taking over the town like an occupying army. There were kids perched on roofs and standing on walls. The atmosphere dripped with tension and there were scuffles between members of rival factions even before the two men faced off. Both were confident and no-one seemed to care at all about the *garda*: they fought right in the open in mid-afternoon. It was also one of the first fights ever to be filmed on video. The two men were called together in the midst of the throng and shook hands: McGinley in a red vest with his hands taped, Dan bare-chested and bare-fisted. They got right down to it, no messing about.

They swapped blows. The bobbing, weaving McGinley had trouble getting past Dan's huge fists and long reach but he was game as a pebble and kept at it. The contrasting styles made for a ferocious fight. Unfortunately the crowd were completely unruly, despite the best efforts of the marshals, and gradually closed in around them. After several minutes it became a real toe-to-toe affair but both men were rapidly swamped by the crowd. Suddenly there was a roar. Hands were raised aloft and after several seconds of utter confusion both men were lifted onto their respective supporters' shoulders. McGinley quickly left the area, saying he would fight Rooney again for £100,000 on Ballinasloe Green at the October fair, while the bemused crowd tried to figure out what had happened. Both had taken punishment – Ernie's face was busted up while Dan had cuts and a black eye – and both claimed victory.

After it was over, a cousin of mine, Peter Maguire, told a reporter on the *Irish Press* that Bartley Gorman could beat both families one after the other. I didn't know he was doing it and to this day I don't know why he said it. Anyway, the paper published the story and my phone number. The first I knew was when my cousin Bessie in Liverpool rang me in a flap. 'Bartley, my Bartley, you are going to get murdered. Why ever have you put that in the paper?'

She told me the story and posted me the cutting from the newspaper. I had a telephone in my mobile home at Fort Woodfield and soon it was ringing off the hook. Every day when I got back there were messages. 'I'm going to bury you, you big, redheaded tramp, and I'm going to beat your brother too,' was one, I believe from McGinley himself. A man called Jake Whaler, a good fighter in Ireland, also said he would fight me. Another time there was a call from a pub. I could hear noises in the background and a lot of Irish voices. Then someone said, 'Go on, say it, say it.' This gruff voice came on. 'Now, Bartholomew Gorman. If you are as good as you think you are, tell me this . . . who is going to win the three-thirty at Galway Races?' Then laughter and they hung up. I ignored the calls. Sam was going to fight them and that would have been the end of the matter. Neither of them could have beaten our Sam.

But something was wrong with my brother, tragically wrong. I was with Peter Sellars one day when Sam came to see him over a bit of business. When he left, Peter and I turned and looked at each other in shock. Sam was a shadow of himself. He had lost weight and his face was sunken. Peter's wife had died of cancer four years before, and he knew even then that Sam might have it too.

A short while afterwards, he went to hospital for an examination on his throat, which had been giving him a lot of trouble. I went with him and afterwards asked the doctor what he thought it was.

'Oh, it's only a small ulcer,' he said.

I walked into the room where Sam was. 'I can't understand all this mither,' I said. 'It's only a small ulcer.'

'You're kidding!' He was so pleased.

That is what the man had told me. A bit later, when the test results came through, I had a phone call from my Aunt Nudi. 'Now, he's not very well, my lad.' She talked round and round but never came to the point. In the end she just said, 'Will you ring Doctor Sharkey up?'

I did. 'It's a small cancer,' he said.

I went into a panic. 'Doctor, what would you do if it was your brother?'

'If it was my brother, I would operate.'

They had found a shadow. The doctor said to me later, 'If Sam Gorman has got a shadow, then that is some shadow.' He also told me there were 200 'species' of cancer, as though it was an alien thing that invades someone's body. I put the phone down and fell on the floor, clutching two pillows to my chest and rocking like a baby. 'My brother Sam, my brother Sam,' was all I could say. I knew it was the end of him.

Sam had cancer of the oesophagus but still didn't know it himself. We couldn't tell him because of his nature: he had four children – Relda, Bridie, Sam and Jerry – and was mental over them, a real family man. It would have broken him up to think he was dying. I discussed it with the doctor and we decided not to tell him.

I went to see the doctor with Sam and his wife. This was an awkward situation, because I had asked the doctor to lie. I sat with the doctor, facing Sam and Relda across the table, and everything the doctor said, they looked at me for confirmation. I was trying not to be emotional but it was hard, acting. 'It is only a small operation,' said the doctor. 'We have to bypass something.' In fact they were taking out part of his stomach and making a new one.

Sam came to my place and stayed. It was a bad time. My mother's brother, Joe Wilson, died that August. He was a holy man who fasted and lived like a monk and sometimes used to train me. 'The man that thinks he can beat this man must be a fool,' he would say. John Taylor carried a fifteen-foot cross into the cemetery and there was a huge wreath made of Welsh leaves to mark his love for that country.

John Fury, my cousin's son, came to Fort Woodfield for a visit. He was ranked the fifth best heavyweight boxer in Britain and was in training to fight fourth-ranked Henry Akinwande in an eliminator for a shot at the British heavy-weight title. He would have been the man for either McGinley or Rooney but was concentrating on his boxing career. I trained with him and his brother Peter, running five miles in the morning, sparring and punching the heavy bag hanging in my field. John asked me to come to his eliminator in Manchester. I didn't want to leave my sick brother but Sam insisted that I go. 'Cheer him on well,' he said. I was sure John was going to win but he was counted out in round three. It was certainly no disgrace. Akinwande, who is 6ft 7in, went on to win a world title.

Sam had his operation soon after. I went into a little chapel and prayed for the four hours he was under the knife. I made sure I was back at the operating theatre when they wheeled him out. I grabbed his hand and said, 'All right, Sam?'

'Oh, my brother,' he said.

We thought he would have five years but he didn't live six months. After the operation, he used to bring his own caravan up to Fort Woodfield and stay at mine for days. He went down to nothing. It was like he had melted. I remember him getting up and saying, 'Holy Mother of God, Holy Mother of God. I know what's the matter with me.' He looked like he had had a revelation.

'What's the matter with you, Sam?' his wife said.

'It's cancer. I've got cancer.'

'Don't be silly.'

He knew then, even though we hadn't told him.

I even had to fight while Sam was dying. A man with a big black moustache came on our ground – I don't think he was a traveller but he knew travelling men – looking for a fight and Sam got upset, so I just went out and steamrollered him. I don't know who he was and I don't want to know.

Sam thought he was getting better. He refused all morphine or painkillers and wouldn't go into the hospital again, though the doctors begged him to. One day he got out of his bed, got dressed, and set off walking as fast as he could down country lanes to try to get life. I was with him day and night. Every morning we would play all his favourite Sixties songs on his cassette. He must have worn out the tape of *I Love You More Than I Can Say*. Towards the end, he declined so much that he never went out. No one saw him for weeks. Then a young man, his pal, died on the camp at Hinckley. When they told him, Sam ordered a wreath and emerged on the day of the lad's funeral, when the ground was black with gypsies. He came out of the trailer with the flowers in his hand, though he hated anyone seeing him so weak, and walked like an old man to the lad's trailer, with all eyes on him. He laid the wreath then slowly walked back to his own trailer and closed the door. That took some doing; he must have had some love in him.

A few weeks later he was lying in a bed in his trailer. 'You was always better than me,' I said to him. 'You was the champ, Sam.' I kissed him and they were the last words I said to him. He was looking up through the window. His son Jerry came in and I went into another room to fetch something. When I came back, little Jerry, five years old, was lying across his dad with his arms around him and Sam was dead.

Ben Smith, a travelling man from Leicester, came in at that moment. He saw what had happened, sighed and took off his cap. 'You didn't deserve this Sam, you didn't,' he said.

It was December 3, 1991. Sam was forty-six. My mother, brother and Uncle Joe had all died within a few yards of each other on the same site at Hinckley and all within eighteen months, as though a gust of wind took them off the face of the earth. I still feel Sam's presence all the time. When I laugh at some remark I feel that Sam is smiling with me.

*

THE NEWS OF my brother's death spread within hours. Many people didn't believe it: to them Sam Gorman was indestructible. Visitors began to arrive to pay their respects. Messages of condolence came from all over the world.

For a week after he died I sat up with him every night. Then they laid out his body in a chapel of rest and had this piped death music in the background. I asked them to turn it off. I was devastated. I remembered when he had had fights as a young man and I was always the one to butt in. They had never closed his eyes and they were looking up. In the hollow was a great big tear and I knew it was for me. I went back that night and cried so much in the trailer that I thought my heart was going to give in.

Ernie Bryan, my dad's cousin, came on the camp on the funeral morning. It was a cold, foggy day. Ernie looked at his sons and then saw me washing in a bowl outside the trailer. I must have looked grim. 'I know my breed,' said

Ernie. 'There is going to be trouble today.' I was so distraught that I paid him no heed. I went into the trailer and put on Sam's beautiful double-breasted suit that he had given me before he died.

Travellers came from everywhere for the funeral; some of the toughest men in England, along with newspaper reporters and television cameras. Someone counted 180 cars in the cortege. They put a photograph over the coffin of Sam squaring up in a boxing pose, while the Lees from the north of England sent a boxing glove in flowers, six feet in diameter, with 'No 1' on it. I bought a pair of six-ounce red boxing gloves, made in California. As they lowered Sam into the ground, I threw the gloves onto his coffin. 'Here you are, Sam. They are not fit to lace your gloves, so let God lace them up for you,' I said.

Big John Fury came up to me at the graveside. 'I know I can never take your brother's place, Bartley, but I'm always here if you need me.' That meant a lot to me.

The tea afterwards was at a club called The Squires. We walked in and they had Christmas decorations up, baubles and gold tinsel. It was inappropriate for a funeral, glittering everywhere like some gaudy nightmare but I seemed to be the only person that noticed. Someone put the television on. I had been talking to BBC Midlands Today in the graveyard and when I saw myself, I looked ill, as though I was in a trance.

Two of Dan Rooney's brothers were there, John and Ned, both fighting men. John was in a tee-shirt. Everyone else was in suits. There were Dorans, Wards, Taylors, Dunns, Willetts, Finneys, Wilsons, Nunns, Kidds, Egertons and many others. Eventually the tea was eaten, the women had left and just the hard-drinking men remained. Some of us moved up to another room and sat around a table with my friend Paddy Doran. Ned Rooney looked at me across the table and that was when it began.

'It was a bad thing what you put in the *Irish Press*, Bartley, that you could beat every Rooney and McGinley one after the other.'

'I never said that, Ned. I would never say that about any breeds. I'd be out of order if I said that.'

'Well, it's very strange. You've been in every paper in England, Ireland, Scotland and Wales and even abroad. You're continually in the Press. I'm asking you a question now. Do you admit you are continually in the Press?'

'Yes.'

'And yet this is the only time that you've never spoken to them?'

'I told you, I never said it.'

'I believe you did.'

'Take it as read, then.' I didn't care what he thought about it.

Everyone had gone silent. There was a table between us and John Rooney was sitting to Ned's right. I had no blood relation with me, and that is an important thing with travellers. The Furys and others had gone.

'Ernie McGinley would be the man for you,' said Ned.

I don't usually badmouth any man but by now I was angry. 'I could knock him out,' I said.

'No way could you knock him out.'

'Well, that's fighting, that's the name of the game.' You have your opinion, I have mine.

I left the table but this played on my mind. I walked back. 'Why don't you think I could knock him out, Ned?'

'That's easy to tell you. My brother Dan is the best man in England, Ireland, Scotland and Wales and he couldn't knock him out, so how can you?'

'Hang on. Your brother Dan isn't, because my cousin John Fury is the best man among travellers.' I didn't brag myself up. I was forty-six now: it was down to younger men to fight it out if they wanted to. But I wasn't going to take much of this.

'No way is he,' said Ned.

'I'm telling you that John Fury is.'

'No way. He could never beat Dan.'

This could have gone on forever. So I said, 'Hang on. I can knock Dan out.'

I knew that would go down like a bomb but I hadn't expected what happened next. As we had been talking, John Rooney had risen to his feet out of my vision. Without warning, he hit me square on the left side of the mouth. He had a fist like a mallet and was wearing a four-ounce saddle ring. I should have gone over the chair backwards, but though I didn't see the punch coming, I am always ready. As I took the blow, my right leg slammed down to brace me, and I kept my balance. I rose very slowly from my seat.

'You are in very serious trouble now, Paddy,' I said. 'Get your shirt off.'

Everybody was stunned. Two top fighters were about to go at it. I was wearing my dead brother's suit and I took off the coat and put it on the bar, then removed my tie, shirt and rosary beads. When I turned around, John had his shirt off. He always claimed to be a better man than Dan and was in the prime of his life, about twenty-eight. I'd had a lot to drink but so had everyone. The club bouncers made no attempt to interfere: they were looking forward to it as much as the others.

I was warming up, moving my body, but as I went towards him, he stopped me.

'Hang on, is this for the title?'

'Yes.'

A human ring formed. We came together, with the head doorman saying he wanted a nice clean fight and all that. I told Rooney, 'I'm just about to teach you a lesson,' and I slapped him hard up the side of the face.

'Let's show how two real men fight,' I said, and pawed him with my left. I was messing about really. He was looking for his range and I pulled him in close with my hand behind his neck, shoulder to shoulder. Every Irishman was shouting, 'Kill him, John.' He had his blood relations and I had none; even my brother John had gone, and this would be the first time Paddy Doran had never shouted for me in a fight, though I could understand it. Still, I wasn't taking things very seriously until Rooney sent in a fierce shot which burst my eye. He still had on his £5,000 red gold ring, set with diamonds. I never wear a ring or a watch.

'Oh, you want it for real now?' I said.

That was when I started to fight. As he rushed in very square with a wide guard and his body exposed, I opened up on him with body shots; I can't remember hitting him to the head once. I was fighting a cross between George Foreman and Ken Norton, not swaying and slipping and using his own energy against him like I used to but fighting flat-footed with a cross-arm defence. I wouldn't let him see my eyes so he didn't know what I was going to do. He caught me with some good right hands because I was a bit drunk but his punches just bounced off me. I backed him up and he hit me a good left hook.

We had a vicious exchange, I hooked off the jab and he stumbled. The bouncer referee wanted to count but Rooney's friends stopped him and pushed their man straight back at me. I unloaded on him. They were causing the man to take tremendous punishment. He set into me again rushing like a raging bull: head down, ready for anything. He had some bottle. There was now nothing but blood, sweat and snot. I didn't realise at the time but I was taking some terrible head shots with this ring and all one side of my face was going black.

John Taylor moved between us. He was Sam's wife's brother, the best fighting brother of the Taylors. He said, 'Take that ring off. You don't have title fights wearing rings.'

Before anyone could answer him, I said, 'Leave it on. Give him a chance, he's fighting Bartley Gorman.'

I was sobering up. In the middle of the room was a decorative wooden pillar with a shelf around it to hold drinks. I put him straight through the pillar and it collapsed: drinks, glasses and all. Rooney pulled the mess off him and raised his arms aloft. 'I'm the King of Ireland!' he roared. Then he charged again. I waited, not budging. There was such a wicked exchange this time that I thought Rooney had broken my jaw. I punched him to the body so hard I could feel his ribs giving in.

This had gone on twenty minutes without pause. When we got in close he was calling me a 'w****r' and I was calling him a 'tramp'. We continued this throughout the fight.

I kept up a running commentary:

– 'Well, at least you can always say you fought for the title.'

– 'Do you know you are fighting the best man in England, Wales and Scotland?'

– 'Don't worry about losing, because you are making history.'

Paddy Doran got mixed up once and shouted, 'Go on Bartley!'

Rooney stumbled over and young Andrew Taylor shouted, 'Kick him in the head.'

'No, I've never kicked a man in my life.'

Rooney had been badly hurt but this was some fighter, feared throughout the country. He generally only has to hit a man once. He got up and this time I felled him properly. Someone else shouted, 'Kick him,' and again I said no. I bent over him, going down on one knee and picked him up with one hand to hit him with the other and he said, 'No more, Bartley, no more.'

I was always a man for the count but on this occasion no-one counted. At that moment the police burst in. They had blocked off the whole of Hinckley. Then Rooney, still game even though I'd won, said, 'I want to finish this fight now.' I said to the superintendent, 'Listen, this is going to go, either in Coventry or somewhere else. Can I fight this man now and finish it?'

'Yeah,' he said. 'Get it finished.'

It was impossible because of the crowd milling around. I was talking to somebody when Rooney suddenly came and hit me. I went to get back at him and more came between us, so I walked away from him to the bar and said, 'Give me a half of lemonade.' I thought, *he has hit me after the fight has finished, on the day I buried my brother*. I saw him standing by the wall with a load of men, walked through the crowd and this time I hit him so that hard to the head it bounced his skull off the wall. How that man took that punch I will never know.

This is gypsy fighting; it doesn't finish nice and clean. I walked away. The landlord wanted us out and the police were ushering everyone outside but before we left the club, Ned Rooney, who had caused it, said, 'Will you fight my brother again tomorrow and I will fight the next man?'

So I pointed to a friend of mine and said, 'He'll fight you.'

Ned stormed over to him. 'Will you, will you fight me?'

This man said, 'No, no I won't.' I won't shame him by naming him but I was disappointed.

So I shouted up then, 'Fetch who you want. I will have my cousin Big John Fury with me, his brother Hughie, his brother Peter and my cousins Michael, Craig and Russell.' This caused near-panic.

The police got us into the street among the cars. There were scores of men and it was agreed we would fight again the next day. I was just sorting this out when Rooney walked through the crowd and hit me *again*. So I went after him and hit him so hard I broke two of his ribs. I heard later he had to go to Grantham Hospital. Despite this, we weren't arrested. The head policeman said, 'You have never disturbed the public, so that is fair enough with me.'

I went into a pub with Paddy Ward while they escorted the rest off to Coventry. I looked down and somehow I was wearing John Rooney's tee-shirt. I must have put it on in all the confusion. I went mad and ripped it to pieces. 'Tomorrow it won't be the day I buried my brother, and I shall demolish him off the face of the earth,' I said.

'Tomorrow, Bartley, I'm with the boys,' said Paddy Ward. 'You better get that into your head.'

'That's good, because he is going to need you real bad,' I replied. I believe in tact but when you are messing in the jungle, if you can't stand it, get out.

I got on the phone to my friends up in Darlington and they were all coming down, while John Fury and his family were going to fly from Manchester to Coventry Airport.

Meanwhile John Rooney had gone to my brother John's in Coventry. They were best friends. Rooney is one of the best uilleann pipe players in Ireland, our John plays the melodeon and that is how they know each other. There they saw another prize-fight between Paddy Doran and my cousin Ginger Stretton. They fought for half an hour before calling it a draw; too much blood had been shed that day.

That night wiser heads eventually prevailed. John Rooney came on the phone to me and we called the truce, otherwise there would have been full-scale war. He later told my brother, 'Bartley would eat McGinley and spew him up again.'

Next day the *Leicester Mercury* reported:

Bare knuckle boxers sparked off a police alert when they squared up to one another at a wake for gypsy Mr Sam Gorman yesterday.

Hinckley Police called in reinforcements from Coalville and Nuneaton and sent a dozen officers to Squires nightclub, Hinckley, when an outbreak of fighting was reported at about 7pm.

About 200 people went to the club after the requiem mass of Mr Gorman, a former boxer who died last Tuesday.

Police reported that about 30 were involved in the fighting incident, but Squires owner Mr Neil Kyle said it was nothing more than a confrontation between two bare-knuckle fighters who had a long-standing feud, although there were perhaps 30 people in the room.

If you are ever in the Grapes public house at Appleby in Cumbria, you will see a wood carving of me fighting Rooney. The carving has a curse on it, by Old Haggard Aggie. They'll tell you all about it in the pub. People come from all over to see it, not just gypsies. I met John again some years later and we shook hands. Then in December 2001, when I was very ill, he and his brother Dan both came to see me. I realised what giants they were: formidable men but nice men too.

I thought I would make that my last defence. I no longer looked for fights. The sudden deaths of my mother, brother and uncle had put me out of the frame of mind and, besides, I had nothing to prove. But I could not seem to live a quiet life.

CHAPTER 14

The American Killer

MOST TRAVELLERS ENCOUNTER prejudice at some time in their lives. My wealthy neighbours in Wood Lane, Uttoxeter, had made it quite clear they did not want me there and nor did many of the town councillors. They claimed my site was unkempt, there were roaming dogs and insufficient screening for my forty-five-foot trailer. It was all nonsense. I offered to fight the entire council in a ring at once – with gloves on if they wanted – and if they were able to beat me I would leave. They didn't accept. My temporary permission to keep a trailer on the site was due to expire in December 1990, so I needed to hit them with something.

I decided to play them at their own game. In November, I submitted plans to build a ten-bedroom mansion, with a swimming pool and tennis courts. 'It will be the poshest house in Uttoxeter so the neighbours will not be able to run me down any more,' I told the papers. 'I am going to build it myself out of tons of old stone I have collected.' I also said I'd put a curse on the planning officer if he didn't pass it. 'As long as we're not turned into field mice by Mr Gorman's curse, a report will be compiled for the committee to consider,' a deadpan council spokesman said.

They agreed to let me stay but would not give me planning permission, which would have made the land worth a lot more. Then I saw in a newspaper the headline, 'Convoy of New Age Travellers passes through Birmingham'. It gave me an idea. New Age Travellers were a big issue at the time and I publicly announced that they could stay on my site. I told the papers my plot could house up to 300 people whom I would teach to live off the land and help to find work on nearby farms as labourers. The chief of West Midlands Police, who just wanted them out of his county, got wind of this and told the 'NATs' – which was what the police called them – that they could stay at Bartley Gorman's place in Staffordshire. Soon after, a big bus pulled up outside my property, driven by an out-of-work landscape gardener with his wife and their German shepherd dog.

'The Chief Constable sent us to you, Bartley,' he said.

'Pull on then.'

Within a month they were arriving from Stonehenge, the New Forest, all over the place. Eventually about 100 came. They were quite a sight: some with dreadlocks, some with fifty earrings in each ear, and dressed in all manner of clothes. One came in with a mobile home forty feet long with one end cut out of it and put together with another forty-footer to make an eighty-foot home. There was a double-decker bus with red and purple spots on, and the men in it only came out at night. They all had aliases and nicknames.

The *Burton Mail* described them as an 'unwanted army' and the council went nuts. They were worried that loads more would arrive when the festival season ended and I was served with an order to evict them within a month. 'It will take an army to get them off because I am going to put up barricades,' I said. 'I am bracing myself for a battle bigger than Bosworth.' I know how to bull when I want to. Someone tried a different tack – setting fire to my £15,000 trailer. Fortunately I wasn't in it at the time, because it was gutted, but I could have been killed.

The NATs themselves had ten campfires going every night and lit up the place like an Indian reservation. They were very artistic people and some of them played in bands with names like the Red Cadillacs and the Mushroom Brothers. They were very good. They would bring a chair out for me and put it in front of the big tent and play. Sometimes half a dozen groups were playing at the same time in different areas, like a mini Glastonbury. The problem was that they liked their music loud, with huge amplifiers. We had murder with the neighbours and the council slapped a noise abatement notice on me.

The NATs were intellectual and some came from wealthy backgrounds – though they did smell bad. There was one lovely girl whose daddy was a millionaire and sent her £1,000 a week. Others' parents brought them bootloads of food. But they were no angels. Once they rammed a police car outside my gates and a breakdown truck had to tow it away. One of them had a scanner and would monitor the police frequencies. There were often fights. Two of them went after each other one day with axes. I didn't interfere. The police came and arrested several of them. I said, 'Listen, this is nothing to do with me. If a man commits a murder in a council house on a council estate, you can't charge the council with murder, can you?'

They brought me gallons of festival wine. Some of it was yellow, some was blue, some orange, some pink, and it had bits floating in it. By God, it had a kick. My Uncle Nack, old Ticker Gorman's brother, came over to stay. He was a man of eighty-four and had seen all the gypsy fighters. The New Agers were fascinated by him: they called him Old Redhammer. Uncle Nack ran out of cigarettes so I asked one of them to roll him a fag. Instead they rolled him a spliff. Nack had a bad stammer and after several deep drags he turned to me and said, 'B-b-bye G-g-god, these j-j-jucks can roll a f-f-fag!' He didn't know what it was but he smoked the lot.

My cousin Booty Kelly also came to stay and had a bareknuckle scrap with one of the best fighters of the NATs for three gallons of wine. I went away for a few days, like a fool, and left a wardrobe full of jugs of this wine in my trailer. 'There's two jars there for you,' I said to Booty. 'Don't touch the other eight in the wardrobe.'

I came back four days later to find fifty NATs in my trailer with Booty and Nack. Arms and legs were sticking out of the windows. They had quaffed all the wine and were so drunk they couldn't speak.

It became a village. They were coming back from Africa, Goa, Spain, all over the world. There were dogs everywhere. Even my Irish traveller friends, who have seen everything, couldn't believe it. Eventually there were about seven council notices on me. I had a licence for only one caravan on the site, so I applied to extend it to 100 caravans. I knew they would refuse but would leave a technicality in there – they always do – and I could home in on that and go for it again. It could have gone on for ten years. John Wren, the council's director of services, finally came up.

'They have to be moved.'

'I'm not moving them.'

'I want them moved.'

'I want a bungalow there.'

'I will give you one if you move them.'

'Take off every notice first.'

'No.'

I knew that if I moved them off with the notices still on, I wouldn't be able to move them back again, and would lose my trump card. In the end they took off all the orders except the noise abatement one. But by then I didn't have the heart to move the travellers because we had become friends. I had lights on the pillars and two signs saying, 'All travellers welcome'.

My friend Malcolm Barrett, a very successful businessman, set up a meeting between myself and Mr Wren at his offices. Malcolm has all these leather swing-round chairs with brandy and cigars and chocolates on the table. Wren tried to lord it over me and said, 'I give you my word you can have a house if you move them, but they must be gone within three months.' I couldn't do it. They had babies there. Some had been conceived and born there.

When I failed to move them, Wren came to see me again.

'I don't want a bungalow, I want a house,' I said.

He replied, 'If you want a house you will have it there and

nowhere else.' And pointed to a spot on the ground which was where I wanted it anyway. We agreed.

Now I had to devise a way to get the travellers off without upsetting them. I knew that Billy Varey, a travelling man who owns a lot of land, wanted planning permission for some farmland in Nottinghamshire. I told him that if he could get the travellers to move onto it, he could work the same trick as me, killing two birds with one stone: I would get rid of the travellers and Billy would get his planning permission. He came and pretended to sell me his land. We had this fake bidding war and slapped hands on me buying his land. Then I told the NATs I was sick of the media bothering me and was moving to this land in Nottinghamshire and wanted them to join me. I stayed there with them for two months but when I left Billy got nervous and pulled out and it is now agricultural land.

In 1993 the council allowed me to upgrade my plans and gave approval for a six-bedroom mock Tudor mansion – yet the truth was that I had no money to build it. I had never made a bean from fighting. I had beaten the system but couldn't cash in. I considered starting up the pirate boxing again and holding an open-air tournament to find the 'heavyweight fighting champion of Great Britain' but couldn't get it going. So when I was approached with an offer that could have set me up for life, it was too good to refuse. There was only one problem: I would have to fight the most dangerous man on earth.

*

THEY SAID JADE Johnson was six foot seven, nineteen stone and black as charcoal. He came from Alabama in the Deep South and had been fighting for money since boyhood. When he was not in the penitentiary he worked as a sparring partner for some of the best heavyweight boxers in America. He was reputed to have killed two men in death matches. Even if half of what they claimed was true, this would be a test like no other.

I was told about Johnson by Marcko Small, a mysterious gypsy whose grandfather, Strong John Small, had been the undefeated champion of south-west England; he would stand on a hill and throw his hat down into the hollow to challenge his opponents. Marcko, a short, stocky man, was the best fighter in Devon, Cornwall, Dorset and Somerset. He could also take out a man's throat with his knife and was known as 'Hangallis', which means a man likely to hang by the gallows. I first got to know him when he wrote to me from jail. He had seen me at fairs, had been following me for years and had even had fights in prison over me.

Marcko was well connected with travellers in the United States and in the autumn of 1994 he told me that a gypsy syndicate was putting forward this black giant to decide who was the bareknuckle champion of the world. I could not turn it down. This was what I had wanted through all of my fighting life: to call myself champion of the world. It would also set me up financially.

The only way to pull off the contest– and make a lot of money – without all getting arrested was to stage it on a ship outside territorial waters. This was an idea I had been kicking around for years. Even old Hughie Burton had once said to me, 'Bartley, I'll fight you on a ship. But what if I knock you into the sea?'

'I would swim out and kill you,' I said.

Marcko knew a former sailor, Denis Browne, and recruited him to find a vessel. It was a full-time job. Denis studied piles of books on maritime law. He said there was a three-mile limit around the British coast that applied to fishermen and a twelve-mile limit outside which you were in international waters. Once we were that far out, it appeared that no-one could stop it.

Trying to find a vessel that was seaworthy, met all the safety requirements and had navigation equipment in order was no easy task. We couldn't just get a heap of scrap because we would have been breaking the law that way. The original plan was to hire a ferry and stage the fight in the hold where they park the cars. Denis was on the phone constantly to people in Holland, Belgium and Germany and eventually found a Dutch company with a 25,000-tonne ferry that could fit up to a dozen articulated lorries down the length of the deck. That would have been more than big enough for the spectators. However, the ferry proved impossible to get, so instead Denis went for a coaster. He said it would have fifteen feet under the hatches which could be illuminated and where we could put up a ring and have spectators around the top and also in the hold, all in suits and ties. For the size of coaster, there would have been a maximum of sixty tickets, and even then no guarantee everyone would have got on.

The cheapest tickets were to be £5,000 and the dearest £10,000. We would have no problem selling them all. Marcko was getting calls booking three and four tickets at a time. We had enquiries from wealthy gypsies, famous rock musicians and film stars. There were to be two doctors on the ship and paramedics in helicopters. We needed a crew of five or six – the engineer, captain, first mate and a couple of able seamen – and a security team. The destination would have been secret. Once the vessel was in position out at sea, they were to telephone to get the fighters on. I was to be flown in by helicopter from England and Johnson from France.

I had never fought outside Britain's shores before. I was once supposed to go to Canada to fight the champion traveller there but said, 'If he thinks he can beat me, let him come to me.' There had also been talk of my fighting Jose Urtain, the Spaniard who boxed Henry Cooper and who was said to be a gypsy man, but he wouldn't meet me bareknuckle.

We deliberately leaked news of the fight to the media to drum up interest and help us sell television and video rights – and it worked. We sent stuff off to the *New York Times*, the *Toronto Star*, the *Irish Press*, Reuters, Transworld Sport, Sky, Granada, Sankei Sports in Japan, Cable Tel Communications, the BBC. Marcko was fielding dozens of letters and phone calls and they were talking about a satellite link-up to the United States.

Denis also had several visits from the local constabulary, who threatened us with the Offences Against the Person Act and the Merchant Shipping Act, but really they were powerless. They could have stopped the ship from leaving port but they'd have needed hard evidence of an offence. What happened in international waters was nobody's concern as long as it was not an act of war or terrorism. Really the Devon and Cornwall police just wanted to ensure that it was not going to happen on their patch – they were afraid that there would be thousands of gypsies coming to watch and they wouldn't be able to cope. 'We'll have all these gypsies hooking up their caravans and coming down into Devon and blocking all the roads,' said one officer. 'Is there any way you can let people know it won't be in Teignmouth?'

Both sides wanted an independent referee so we decided to ask Muhammad Ali. We approached him through the Irishman Paddy Monaghan, a good friend of Ali's who ran his fan club in Britain. Paddy wrote back to say, 'I've been talking to Muhammad over the phone and I'm sorry to have to tell you he will not be able to accept Mr Gorman's kind invitation because of the sad news that his mother has recently had a stroke and he feels the need to be by her side as much as possible. I am sure you will understand.' I suspected also that he didn't fancy going out on the ship.

I would be fighting with Jem Mace's original silk around my waist. I had acquired this gypsy treasure from a pub landlord who had bought it off Mace's granddaughter. It says: 'The original silk of the Swaffham Gypsy – Jem Mace – Bare Knuckle Heavyweight Champion of the World, Champion of the Gypsies.' The landlord had it hanging on the wall behind the bar in the Queensberry Arms in Teignmouth and I was desperate to have it, so I went in with my best suit on and with big gold rings on each finger and said to Marcko, 'Say nothing, leave this to me.'

Marcko introduced me as the champion of the gypsies and this landlord, an ex-boxer, fell hook, line and sinker. He thought I was a multi-millionaire dealer, as I was flashing gold-plated watches and a gold-plated chain, and ordering double whiskeys. We chatted about boxers as I smoked a big cigar.

After a good while I said, 'What would you ask for that?' He wanted £2,000. I said, 'Would you take this watch for part exchange?' I said it was worth £1,000. He said he would, so now I had to give him another £1,000. I opened my pocket and pulled out another watch. I told him I had paid £2,000 for it (I had actually paid £100 each). So I said, 'Instead of parting with my money I will give you the two watches for it.'

'It's a deal,' he said.

'Put them in a safe and don't let them see daylight,' I said. I couldn't get away quick enough.

We put a lot of work into arranging the Johnson fight. The plan was to have it just before Christmas, weather permitting. Marcko was talking to the Americans and I was given to believe a lot of people were willing to back the fight and put money into it. Some even paid upfront to be there. Finally Denis was quoted £48,000 for a vessel for three days. He was a week away from getting a boat. I would make enough to retire on and Johnson would get a very good pay packet. Everything was going great.

Then it all went bump. Marcko became quiet and withdrawn. At the same time, he seemed to be walking around with money. One story was that Johnson was worried that the ship would be unsafe and he would end up drowned, so the fight had to take place somewhere else. We discussed having it on a remote beach but it would have been impossible to escape police attention. Weeks went by and I heard nothing. The trail to Jade Johnson went cold.

And so the first world heavyweight bareknuckle fight since John L. Sullivan fought Jake Kilrain never happened. Through it all, I never once met or spoke to Johnson. Some people have since doubted whether he ever existed. I am sure he did, though Jade Johnson may have been a pseudonym; if you enter death matches, you are not going to fight under your real name. So I never fought the American Killer, and have heard nothing of him from that day to this. But if you ever come across a nineteen-stone man-eater from Alabama called Jade, give him my regards.

*

THE PUBLICITY OVER the Johnson fight had put my name back into the limelight and all the tribes started coming out after me. They thought I no longer had the backing now Sam was dead. They were wrong: I had my cousins' sons, the Furys, to see me fair play. The Furys had been close to my family for over 100 years – from the days of the legendary Black Martin Fury – and had intermarried with the Gormans. Big John Fury was, by the mid-Nineties, the best man in the country, now that I was getting older. They were one breed that no-one wanted to mess with.

I was sitting having a quiet tea with my Uncle Pat in Burton-upon-Trent one day when the phone rang. My brother John was at Coventry Pot Fair, a big gypsy gathering, with 200 Dochertys, the most powerful of the Irish travelling clans in Britain. He was drinking with Par Docherty, who was shot dead in Birmingham a couple of years ago (he managed to stagger to his Shogun shouting, 'Mammy,' and died in his mother's arms). 'There's an English travelling man at the Pot Fair who wants to fight you,' said John. It was a fellow from London called Bugsy Price. He'd been after fighting me for some time and wanted to challenge me for the heavyweight championship even though I no longer claimed it; as I have said, I considered John Fury to be the top fighter but he was concentrating on his boxing career. The Prices are all blond and are one of the biggest breeds in England. This Bugsy had an eagle tattooed on his chest, with the wing tips reaching his shoulders, and had done time for shooting his own father-in-law.

'I'll be over soon,' I said to John, to get rid of him. I had no intention of going; it was a nice quiet day and I was dressed up and relaxed. But he phoned that many times I got sick of it. In the end I thought I had better go because otherwise John might get hurt but I was determined to avoid another Doncaster.

I rang Michael Fury. 'A man wants to fight me in Coventry, Mike. Will you see me fair play?' Michael came straight away in a minibus with his sons Craig and Russell, two heavyweights, and was joined by John, Peter and Hughie Fury, Poppy O'Neill, Podge Gorman and a couple of others. They arrived within two hours and I jumped in the motor with them.

Meanwhile, our John and the Dochertys had heard this man with a London accent outside the pub shouting, 'Where's Bartley Gorman?' It was the Prices with a group of Lees. Every Docherty went outside and attacked them. They smashed up every motor in less than two minutes in a show of power.

When I arrived, my brother was in his forty-foot mobile home discussing the situation with twenty men. Big John Fury opened the door and said, 'Excuse me men, we have got some business to talk about, will you kindly leave.'

They all left immediately. As they were going, one of them got me by the arm. It was old Tucker Dunn, a good fighter who had shown me how to put a man's eye out by raising your middle lower knuckle. 'Don't go down there tonight, Bartley,' he whispered. 'They have got yoggers.' Guns.

I took heed. 'We are not going down tonight,' I said. 'We'll go in the morning.'

We stayed on a camp and they kept me up all night. At four o'clock the next morning, I dressed in a blue and red tracksuit over a hooded sweatshirt, pulled on my white boxing boots, and climbed into the front seat of Michael's white minibus with John Fury. I didn't even know where we were going.

After twenty minutes or so, we pulled onto what looked like a piece of common ground and cut the engine. Gypsy trailers were parked haphazardly and between them were Shoguns and Mercedes with shattered windscreens and headlamps – the cars that the Dochertys had attacked. I walked onto the ground with the others behind me, my face hidden by the hood, like a phantom. All the curtains were drawn and nothing stirred but gamecocks and a few grey-hound dogs, some with the mange, sloping about like jackals. There were discarded water cans among the smashed-up vehicles. I could see death here. I had at least fifteen men with me but there were about 100 on this ground.

'Bartley Gorman has arrived,' I shouted. 'Where is the man with the tattoo?'

No-one came out. I could see curtains opening a little, then closing. A couple of men climbed out the back of their trailers. There was more than one on the site with a tattoo and they thought I was after them. One man shouted, 'Jel, jel,' – which means 'go' – jumped out of a trailer window, ran into barbed wire and ripped off one of his testicles. They tell me his wife is after me to this day.

'Let's get this thing on,' I yelled.

After ten minutes, with the sun beginning to rise, I decided he wasn't coming out and went back to the van. The Furys and Mitchell Barney were walking slowly around (the Barneys are a dangerous fighting breed from Southampton). I took off the tracksuit top and pulled down my hood.

All of a sudden, one shouted, 'He's here, he's ready for you!' and a man appeared, stripped, with six or seven others around him. This was a very dangerous situation. I just wanted to be a clever, scientific fighter, like Jack Johnson: I didn't want him to be here. But there was no turning back. 'Take me over, Mike,' I said. Michael Fury started the engine and I hung from the side of the Transit as he drove. We passed a young girl running, holding a small child. 'No need to run, we don't hurt children,' I shouted, but it sickened me that we should even be here, frightening youngsters in the early hours.

Price was there, fists clenched and ready. He was about forty-two, and I was now fifty. Michael gunned the engine, then threw the van into a spin. As it turned side-on towards Price and his men, I jumped straight off, ploughed through his guard and started throwing bombs at his head. No-one said 'title'; we just fought it out. He was stocky, about 5ft 10in and 14st 8lbs, and he was hard. I battered and smashed and battered and smashed, knocking him backwards.

'Go on Bugsy,' shouted one of his men. 'Cor him.'

'Carib,' shouted our lot.

He was a tough nut to crack; these gypsies have been there before. He had a good style and caught me with a right hand flush in the mouth. I stood back with my hands down, spat blood, then bulldozed him to the floor. While he was down, some relation of his started rowing with Mitchell Barney and Mitchell ran him into a trailer.

As I stood over Price, who was out, his wife ran out with a twelve-bore gun and pointed it straight at me. She was a beautiful gypsy woman. She screamed, 'I'll kill you, you bastard,' and pulled the trigger . . . but nothing happened. The safety catch was on.

I quickly grabbed the barrel in my hand to point it away from me. 'Let go, love, let me see if there's anything in it,' I said soothingly. She wouldn't let go; her knuckles were white. To my great regret, one of the men with me hit her and knocked her to the floor. I got the gun in my hand and it had two cartridges in it. I said, 'Let's go,' because there were now more men running towards us with weapons. I backed over to the motor, we got in and Michael drove off. Price and his wife were left lying there.

I showed them the cartridges in the van. 'Look, I have had enough,' I said. 'I don't want this any more.' I was determined that this would be my swansong. I smashed up the gun and threw it in a canal five miles up the road. It turned my stomach. All because someone wanted to fight me.

Yet not long after, Michael Fury rang me one lunchtime. 'I'm coming to see you. I'm with John, Pete, Hughie, Craig, Russell, Mitch Barney, Poppy, Podge and some others. I'll be over by five o'clock.' That was all he said. I knew something was up.

The minute they arrived, Big John walked in and said, 'There a juck that wants a carib with you, but if you don't want to fight him, I'll fight him for you.'

I was forlorn; I thought I had finished with all this. 'No, no, I'll fight him,' I said. 'Who is this man?'

'Ogie Burton.'

Ogie was the nephew of Big Just and the brother of Wick-Wack Burton, one of the men who had tried to slaughter me at Doncaster. Wick-Wack was the one I had flattened and Ogie, I later found out, had wanted to fight me for years because of the stitches I had put in his brother's eye.

Well, when they want to fight you, you have to fight, in 'town, field, fair or market', as they say. We went over to a very rich camp at Hopton, near Stafford. This was another situation where anything could happen. There were some tough men stopping there: Billy Thompson, who is known as 'the Iceman', and Bill Fuller, a Londoner who has never been beaten. It was just getting dark when we arrived.

'There is his trailer, Bartley.'

'You go over,' I said to Hughie Fury.

I stood in the shadows wearing my Charles Bronson cap. Hughie knocked on the door and said, 'Are you in, chap?'

Ogie Burton appeared in the doorway, holding a kettle iron. 'What's the matter, like?'

'Do you want to fight Bartley Gorman?'

Burton immediately uttered a disgusting insult about my mother, which does not bear repeating. This is a man I had never met.

I walked out of the shadows. 'Are you talking about me?'

'Are you Bartley Gorman?'

'No, I'm Bartholomew Gorman.'

He said the insult again. So I cursed him. This had gone personal; it was out of hand. He went to swing the kettle iron at me and I hit him with one of the hardest right hands I have ever thrown. It sent him into his trailer, where he smashed into the pots and pans and lay among them. That was the end of my title fight with Ogie Burton.

Then John Fury went berserk. He ran at a trailer and nearly turned it over, then challenged out the entire ground, 150 travelling men. Top fighters were on that ground but none would take him on. Someone must have rung the police, because dozens of them arrived and surrounded the camp. Our work was over, but before we left I said to Burton, 'I want you out of Staffordshire within twenty-four hours.' And he was.

About two years later, a rich gypsy called Reilly Smith had some bother with Ogie Burton and had 100,000 leaflets printed up saying that, having beaten Ogie with one punch, Bartley Gorman now wanted to meet him again, face-to-face. It had nothing to do with me but Reilly went up in a helicopter at Epsom and dropped them over the racecourse and also put 10,000 out at Appleby.

CHAPTER 15

The Outlaw

GYPSY FUNERALS ARE among the most dangerous places on earth. They draw together factions who may not have seen each other for years, people with long memories and sometimes scores to settle. While for house-dwellers funerals are solemn occasions, marked by restraint and respectful grief, travellers wear their emotions on their sleeves. Their anguish is public and heartfelt. There is often heavy drinking afterwards, and tension in the air. It is worse when people know that top fighters are going to attend: there are always those that see it as the chance for a challenge. Men have even been shot dead at burials.

In June 1995, my cousin Billy 'the Bat' Gorman died. On the day of his burial, at Arnold in Nottinghamshire, I was feeling unwell but because he'd been a good pal of mine I asked my daughter Maria to drive me there. There were the usual crowds of people: most of my relatives, of course, along with the Fury brothers and lots of other travelling breeds. After the church service, we went to a big cemetery. They carried the coffin to the grave but there was a delay as they tried to get it into the ground – the hole was a little small, and they had a struggle to lay it down. Some people later said this was Billy sending me a message from the grave.

As we stood waiting in silence in our suits and black ties, I sensed someone watching me. I turned my head slowly and looked to my left. Standing on slightly higher ground, outlined against a clear sky, was a man in a long black Melton coat, his hands in the pockets. He was staring at me. I tried to make out his face against the light. His nose was like a piece of putty and he had a bald head with lank blond hair over his ears. He eyed me like a gunslinger, emotionless. I know a proper fighter by the smell of him and could tell he was someone to be reckoned with. *But who was he? How come I don't know him?* I turned my head back to watch them bury Billy but made a mental note of this man.

We retired for the tea to a large pub in Arnold. It was soon packed with travellers. I sat with my cousin Booty Kelly, some of the Furys and a prizefighter called Joe Walton. Joe and I had had a dispute but on the day he came over, shook hands and we settled it. We tucked into a spread and the serious drinking started. Someone – as usual – shouted to me about Bob Gaskin but I didn't want to talk about that man.

The stranger in the Melton coat was across the other side of the pub, looking like the Outlaw Josey Wales. After a couple of drinks, he lay across a table on one elbow, among the pint pots, the kind of thing I used to do. He was laughing.

'That's Henry Francis,' someone said.

Now I knew him. Henry had been making waves on the fighting scene for some time. I first remembered him in the crowd when I was going to fight Johnny Mellor in 1986. He was a young man then and I barely noticed him. A few years later, he had come on a ground where our Sam was and asked for some water. 'I don't like that man,' Sam said, which was unusual for my brother. There was something threatening about Henry.

As a young lad he would hang a ball from a clothesline and spend hours butting it. He could throw three or four headbutts in fast succession, overwhelming opponents before they had got over the shock of the first one. Some called him 'the Woodpecker', others 'the Heat'. He preferred the nickname 'the Dynamite Kid'. Just as I had cut through the ranks of the travellers on my way to Hughie Burton's crown, so had he beaten some of the best men of his day. He defeated an Irish fighter called Johnny Cash when he was barely fifteen and then went through all of the Gaskin brothers, including Bob. His notoriety grew so quickly that the Irish traveller Blond Simon Docherty brought Ernie McGinley over to fight him when Henry was only eighteen, while McGinley was about twenty-six and a trained boxer. Simon paid McGinley £3,500 and a horse. The Irish contingent turned up early in the morning at the camp where Henry was stopping and called him out. Henry had no-one with him and was also under the weather with the 'flu but he got straight up and fought. In a terrific fight, Henry ballooned Ernie's head with butts – they say his face looked like a sheep's head at the end – but Ernie was a strong, fit man and landed plenty of punches of his own. After fifteen minutes, the teenager gave best for the only time in his life. 'McGinley can take it but he can't give it,' Henry later told me. 'I hit him a good few times and he was like a trunk, and getting stronger all the time. But he had all these men with him and I was on my own, and my mother was screaming for me to stop, so I did.'

Henry broke Dinny Kelly's leg at Doncaster, beat Booty Kelly several times and won a long, vicious fight with a Pole. He even fought a man on an aeroplane flying back from South Africa. He was undoubtedly the most dangerous knuckle man of the Nineties and many were afraid of him.

I went to the bar to buy a round. As I waited to be served, Henry appeared next to me. 'W-w-want a d-d-drink, Bartley?' He had a bad stutter. Always look for a man that stutters and a man with a walleye, because they can usually fight.

'Thanks Henry. I will.'

He bought me a drink and I bought him one. It gave me an opportunity to study him more closely. He looked just like an outlaw and that is what I nicknamed him: the Outlaw. He was in his early thirties and I was fifty-one. He never stopped talking about fighting and he knew all about me. He was fanatical about me. 'You turned John Rooney white overnight,' he said. Apparently Rooney's hair had changed colour after we fought, like a man with shell shock. Then he added, 'I can beat Dan Rooney any day, Bartley.'

I just went, 'Mmm,' but I knew then that I was right in my estimate of Henry, because nobody said things like that lightly. Dan Rooney was one of *the* top men. Still, I was more or less taking a back seat from the fighting and was pleased the ball was in other people's courts. He was being very friendly and clearly thought the world of me.

The guests began to filter out. I stayed because I was drinking, and once I'm drinking, I'm drinking. Wild horses wouldn't get me out. Maria got a lift home with a friend and left me the van. As time went on, there was just a handful left: Booty Kelly, a terrific drinking man, his brother Dinny – whose leg Henry had broken in a fight – and my cousin Black Bart. Francis was with some tattooed hardmen with cropped hair.

When I went to the gents, Dinny came in after me. It was about 7pm. 'Our old soblia is going to carib with this juck because the juck's come here to carib him, so see him fair play, soblia,' said Dinny. He meant that Henry Francis had come to fight Booty.

'Don't be silly,' I said. 'The man just wants to enjoy himself.'

But once a seed is set with me, it is set. Back in the bar, Henry never stopped talking about fighting. They were all at it now. It was nothing but fighting, instead of having a song or a laugh. Booty hurt my feelings by saying, 'John Fury could have beat your Sam any day.'

I didn't respond, though it made me sad. I knew John Fury would never have put himself above Sam: he thought too much of him. Whether it was the cause of what I said next, I don't know. Perhaps I just wanted to see how fast Henry's guns were after all the talking that had been done, or perhaps I knew it was going to end in trouble and decided to get it over with. Anyway, Henry was sitting on my left side and kept on about fighting and so I said:

'I'll fight you, Henry, if you want.'

'Okay then.'

He never hesitated. Henry would fight a bear at the drop of a hat.

'Come on then,' I said.

Out we walked into a big car park – Booty, Dinny, Black Bart and these hardcases with Francis. All England would have wanted to see this, the travellers' equivalent of Mike Tyson and Muhammad Ali strolling into a parking lot to settle the world heavyweight title.

I had on Sam's £500 grey suit that he gave me on his deathbed. Under a tree I took off my coat, tie and shirt. Henry stripped off. He was not very tall and had a white body, a thick, round neck, sloping shoulders like a bottle of Guinness and huge thick thighs. He weighed about fourteen stone. I was fifty-three but still hard and at least a stone heavier than Henry. 'When Bartley stripped off I thought John L. Sullivan was in front of me,' he later told a friend of mine.

I was about to move in on him when he stammered, 'N-n-no. We won't fight, Bartley. But p-p-put it in the papers that we were going to fight anyway.'

'Yeah, yeah, okay.' I never pressed it. I picked up my clothes and put them back on. Then Booty started to go mad. 'You fight me now,' he shouted at Henry. Booty had been all over America illegal gamecock fighting and was a very tough man; they call him 'Scrap Iron' Kelly.

Henry said, 'I'll k-k-kill you Booty if you mess with m-m-me.'

So I said, 'Put your coat on Booty. This man's just said he'll kill you. Why don't you take notice?'

I should have gone then: how could it be peaceful after that? Instead we went back in the pub and started drinking even more heavily. The pub was starting to fill up with evening trade and Booty ripped off his shirt and stalked around like a bull terrier, challenging everybody out. He and some of Henry's men also started smoking spliffs. I don't mess with drugs but they gave me one when I was drunk and I smoked some of it. My head started to go fuggy and my legs wobbly.

I said to Henry, 'Do you want to come back to my place? You can stop there as long as you want and we can have some drink?'

'No, my wife will kill me.'

'Come on, man, don't be so petticoat government.' That's what we call people who are under the thumb.

Eventually we decided it was time to go. Henry said, 'Let's go down to Bulwell (a site with lots of Irish) and I'll fight Ned Rooney.'

'No,' I said, 'I'm not going down there, there'll be murders.'

I staggered out to my van, paralytic drunk. It was about 8.30pm but still light, a bright June evening. Booty got in with me and we waited for Dinny and Black Bart. Henry pulled round in a blue Transit from the other side of the car park, flashed his headlights and shouted out of the window, 'Come on, I'm going down to Bulwell. I want to fight.'

Now Will Braddock had warned me 100 times, *They will come for you when you are drunk, my lad*. I was too arrogant to listen. I shouted back to Henry:

'If you want to fight, I'll fight you. I've told you.'

I came out of the motor flatfooted, still in my suit. Francis got out with a tee-shirt on. I walked up to him and slapped his cheeks, saying, 'Pat-a-cake, pat-a-cake, baker's man, bake me a cake as fast as you can.'

That was all the provocation Henry needed. He flew at me. I walked straight into him, punching, but I was too drunk. He swayed to avoid my cumbersome shots and came up the side of me. We clinched and Henry butted me full force. He had a head like a rock and I pulled away.

'No headbutting.'

No use saying that to him. I didn't know that he was the best headbutter in the country, and with the King of the Gypsies in front of him, drunk, he wasn't likely to let up. He butted me continually like a jackhammer: I bet he butted me thirty times. Any two would have had most men away.

I needed room to fight. I pushed him back with my right hand and hooked him hard and sent him up against his blue van. This was my chance. I went in to finish him but I had trouble focussing my eyes from the drink and the effects of his butts and couldn't get the bull-hammer going. I was too slow and flatfooted. I swear he went down on all fours like a cat and bounced straight up inside my guard like a serpent and hit me again with his head.

In the melee the two of us somehow got tangled and ended up on the floor, I'm ashamed to say. While we rolled over he was still nutting me.

'Carib! Carib!' yelled Booty and Dinny.

Henry struggled up just before me and as I went to get up with him I grabbed both of his thighs and pulled and he went over and his arse hit the floor. Booty Kelly shouted, 'I'll give you headbutting. Call yourself an effing fighter? Put your hands up and be a man.' And with that he ran in and took a flying kick straight into Henry's head. It was so hard that the sole of Booty's shoe came off with it.

Henry took it. Then he rose on one knee and gave Booty a look like death. 'I'm going to kill you, Booty,' he hissed. He got up. I had taken heavy punishment and my face was swelling, while blood was coming from Henry's mouth and nostrils. I had thought he would be just another notch, but no he wasn't. Henry squared up in front of me. I was flatfooted with a long guard.

'Carib, soblia,' shouted Booty.

As the words left his lips, Henry suddenly exploded sideways and butted Booty with all his might. There was a horrible thud as Booty was sent flying backwards. Then Henry and I continued to fight. This had now gone on for eight minutes and someone must have rung 999, because police vehicles came from everywhere: motorbikes, panda cars, vans, the lot. The first man they got was me; two big officers grabbed me on either arm. Another came running up between Henry and me with his walkie-talkie crackling. They dragged me away to one side and asked me my name. 'Tom Lee,' I said.

Francis came up, pushed a policewoman out of his way and, while the officers were still holding me by my arms, hit me with his head flush on the nose. The bone crunched. I went mad trying to get free but two more officers came and restrained me. Henry jumped up on a wall. They didn't seem to go after him, just me.

That was the end of it. The police put it down as just another drunken gypsy brawl and eventually let us go, making sure that Henry went one way and I went the other with my friends. I got in a cab and went straight to John Fury to see fair play but I was in no condition to resume the fight the following day. I felt rough with the drink and even worse with injuries: both of my cheekbones were broken and my nose was cracked in three places but I refused to go to hospital. I was still bruised three weeks later and my cheeks hurt to this day if I press them.

Afterwards I vowed that I would not talk to Henry again until I fought him. He said, 'I don't have to fight Bartley Gorman to be his friend.' He also said I hit harder than any other man he had fought but he did brag that he had 'handled Bartley good'. Even the Gaskins went mad when they heard of it, that a man of thirty-three should fight a man of fifty-one. They won't have me talked about. But that's gypsy fighting. The matter was never settled and I would not see Henry for another six years. Then, in December 2001, he visited me when I was very ill. It was good of him to do it and I told him that I bear him no ill will – he reminds me a little of myself when I was younger.

*

A FEW WEEKS after my fight with Henry, I was filmed for a Channel Four TV series called *Battered Britain*. The ten-minute short was made by Shane Meadows, whose dad Artie had boxed on my pirate shows twenty years earlier. The film showed me punching the bag in a field, singing old songs and talking about my life. I explained how it was very difficult for a champion prize-fighter to find any peace, and how the challengers would not leave you alone, especially as you got older and, in their eyes, more vulnerable. Shane went on to make the feature film *TwentyFourSeven*, starring Bob Hoskins.

The world generally seemed to be getting more and more violent, and I was sick of it. Even my daughter Maria was a victim of it. She had been for a night out with a friend and was coming out of a takeaway when a lowlife toe-rag punched her for no reason and smashed her jaw. The first I knew of it was when I saw my beautiful daughter lying in a hospital bed with a face like a balloon. I soon had a name and searched high and low for this man. I even told the police exactly what I would do to him. A man was charged but was acquitted in court.

Not long afterwards, I was in town with Shaun and Maria when we saw this man and a scuffle broke out. I hit him a few times – I wanted to break his jaw – but he ran like a greyhound and got away. I ended up at Stafford Crown Court in November 1996. The prosecution said I had meted out 'rough justice' to him but I pointed out to the court that, as a bareknuckle champion, if I had gone to town on him he would be unrecognisable, and I was acquitted. Shaun admitted assault and was ordered to do community service.

The Henry Francis brawl was not my prize-last. Some time after, Marcko Small rang me up and said a gang of travellers, Lees and Prices, had moved down to the south-west and one of them was challenging out all of Teignmouth and Torquay, walking around with no shirt on threatening the bouncers. Marcko went to their stopping place to fight the man but was told, 'You may be the champion of Cornwall but I don't want to fight you, I want to fight Bartley Gorman, the champion of England.'

Marcko called me and down I went. Why? I don't really know. Gypsy pride, I suppose. I was still vexed at the way my fight with Henry Francis had turned out and wanted to prove something. They also intimated that they would come up to the Midlands to find me if I didn't go down. I took no men with me as Marcko knew lots of rough characters from local pubs who would see fair play. He was also friendly with a crowd of Russian sailors who were desperate to see a bareknuckle fight. They even wanted me to fight one of their own men on their ship in dock. I went on board with Marcko but the captain wouldn't allow it.

Marcko fixed up the gypsy contest and we met the Russians on the railway station car park in Teignmouth. I was small compared to some of them and was glad they were there. Two Transit vans headed for a Dartmoor beauty spot called Badgers' Holt. Lee's mob arrived in eight cars. We walked from a public car park through fir trees with a morning mist among them. You could imagine a pack of wolves coming out of there. Beside us was the River Dart, with great stepping stones across it and a stone bridge. We went down a steep hill with wild ponies grazing and walked as far as we could by the river until we got to a good place. Marcko did the talking. The Prices and Lees were wondering who these foreign men were with us, while the Russians were very excited.

I had heard of Freedom Lee before: a good fighter. He was a heavyweight, blond-headed, younger and slightly taller than me, aged about thirty. I didn't give him a chance to get going but feinted and knocked him straight down with a bull-hammer. His feet went up in the air and he sat down hard. He wasn't unconscious but he couldn't get up: they had to carry him to the car because his legs wouldn't work.

The irony is that none of my fights raised as much heat as my announcement in the summer of 1997 that I was going to have a hedgehog barbecue on my land at Fort Woodfield. I said the *hotchy witchies*, as gypsies call them, would be grilled on wooden skewers, marinated in honey and stuffed with shrimps. The story went around the world — a friend even sent me a copy of the *Bangkok Post* with it in. It was also in every English national newspaper and most of the local ones. One wildlife campaigner called it 'plain murder', which I thought was a bit strong. The fact is that gypsies have been eating them for years. Some retired major who was head of the Hedgehog Preservation Society said it was disgusting but the RSPCA pointed out that it was not an offence to kill and eat hedgehogs. The League Against Cruel

Sports said they wanted the police to take away some of the hedgehog carcasses to see how they were killed. The Meat and Livestock Commission got involved. The whole thing was ridiculous. I pointed out that if I really planned to eat hedgehogs I would do it in winter when they had fattened themselves up for hibernation. I actually did it to raise awareness of my anti-abortion views, to prove that people cared more for animals than for unborn children. All the soldiers in the world wars didn't die to have their grandchildren murdered at the hands of professional men who call themselves surgeons. People call me a gypsy, but a doctor – a professional man – will kill four or five babies a day, take off his white smock, wash his hands, go home, have his tea and tell his own children a bedtime story.

This book has largely been about the fighting side of my life. But I also have strong views on many things. If I had not been a fighter I would have liked to have been a preacher. Not everyone may agree with my opinions – I admit I'm a great one for argument and debate – but if a man cannot stand up and speak out for what he believes is right, then what use is he?

CHAPTER 16

The Unforgiven

IN NOVEMBER 1997, the *Daily Mail* ran a long feature about my life under the headline 'FINAL BELL FOR THE GYPSY KING'. One of their writers spent a day with me at Fort Woodfield. He described me as having 'beaten-down eyes, a Joe Bloggs T-shirt and an unshiftable aura of melancholy.' As descriptions go, it was pretty accurate.

Bareknuckle fighting might seem glamorous. Champions are lionised by their followers, feted by their community and are a magnet for women. But the life brings with it too much pain. And in the world of the gypsy prize-fighter there is no such thing as retirement; they won't allow it. My grandfather still fought in his sixties and so did Big Just. Atom Bomb Tom Lee was attacked by a mob and never recovered. A band of tinkers ambushed John-John Stanley and shoved two pool cues through his arms.

I remember in the Nineties watching a Clint Eastwood film called *Unforgiven*, which showed the old Wild West gunslingers as they really were: not sharply dressed and heroic but scruffy, mean, drunken men who couldn't shoot straight. Prize-fighting was the same: not the vision you see in old prints of two trained athletes with their fists aloft, squaring up in a neatly pegged-out ring with seconds and an orderly crowd of toffs, but often little more than vicious brawling.

One who did manage to turn his back on fighting was

Dan Rooney, who became a born-again Christian, hung up his gloves and now preaches God wherever he goes. Though I had never met him, he rang me one day and said he was coming to see me. He arrived with two Irish travellers, both as big as him. These men were saying, 'Bartley, you were a legend,' and all this, and I felt a bit sorry for Dan, because he was supposed to be the man at that time. I told him, 'I said some things to your brothers about you Dan, because they mentioned your name to me. But whatever I said, I am sorry now because it was in the heat of the moment.'

He shook my hand and said, 'Thank you, Bartley.'

Though he had rejected his former life, I did give him one word of warning: 'If ever you fight Henry Francis on a field on your own and you can't beat him, he will kill you. He's a psychopath.'

Dan wanted me to become born-again, something that has become very popular among travellers. He took me to a big Christian convention in Staffordshire. Everyone was looking at us, the two great fighters; there must have been twenty video cameras on us. Dan did not need to convert me; I have been a practising Catholic all of my life and the older I have got, the stronger my faith has become.

Instead of fighting, I was putting my energy into things I felt strongly about. I stood for election to Uttoxeter Council under the slogan: 'Be independent! Vote Gorman.' I wasn't elected but I did pretty well. Through my friend Marcko Small in South Devon, I also got involved in a dispute with the Archdeacon of Exeter. They wanted to build an extension on a beautiful little church in Bishopsteignton which would have meant digging up forty graves, including those of gypsies. Marcko and I said we would bring gypsies from all over the country to blockade the village, the villagers all gave us their backing and the Church backed down. I regret it now because Christ once said, 'Let the dead bury the dead.' I should have let the extension go on, for the living.

One of my dreams is to put up a memorial to the gypsies who died in the Holocaust. The genocide against travellers has received little recognition. I also campaigned to get more legal sites for travellers, as there is still a shortage of official places. Gypsy people are at the end of their tether. Many would welcome the chance to buy or rent their own sites and manage them properly under licence, but district councils are not prepared to meet their responsibilities and find suitable sites. Travellers are being forced onto the road where they come up against prejudice and new laws aimed at stopping 'travellers'.

Early in 1998 I even started to campaign for the release of Reggie Kray, the gangster. I had never mixed with London villains, never cared for them or their world, but one day out of the blue Reg sent a letter to the *Black Country Bugle* to be passed on to me. The *Bugle* had run a series of stories about my fighting past and someone had forwarded copies to Reg in prison. His letter was addressed to 'Bartley Gorman, King of the Gypsies' and arrived from HMP Maidstone in Kent. His spidery handwriting was almost impossible to decipher but the picture at the top of the letter – of twins in boxing gear – was unmistakeable:

Be Strong. Peace.
Bartley
I read of your career in the Bugle and I've heard your name in the recent past. I admire all you stand for and I admire you as a man.

I have something in common. I used to fight as amateur and pro and I also have gypsy blood in my veins which I am proud of. My late brother would have been pleased I have written to you. Hope you don't mind me calling you by your first name.

I would like to see you for a visit in the near future if you could. No offence taken if you are reluctant. You can phone or visit any time.
God Bless
Friend
Reg Kray

Reg had been sentenced to life imprisonment for the murder of Jack 'The Hat' McVitie in 1969, with a recommendation he serve thirty years, and was coming to the end of his tariff. I visited him and found him a nice man. Although he had no remorse for the crime he'd been convicted of, he was reformed and certainly no threat to anyone. You could tell he was a fighter; he wasn't big but he was fit and he had that look about him. Once or twice I caught him weighing me up. He also put his hands on my shoulders to test me and said, 'You could have beat Roy Shaw, couldn't you?'

I just smiled and said to him, 'You've got the hands of a prize-fighter.'

I met him four or five times altogether after he moved to Wayland Prison in Norfolk. He kept up lots of correspondence with people outside and had a proposition for me: he wanted to fix up a bareknuckle fight with Earnie Shavers, the former heavyweight challenger from America who was once voted 'Puncher of the Century'. Shavers – who despite his ferocious reputation is said to be a very nice man and a Christian – had ended up working as a doorman in Liverpool and speaking on the after-dinner circuit. He had been approached and apparently expressed some interest. I said I would do it. Even though my heart was no longer in fighting, I could never resist a big challenge. I like history: leave your mark. That's why I would have fought Shavers, but it never came off. I don't think Earnie was really keen. I was, however, presented with something called the Ronnie and Reggie Kray Twins Fighting Trophy. A fellow prisoner had made it specially for Reg and I went down to a function at the Princess Alice pub in the East End of London to collect it from his wife Roberta.

When Reg's thirty years were up and he had still not been let out, I wrote to the Queen saying, in part, that 'the penalty meted out to Reg Kray was extremely severe, to say the least, and calculated by a formula which no longer applies in an era when justice tempered with mercy appears to be ten years (inside) for sadistic child killers . . .' I was referring to the well-publicised case of a paedophile gang who had killed children and yet were out within a far shorter time than Reg. I received a reply from the senior officer at the HM Prison Service Lifer Review Unit, explaining that the judge had made a recommendation of a minimum term and that at the end of that it was up to the Home Secretary, under the advice of the Parole Board. 'Moreover, as part of the process of reintegration into society, mandatory life sentence prisoners are normally required to undergo a lengthy period of testing in an open prison before they are released on life licence.' Anyway, they didn't let him out.

Reg's brother Charlie died in the spring of 2000 and he phoned and asked if I would go to the funeral in London that April. He was brought there in a convict-carrier and when he stepped out of it I was the first man to greet him. He was not well himself and six months later I was attending his own funeral. Half of the East End turned out for it and most of the country's media. Reg was buried next to his twin Ronnie. I was standing there with people all around, looked down at Ron's grave and saw a hand on the gravestone. I looked up and it was Roy Shaw. We had never met before. I tapped him on the shoulder and he gave me a handshake and then a handclasp. He looked very fit and left in a £180,000 Bentley. As I say, I don't mix in gangster circles but I also met Dave Courtney, who said, 'Hello champ.' I later thanked him for calling me that and he said, 'Bartley, I never say something unless I mean it.'

There has been a resurgence of interest in the underground fighting scene, with books by Lennie McLean, Roy Shaw and others, television documentaries and even Hollywood films. I get no end of requests to appear on TV programmes, most of which I turn down. Rarely, however, do any of these programmes touch on the top gypsy men, who are still very secretive. So, for the first time ever in print, here are some of the best today.

JOHN FURY

Big John is the most respected fighter among all travellers, a handsome, black-headed giant, six foot four and touching twenty stone when not trained down. He is married to a daughter of Oathy Burton, Hughie's older brother. John has avoided the bareknuckle scene to concentrate on his boxing career. His brothers and cousins are fighters too.

I went to see him boxing at Cat's Whiskers in Burnley in 1987 and had a dispute with the promoter over my ringside seat. He tried to make me move, embarrassing me in front of a lot of travellers. I told him I would fight six of his bouncers in the ring. Big John got involved and announced from the ring with a voice as loud as thunder that he would fight any man in the arena for a packet of cigarettes. Needless to say, no-one took him up.

He had a fistfight with one gypsy fighter and put him in hospital. When my cousin Booty Kelly criticised him for it, John beat Booty so badly that he lost control of his bowels. All in all, not a man to mess with.

HENRY FRANCIS
Henry may be the most feared gypsy alive. A fighter to his bootstraps, he is touching forty now but has his own gym and is naturally fit. He was once blasted with a shotgun and still carries 38 pellets embedded in his neck and back. He was also badly stabbed in a black club in Nottingham but fought his way out. Most recently he had a couple of savage fights with a man in the Midlands that left both of them missing parts their ears. Whoever he beats, he really messes up. But he is good friends with most of the other top men and so unlikely to fight them.

In the mid-Nineties he fought a Londoner called Jimmy Stockin at a country and western day in Peterborough and put him in a terrible state. According to Henry, they had a fall-out over a game of pitch and toss and Stockin pushed him, saying, 'Don't mess with the best because the best don't mess.' It was the wrong thing to say to Henry. They cleared an area and Boxer Tom refereed. The only person there rooting for Henry was an Irish girl, Belsie Docherty, but she shouted up just the same. Henry hit Stockin and stuck the nut in a few times and that was the end of him.

Towards the end of 2001, I became very ill and had to go into hospital. Henry came to see me. 'B-b-bartley,' he said, 'you were the greatest of them all. When I was eighteen you were my hero. I always wanted to be like you, and now I am. You're still the b-b-best man in the country and I'm the second best.'

At the time, I was too weak even to hold a drink up to my lips, so it was kind of him to say it. He later told a friend of mine, 'Any man who calls Bartley Gorman, I'll do him in.' I wouldn't ever want him too, but that's Henry.

LEWIS WELCH

Lewis, who was thirty-two in December 2001, once told me he would fight any man in the British Isles. He was undefeated as a pro boxer but packed it in when he was only twenty-one to go bareknuckle. He is 5ft 11½, built like a tank and has never been beaten. He lives in Darlington, the toughest travelling town in the country, and his family are very influential at Appleby Fair.

Lewis's dad Billy was a good fighter – he went to Doncaster in 1963 to challenge Hughie Burton but Hughie wasn't there – as were his uncles. Lewis himself went to Appleby one year with 100 men to fight James MacPhee but the big Scotsman didn't turn up. There was also talk at one time of him fighting the boxer Henry Wharton but it never happened. Lewis trains seven days a week and his friends say he eats more than three pigs. For all that, he is an absolute gentleman; spend a night in his company and he won't mention fighting once. I have always been made very welcome by him when I have been up to the north-east.

TERRY WARD

The nephew of old-timers Sam Ward and Jim Crow, Terry is in his mid-forties and is another Darlington man. His hands are greased lightning and he is known as 'The JCB' because he hits like an earth-mover. A former light-heavyweight boxer who packed it in to go bareknuckle, he had the muscle in one of his arms virtually chewed off in one fight and still carries the scars.

He had an incredible fight against a giant Rastafarian called Winston Garfield who is 6ft 7in tall and 23 stone and has a 56in chest and a 23in neck. He travelled up from the Midlands to challenge Terry in a money fight. Garfield's second, who was 6ft 3in himself, went into the Greyhound pub in Darlington to say he had come to fight The JCB. One of Terry's pals got on the phone and said, 'There's a man who's come to fight you and if he's anything like the lad he has sent with the message, he'll take some handling.'

They fought the next morning at the site on Honeypot Lane. They were expecting Terry's opponent to turn up with a big team but he arrived with just his second, so he was obviously confident. 'All I can do is put my eggs in one basket,' said Terry when he saw the size of him. Garfield threw a left hook that would have killed Terry but he ducked under it and unloaded body shots without let-up. His wrists were sinking into the guy's body and in the end Garfield flopped to the floor and didn't get up.

*

THESE ARE FOUR of the best men but there are many other good men. Henry Arab, from Stanley, near Newcastle, has knocked out that many teeth that they call him the 'Dental Surgeon'. He doesn't care for man or beast. He fought Bob Gaskin twenty years ago after Gaskin spat in his face in a bar. Arab knocked him out, dragged him across the road to a pump and pumped water onto his face. He also knocked out Johnny Love, said to be the best man in Essex, at Appleby Fair. Ivan Botton, the champion of Nottinghamshire, is also in his forties and recently beat one of the Prices at Newark. One of his sons is a pro boxer. Big Dick Smith from Barnsley is the top boyo over Yorkshire way, and in Lancashire there's Eric Boswell.

There have also been some very successful gypsy boxers recently: Gary Cooper was British champ in the Eighties and Henry Wharton was British, Commonwealth and European champ in the Nineties. Charlie Moore, from Darlington, won nine amateur titles and was unbeaten as a professional until he packed the game in. He told me, 'I couldn't go on boxing because I know how tame it is compared to our bareknuckle fighting.' There's Mark Baker from Kent, Henry Brewer from Bradford, whose grandad is a Price, and the flyweight Terrance Gaskin. Trainer Darkie Smith's lad Stephen recently won a version of a world title. Sam Gorman, my brother Sam's son, is a top young prospect and was National Schoolboy Champion. My own son Shaun never became a fighter: instead he plays rugby union for Uttoxeter. He's built like a bull and, believe me, he can look after himself.

Challengers were nowhere to be found when Sam and I were looking for them in the late Sixties and early Seventies. Now they are all fighting men. Yet the last two really big contests in England were between me and John Rooney and me and Henry Francis. John Fury and Henry, who could fill Wembley if they ever fought each other, are friends. Other top men won't fight each other today: either they are very good friends or they are scared of each other. You don't get anyone these days saying, 'I'm the King of the Gypsies.'

*

IRELAND IS ANOTHER matter. There are estimated to be 11,000 travellers in the Republic, where they have been treated as second-class citizens for centuries and even now can be refused a drink in a pub. Lynching still goes on in Ireland: these travellers they occasionally found hanged, 'suicides', for interfering with women and suchlike.

They are also terrible for feuding with each other. In July 1994 there was an attack on the house of Joe Joyce, The Hulk, in Athlone by men with guns, allegedly because he wouldn't fight another man. The McDonaghs and the Wards have also been feuding for most of the 1990s. In June 1996 there was carnage following a funeral at Tuam in County Galway. It started when someone stood on a gravestone to get a better view and was told to get off. A riot erupted and seven people ended up in hospital. The next day a mob went on the warpath in Tuam armed with slash hooks, iron bars and hatchets and smashed up a house and two vans. It led to the trial of thirty-five travellers on charges ranging from assault occasioning actual bodily harm to possessing offensive weapons.

At the sixteen-day trial, it was claimed that Bernie Ward was King of the Travellers. But his lawyer said, 'Mr Bernie Ward does not claim to be king of the travelling community and he has no interest in being king,' adding that he was announcing Ward's abdication for the benefit of anyone who believed he was king. His denial was somewhat undermined when it was revealed in court that a picture of Bernie, stripped to the waist with his fists clenched, was displayed in the window of a shop in Ballinasloe and videos of him fighting were on sale. He had also acted as referee at several bareknuckle fights filmed on video.

In February 1998 the *Daily Mirror* reported that an illegal bare-knuckle fight was postponed in England following a tip-off to police. 'Hundreds of Irish tinkers had converged on Manchester for the bout in which two men fight until they drop,' said the report.

Gypsies had travelled from all parts of Britain and Ireland for the UK title fight. The winner would have collected a purse of £5,000.

Members of the police Tactical Aid Group were called in and a helicopter hovered overhead. Although the bout had started when cops arrived there were no arrests as the fighters melted into the crowd.

One officer said, 'It was impossible to tell who the contestants were but there was a lot of money around. The road was lined with top-notch cars including Shoguns and Mercedes.'

Illegal bare-knuckle fighting is still popular among

travellers and Manchester has traditionally been the venue for many organised fights.

Three months earlier, Jimmy 'the Boxer' McDonagh had beaten Paddy 'The Lurch' Joyce near Drogheda, knocking him down five times in ten minutes. A few months later McDonagh, who is 6ft 2in and 15st, won a fight for a £20,000 purse and the title King of the Travellers in a field in County Louth. But in May 1998 he was attacked by five hooded men outside a bar in Dundalk and shot in the back of his leg. He had been due to fight the following month. I don't know what the shooting was about but one of his relatives told the newspapers, 'He was only into the bare boxing, and that's fair. There are no weapons or anything. Ask anybody about Jimmy and they'll tell you he is a lovely person. Even the guards have loads of time for him.' By November 2000, Jimmy McDonagh was back in action, beating David Nevin after a very long fight for £30,000 a side.

The video tapes of these fights are big business. Some are shipped out to bars in the holiday resorts of Spain and the Canary Islands, where they advertise them as 'Irish Travelling Community Bareknuckle Fighting' to pull in the customers. There is money to be made, but the scene is wild and unpredictable. In 1998 Francis Barrett, who became a national hero when he boxed in the Atlanta Olympics and carried the Irish flag at the opening ceremony, was stabbed for refusing to take part in a bareknuckle fight while visiting his family in Galway.

The gardai in Tuam brokered a peace agreement between the Wards and McDonaghs in September 1998 but the following month the gardai seized a large amount of weapons at a funeral and there were a number of clashes around Ballymote in County Sligo. In May 1999, the feud grew even worse when a man was shot dead and another wounded as a crowd of 200 travellers waited outside a graveyard in Ballymote for a funeral. In July that year, extra gardai had to be drafted in for the funeral of another traveller, Bernard

Lawrence, in Kells, County Meath. The police established checkpoints and most of the pubs were closed.

There were other feuds as well. In December 1999 a fight to find the King of the Travellers of the Midlands was arranged for Longford in Ireland but police in riot gear and armoured patrol vans sealed off the town with roadblocks. The two sides had previously agreed a truce but it was understood that had broken down and police had information that guns, machetes and other weapons were going to be brought in. 'Our information was basically that the King of the Travellers' dominance was being challenged,' said a garda. 'There have been a number of fights around the country in recent months and this was due to sort it out once and for all. Over three hundred people were due to attend the fight in a field just outside Longford town. But our information indicated that the King of the Travellers was actually going to be shot during the fight.'

In May 2000 police seized weapons including slash hooks at yet another family funeral in Kildare. And in July 2001 there was a huge and violent fight between four different factions on a playing field at a council estate in Galway. Only the arrival of dozens of gardai prevented it from being even worse. The gunplay is not unknown in England either. In the summer of 2001 there was a shooting at a travellers' camp in York after a fight following a wedding.

Who needs that? To me, bareknuckle fighting was an honourable pursuit, as much a gypsy sport as hare coursing, fishing or lock-jumping. I was attracted to the romance of it, not the violence. When it all got too dangerous, I lost interest. 'Bone, steel or lead' is how they settle it now. I was once told that a gang of ten men were waiting for me at Stow-on-the-Wold Fair with chainsaws ticking. Where is the honour and glory in such barbarity? I have come to the end of the breed business for good. It leads to too much bad blood.

I was born into a violent inheritance but times have changed. When I was young there was only a murder about twice a year. Now they are common. My grandfather, the best of them all, told me he would never lift his hands to another man if he had his time over again, and I agree. Being a fighter gives you a terrible feeling. You are lonely even in a crowd. I wish I had never had that life.

I have seen a lot of death. It is true what the writer said about me several years ago – I do have an air of melancholy. So many of my old boxers had died: John Peaty, Dave Smith, Alan Wilson (who was murdered in Rhyl), Rodey Shaw, Bowie Barsby, Beaky Smith, Guy Harrison, Gandy Hodgkinson and, of course, our Sam. Others involved who had gone included Mick Mould, Harold Groombridge my co-promoter, referee Percy Slater and my timekeeper Fred Parker. It is unaccountable.

My parents are dead. So are Bob and Will Braddock, Hughie and Oathy Burton, Big Tom Lee and so many others. Nelson Boswell, who refereed my fight for the title, passed away in a chair after asking his mother for a cup of tea. My friend Steve Plant burned to death in his trailer. My good pal Les Oakes died when he was hit by another vehicle while adjusting a load on his van. Les was the king of the antiques dealers, had the largest collection of horse-drawn vehicles in Europe and always had a pound to lend, a pound to spend and a pound to give away.

The deaths of friends make you look at yourself. I'm a man born out of time because my values are of bygone years. I can't get my head around the values of people today. Religion has gone, the people have lost God. How can they win without God? I believe I must go to church to have grace. You can't see love but it is there and grace is the same, a force like love. If I keep going to church I believe it will give me that little bit more grace to get better.

My fighting days are over and so are my travels. I eventually sold Fort Woodfield and bought several acres with a stream running through them beside the McDonald's restaurant on the A50 at Uttoxeter. There I planned and built my own house, called 'Bangalore'. I was also very proud to be honoured by my adopted hometown when in September 2000 they unveiled a large monument in the town square in recognition of prominent Uttoxeter citizens. There, alongside the likes of the Earl of Shrewsbury and Joseph Cyril Bamford of JCB, was the name 'Bartley Gorman, bareknuckle prize-fighter'. It did make me smile.

I have many blessings, not least my three lovely grandsons: Nathan, Samuel and Bartholomew Gabriel. I hope they will grow up to be healthy, happy and good. I hope that they will know an oak leaf from an ash leaf and not be mesmerised by computer games and other rubbish. And I also hope they will never want to fight.

For what is a so-called hard man? Not the men who think they are, who swagger and bully, that's for sure. However tough you are, there's Someone tougher, and fitter, and braver. On every sprawling estate in Britain, from Cardiff to Newcastle and Edinburgh to London, there are real tough men. They probably sit quietly of an evening watching television, dangling their children on their knees, never looking for trouble.

I know gypsies will continue to fight, as boxers, on camps, at weddings and funerals and horse fairs, in pubs and clubs. Any night of the week there'll be gypsy boys training in makeshift gyms with no electricity or sinks or showers, punching the bag and skipping rope and sparring and dreaming of glory. Many will never make it to the senior ranks or the pros. Instead, they'll go bareknuckle, as they have done since time immemorial.

I would just remind them that the most important word in the language is not 'fight'. It's 'love'.

*

IN THE AUTUMN of 2001, while in the final stages of finishing this book with my friend Peter Walsh, I was feeling very ill. I thought it was a 'flu virus, but I could not seem to shake it off. After several weeks, it suddenly became much worse. I was admitted to hospital and, after various scans and biopsies, was told I had a serious cancer of the liver. I quickly became so weak I could hardly walk and there were several occasions when I did not think I would survive another night.

Eventually I moved to a specialist unit at the Queen Elizabeth Hospital in Birmingham. They carried out more tests and put me on regular doses of morphine for the pain but after a couple of weeks they made it clear there was little more they could do for me. They suggested that I would be more comfortable at home, with a Macmillan nurse to visit me. I knew what that meant.

So rather than give in, I decided that – with God's help – I was going to beat this hideous thing that had struck down my father, brother and uncle. My girlfriend Ann – who never left my side night or day – and some close family and friends booked me into a private clinic near Frankfurt, Germany, and I was flown there, accompanied by a male nurse, on the Saturday before Christmas. It was a hellish journey but I felt it was my only hope. The clinic pioneers unorthodox alternative treatments, including injections directly into the tumour. I won't go into detail: suffice to say that the pain is unimaginable. Anything I suffered in a fight was a picnic by comparison.

I did realise for the first time the friends I had: all of those people that came to visit me. I will not list them all here, as it would be too long, but they know who they are and I thank them all. Even old opponents like John Rooney and Henry Francis have put their arms around me and kissed me and prayed and wept by my bedside. I have discovered how much love I have in me. I don't want to carry any hate in my body and soul, only love.

I hope that when you read these words, I will also be reading them: sitting up in bed, enjoying my own book and recovering. I have been going through a black desert and I now know the true meaning of the phrase, 'Deliver us from evil'. I have resolved that if I come through this terrible ordeal – more horrible than I can describe – I will devote the rest of my life to doing good. I hope it is something I can live up to. Since being in hospital I have longed so much for the green fields and hedges and blue skies and God's earth. I feel weak but at my weakest I am at my strongest, because my strength is in Jesus Christ.

Please God, I will give it my best; for if nothing else, I am a fighter.

My Fight Record

This is my illegal fighting record as far as I have been able to recall it. There are no record-keepers at gypsy fights and I have had to rely on memory, so some of the dates may well be inaccurate. I have not included all of the street fights or bar brawls I engaged in, as these would be too numerous to mention.

W means Won, D means Drew, S means the fight was Stopped or broken up before either man won, and TF means Title Fight.

Born	1 March 1944, at Giltbrook, Nottinghamshire	
1956	Began amateur boxing in Bedworth, Warwickshire	
1956	My first bareknuckle fight, against Pete Taylor, at Polesworth, Warks. I later engaged in bareknuckle and illicit gloved fights with Peter Lee, Freddie Turnbull, Harry Smith and John Green. Few of these were allowed to go to a conclusion, as we were children	
1960	Dave Bryan North Wales	W
1960s	Throughout this decade I had numerous now-forgotten fights with construction workers and gypsies on camps and boxed as an amateur	

1963–4	Unknown	Uttoxeter, Staffs	W	
1966–7	Numerous fights against American GIs around Uttoxeter			
?	Joe 'Blood' Gorman	Uttoxeter	S	
1967	Leefoy Price	Norfolk	W	
1967	Mark Ripley	Kent	D	
1968	Unknown	Fakenham, Norfolk	W	
Aug 1971	'Mad Dog' Upton	Cheadle, Staffs	W	
Sept 1972	Went to Doncaster Racecourse to challenge Uriah Burton for the title but he failed to show up			
Autumn 1972	Jack Fletcher	Hollington, Staffs	W	TF
?	Henry Quentin	Buxton	W	TF
?	'Big John'	Ladybower Dam	W	TF
?	Pete Collins	Hinckley, Leics	W	
?	Pat Brennan	Hinckley, Leics	W	
Sept 1976	Wick-Wack Burton	Doncaster	W	TF
	Bob Gaskin	Doncaster	Attacked by mob	
1977	Issued leaflets challenging every gypsy man in the world			
1970–80	Unknown farmhand	Peak District	W	
1980	Mexicana Webb	Coventry	W	TF
1980	Don Halden	Kingstone, Staffs	W	
?	Unknown	Ripley, Derbys	W	
1980	James Preece	Longrake Mine	W	TF
?	Felix Rooney	Cheadle, Staffs	S	TF
1982–3	Liam Galloran	Hanley, Staffs	S	TF
	Rodey Shaw	Uttoxeter	W	

Mid-1980s	Rcd Bob McGowan	Coventry	W	
1986	Staffordshire Wolfman	Staffs	W	
Nov 1986	Johnny Mellor Prevented	Uttoxeter		
?	Scotsman	Cannock	W	
?	Lee Harbour and Gerry 'Flash' Doran (fought at same time)	Uttoxeter	W	TF
?	Phil Leah		W	
Autumn 1991	Unknown	Uttoxeter	W	
9 Dec 1991	John Rooney	Hinckley, Leics	W	TF
1994	Jade Johnson		Fell through	
?	Bugsy Price	Coventry	W	TF
?	Ogie Burton	Hopton, Staffs	W	
June 1995	Henry Francis	Arnold, Notts	S	
1997	Freedom Lee	Dartmoor	W	

The Gypsy Greats

This is a list of the great fighters said to have gypsy blood, from the 18th century to the present day. Again, it has been difficult to compile because of the lack of written records but I have tried my best to include as many of the very best men as possible. Apologies if I have unknowingly left out anyone who deserves to be in.

Early 1700s
Prince Boswell

1780s–90s
William Hooper (Hooper the Tinman)
Arthur Smith
The 'Slashing Gypsy' Jack Cooper

1810s
George Cooper

1820–40s
Harry Lee
Thomas Britton
Arthur M'Ginnis, King of the Tinkers
Jem Ward, the 'Black Diamond'
Nick Ward
Ambrose Smith

Farden Smith, 'King of the Gypsies'

1850–70s
Jem Mace. The champion of England at several different weights, Mace beat Tom Allen for the world title in Louisiana in 1870 and later toured America, Australia and New Zealand showing his skills. He became known as the Father of Modern Boxing. Other top gypsy fighters of his day were his cousin Pooley, Louis Gray and Posh Price. Jem Mace died in 1910 and lies in an unmarked grave in Anfield Cemetery, Liverpool.

Bareknuckle fighting became strictly illegal in Great Britain from the middle of the 1800s but survived underground among the 'mountain fighters' of the Welsh mining valleys and, more importantly, the English gypsies and the Irish, Welsh and Scottish travellers and tinkers. No records exist of their contests and the list below is the first that anyone has ever attempted of the great fighters of the past 150 years. It is by no means exhaustive and many may dispute its findings. All I can say is that this is how things have been handed down to me by personal recollection and reminiscence.

Champion	Contenders
Mid to late 1800s Bartley Gorman I	Jack Ward, King of the Tinkers (Ireland) Caleb Wenman (Somerset) Moe Smith (Cheshire) Jack Hearn (Wales)
1900s–1920s Bartley Gorman II	Black Martin Fury (Ireland) Billy Elliott (Scotland) Wiggy Lee Matt Carroll (Ireland) Chasey Price, 'the Blackbird' (Wales) Tom Daley (Ireland)

Andy Riley (Ireland)
Ben Smith (Midlands)
Zachariah Lee (Wales)

1920s–30s
Disputed

Jimmy O'Neill (Lancashire)
Benny Marshall (South Wales)
John Ward, 'King of the Tinkers' (Ireland)
Strong John Small (South-east coast)
Leonard Smith (Cornwall)
Edmond Penfold (Cornwall)
'Isle of White' Jimmy Willett
Lofty Cooper (Hampshire)

1930s–40s
Disputed

Ticker 'Tiger' Gorman (West Midlands)
Reilly Smith (Leicestershire)
Johnny Winters (Nottinghamshire)
'Whiteface' Tommy Allen (Midlands)
Chris Wriles/Royals (Worcestershire)
Billy Turnbull (Newcastle upon Tyne)
'Battling' Bartley Gorman III (Wales)
Sam Price (Wales)
Billy Rogers (Cheshire)

1940s–50s
Disputed

Big Jim Nielson, the Black Panther
Oathy Burton
'Atom Bomb' Tom Lee (Lancashire)
Sam Ward (Darlington)
Jim Crow (Darlington)
Bob Braddock
Black Bob Evans (Wales)
Lawrence Ward, 'King of the Tinkers'
(Ireland)

1950s–60s
'Big Just'   Barney Docherty (Ireland)
Uriah Burton   Big Tom Roberts
                    Caley Botton, 'Big Chuck'
                    Wisdom Smith (Warwickshire)
                    Willie Biddle (Coventry)
                    Tucker Dunn (London)
                    Levi Silks (East Anglia)
                    Billy Welch (Darlington)
                    Oliver Ayres
                    'Big Daddy' Walter Harrison (Cheshire)
                    Old Bobby MacPhee (Scotland)
                    Ludlum Gaskin

1972–92
Bartley Gorman V   1970s
                    Mark Ripley (Kent)
                    Simon Docherty (Ireland)
                    John-John Stanley (New Forest)
                    Boxer Tom Taylor, Sam Gorman
                    Johnny Frankham (London)
                    Jack Fletcher (London)
                    Les Stevens (Reading)
                    Bobby and Jackie Lowe (Scotland)
                    'Cutthroat' Bob Gaskin (Yorkshire)
                    Eric Boswell (Lancashire)
                    Nigger Smith (Yorkshire)
                    1980s
                    Dan Rooney (Ireland)
                    John Rooney (Ireland)
                    Ernie McGinley (Ireland)
                    Joe Joyce, the Hulk (Ireland)
                    Bobby and Jamesy MacPhee (Scotland)
                    Joe-Boy Botton (London)
                    Big Philip Reilly (Selby)
                    Charlie Cooper (New Forest)
                    Henry Arab, 'the Dentist'

1992–date
Unclaimed

Big John Fury
Outlaw Henry Francis (Notts)
Terry 'JCB' Ward (Darlington)
Lewis Welch (Darlington)
Ivan Botton (Notts)
Bernie Ward (Ireland)
Jimmy 'the Boxer' McDonagh (Ireland)
Dick Smith (Barnsley)
Charlie Moore (Darlington)
Jimmy 'the Bull' Ayres
John Nevin (Ireland)
Joe-Boy Gaskin (Yorkshire)
Eli Frankham (London)

The Great Gypsy Fights

Many of these great fights involving gypsies are described in more detail in the main text.

Prince Boswell v George Taylor
Boswell was the first Romany fighter that we know of and was supremely talented. He fought Taylor, a leading English pugilist, several times, winning at least once.

William Hooper, the Tinman v Will Wood, June 1795
The experienced Wood held his own at first but Hooper won after fifty minutes of hard battling.

George Cooper v Dan Donnelly, The Curragh, Ireland, 1815
Cooper and Hooper were both believed to have gypsy blood. Neither was a champion but both were top men of their day and Cooper gave Irish champion Donnelly a famous fight.

Jem Mace v Farden Smith, 1850s
Recorded by Mace in his book *Fifty Years A Fighter*. Mace went on to win the heavyweight championship of the world. Of course, he always denied being of gypsy blood.

Bartley Gorman I v Jack Ward, Donnybrook Fair, Dublin, 1854
My great-grandfather was not known as a fighter until he bested Ward, the notorious King of the Tinkers.

Pooley Mace v Louis Gray. King's Lynn, Norfolk, 1862
Pooley, Jem Mace's cousin, was a half-bred gypsy while Louis was a Romany from the Norwich area. Gray drew first blood but took terrible punishment to the face and by the seventeenth round was semi-conscious and unable to continue.

Jem Mace v Bartley Gorman I, Dublin, 1864
An impromptu challenge in a Dublin saloon led to a cobble-stone bout between these two great knuckle men. It was broken up by the garda.

Bartley Gorman I v Caleb Wenman, Black Patch, Birmingham
One of the most brutal of all fights, it resulted in Wenman losing an arm and my great-grandfather having to wear a collar around his neck for three months.

Bartley Gorman II v Chasy 'Blackbird' Price, Wales
My grandfather beat the gigantic young Price in quick time but said that he would not have fancied fighting him years later, when Price had grown so big he could dangle Bartley II on his knee.

Bartley Gorman II v Matt Carroll, Dublin
A fight which took place at the harbourside saw Bartley II vanquish Carroll after a very close fight and also knock out his sister!

'Strong' John Small v Edmond Penfold, Exeter
Both were unbeaten when they met and Small prevailed after a heroic tussle. John Small never lost a fight. He was the only man ever to beat Penfold and also beat the brothers Tom and Jimmy Duckett and several members of the James family.

He was a Devon man and fought Tom Duckett twice. After beating him on Duckett's home ground, he said, 'I can cor [fight] just as good in Bristol as I can in Devon.'

Reilly Smith v Charlie Bacon, Six Hills, Leics, c1936
Smith was a heavyweight boxer while Bacon was a young bull. They fought twice after the Bacon family had a dispute with the Elliots, who were relatives of Reilly Smith. Bacon apparently won the first one in a big upset at Cambridge Fair but Smith beat him at Six Hills and it was left at that.

Crooked-necked Robin Winters v Tommy Woodward
Winters – also known as Wry-necked Robin because he had one shoulder higher than the other – and Woodward (pronounced Wothard) had one of the great fights of the mid-1930s. Woodward once jumped in the ring at a big police boxing tournament in Liverpool and said, 'Bring out your best heavyweight policeman and donate what I win to your nearest charity.' But they wouldn't let him fight. They were true sporting men in those days.

Johnny Winters v Whiteface Tommy Allen, Walsall and Doncaster
Two great fighters from the Midlands. They fought twice and Winters, the bigger man, won both times.

Sam Price v Johnny Winters
They fought twice and Price won at least one of them. They say he was the best Welshman ever. He must have been good if he beat Winters, who never took a backward step. Winters was still alive at the time of writing but Price died a few years ago. Top modern fighters like Henry Francis and Dan Rooney were at his funeral.

Little Tommy Lee v Charlie Whitehead, Manchester
The Lees could fight. There were three brothers: Jack, Saley and Little Tommy. Charlie Whitehead was said to be the best man in Manchester when they fought. Tommy fell and broke

his ankle and Whitehead said, 'Let's call it a day.' Lee said, 'Prop me up against this wall,' so they did. Whitehead came at him and Lee sparked him out.

'Atom Bomb' Tom Lee v Oathy Burton, Manchester
Said to have taken place in a bomb crater. There were no witnesses but Burton, older brother of the famous Hughie said that after a brutal fight, Lee hit him with a half-brick.

Tom Lee v Joe Stretton, Rugby, Warks
They fought in a bull-ring at a cattle market. It was a good fight but the Atom Bomb was too powerful for Stretton, whose son Ginger is a friend of mine.

Black Bob Evans v Billy Rogerson, Wrexham Horse Fair
A hell of a fight until one of the Evanses hit Rogerson on the sly and everyone piled in. The Rogersons were Nantwich travellers and Billy was the best man in Cheshire and Shropshire, while Black Bob was the best man in Wales. Blondie Bill Evans, Black Bob's brother, was the best man in Anglesey.

Tom Brazil v Jimmy Frankham
Said to be one of the great fights. Jimmy was the father of Johnny Frankham, who became British light-heavyweight boxing champion. The Brazils are a well-known gypsy breed: my uncle Ticker once beat one of their best men.

'Big Chuck' Caley Botton v Willie Biddle, Coventry, 1950s
Caley made his name when he beat Biddle, who was a showman and one of the best men of his day, at the annual Pot Fair.

Caley Botton v Wisdom Smith, Stratford-on-Avon, 1950s
According to Caley, he and Smith fell out over a family dispute. Smith was a millionaire but also a respected fighter.

Barney Docherty v Big James Friel, Donegal, Ireland 1950s
A classic fight between two of the toughest men in Ireland. Barney won and later set off to England for a death match with Hughie Burton but died in mysterious circumstances on a train. His son Simon was a top fighter.

Uriah Burton v Big Jim Nielson, St Boswell's Fair, Scotland, c 1960
Burton won the title 'King of the Gypsies' in controversial circumstances. Those who were present say he forced Nielson to give best by throwing him to the ground and biting off one of his nipples.

Uriah Burton v Big Tom Roberts, Epsom Derby
Roberts was a boxer and a giant man but Burton was too savage for him.

Bartley Gorman V v Jack Fletcher, Hollington Quarry, 1972
After Hughie Burton failed to meet me the previous year at Doncaster races, I fought and beat Fletcher for Burton's crown.

John-John Stanley v Boxer Tom, Watford, 1972
Two of the best men when I was in my prime, though I fought neither of them. Their battle was a marathon affair and said to be one of the greatest ever. They remain good friends and can still look after themselves today.

Bob Gaskin v Simon Docherty, Appleby, 1976
Gaskin and Docherty fought three times, with Simon winning two of them. When they fought at Appleby, Simon also took on and beat Gaskin's brother Kevin.

Bartley Gorman V v Bob Gaskin, Doncaster Races, 1976
The most infamous mob attack among all travellers, it became known as the Massacre on St Leger day.

Bartley Gorman V v Mexicana Webb, Coventry, 1980
An impromptu challenge in a pub, I dislocated my shoulder in this fight but still won.

Dan Rooney v Joe 'the Hulk' Joyce
Joyce had beaten Anthony Donnelly in Ireland to claim the title King of the Travellers. He was a big man, well built, and got his nickname when he crunched five or six lads at a wedding in London and the police had to powerhose him. All these people were shouting, 'He's the Incredible Hulk!' He was no fancy dan but he would get in and hit you and that was all he needed. Big Dan was the up-and-coming man when they fought and won when Joyce broke his ankle.

Ernie McGinley v Henry Francis, Yorks, c1982
McGinley was given a £5,000 horse to challenge Francis. Henry was sitting on the steps of his trailer picking his toes when McGinley showed up to challenge him.

Dan Rooney v Ernie McGinley, Crossmaglen, Ireland, 1991
For the Championship of All-Ireland. This was the first gypsy classic to ever be recorded on video. It was stopped when the crowd became too unruly and both men claimed victory but it is generally accepted that Rooney was having the better of it.

Bartley Gorman V v John Rooney, Hinckley, Leics, 1991
My victory over John, younger brother of Big Dan, is commemorated by a famous wood-carving in the Grapes public house at Appleby.

Bartley Gorman V v Henry Francis, Notts, June 1995
My last epic fight and yet another spur of the moment encounter, again after a funeral.

Jimmy McDonagh v Paddy 'The Lurch' Joyce, Drogheda, Ireland, Nov 1997

Another fight recorded on video. It was not a great one but McDonagh is a top man now.

Tribute

Bartley Gorman died in the early evening of Friday, January 18, 2002, at a hospice in Derby. He was fifty-seven. He had fought a short but typically heroic battle against cancer and was surrounded to the last by close friends and family, and much love. Many hundreds of people, gypsies and non-gypsies, attended his funeral a week later in Uttoxeter, his adopted hometown, and his burial at a small cemetery in nearby Rocester. It was a bleak, wet day, and a sad one for those who knew this remarkable man.

This book has concentrated on Bartley Gorman the bareknuckle prize-fighter, for it is that which made him famous. But there was much more to him. He kept largely silent about the family that he loved, in order to protect their privacy. He never mentioned how he would suddenly appear at early morning Mass on a midweek day in some small country church, or his uncountable small acts of kindness and charity, or his long conversations with friends about religion, philosophy and life. He had many facets, some of them more important to him than the fighting which made him a legend. As his cousin Malcolm Wilson told his funeral congregation, 'We all knew he was a great fighter but he was also funny and he was clever. He could argue. He was kind and, above all, he was loving.'

I learned that in the all-too-brief eighteen months I knew him. He was a unique man, a one-off. I shall miss his late-night phone calls, the photographs and newspaper cuttings that would suddenly arrive in the post, the long conversations over endless mugs of milky tea in his trailer, the shared meals in the Little Chef at Uttoxeter or at various pubs and the regular tussle to stop him picking up the bill.

Everyone who knew him will remember different things about him: his stubbornness on points of principle; his playfully wicked sense of humour; his quick wit; his love of argument and debate; his veneration for anything old and for nature; his constant gift-giving; his love of small children, whom he would shower with treats and sweets and who brought out the barely disguised child in him.

Shortly before he died, he told me he wanted to make one thing clear. 'The people in my life that ever did anything against me, even the men that attacked me at Doncaster, I forgive them all. Every one. Because if I can't forgive, then I'm not worth anything.'

Bartley need have no worries on that score. Goodbye, my friend.

Peter Walsh, February 2002